The Truth About Westminster

PATRICK DIXON

KINGSWAY PUBLICATIONS
EASTBOURNE

ISBN 0 85476 685 5

Designed and produced by
Bookprint Creative Services
P.O. Box 827, BN21 3YJ, England for
KINGSWAY PUBLICATIONS LTD
Lottbridge Drove, Eastbourne, E. Sussex BN23 6NT.
Printed in Great Britain.

To Sheila, with thanks for many happy years.

Contents

Acknowledgements 9

Introduction 11

1 MPs Available for Hire 17

2 Buying and Selling MPs on a Large Scale 40

3 MP Fiddles and Some Reluctant Lords 62

4 The Power of Patronage 78

5 The Truth about Party Funding 94

6 Sex, Money and Power 121

7 Whipping and the Death of Conscience 128

8 Secrets of Ministers and Civil Servants 148

9 Trade Scandals and Arms Deals 180

10 The Changing Culture 215

11 Rebuilding the House 239

12 Christians in Politics 287

Notes 303

A Short Bibliography 317

Acknowledgements

I am indebted to more than seventy individuals with several hundred years of cumulative experience between them of public and political service, whether as Ministers, back-benchers, Peers, civil servants, party officials and others. Some have been willing to be identified and are described in the positions they held at the time of writing, while others have chosen to remain anonymous, but all have contributed invaluable insights, comments and background, or have helped debate the issues.

I am also grateful for the co-operation of the Cabinet Office, and of the librarians of the House of Commons, House of Lords and Westminster Reference Library, who have all helped locate important information. All sources are acknowledged except in the case of some anonymous comments made in interviews.

I have appreciated comments and perspectives from a number of people who have read part or all of the book at various stages. In particular I would like to thank His Honour Judge Christopher Compston and Christopher Graffius, together with Araminta Whitley at Peters Fraser and Dunlop. I would like to thank the people at Kingsway, and in particular Rachel Ashley-Pain, for helping produce the book so rapidly from text to publication.

Thanks are also due to Sheila, my wife, for her support and encouragement, comments and corrections, as well as substantial help with the analysis of House of Lords voting patterns; and to John, Caroline, Elizabeth and Paul, who cheerfully put up with the long writing process.

Introduction

'*Most people regard us as corrupt. They assume we've got our fingers in the till and they also assume we've got our leg over our secretary.*' Jerry Hayes MP (1953–)[1]

'*The perception of this House has gone down and down. If it doesn't command the confidence of the people, that is a serious threat to our democracy.*' Tom King MP (1933–)[2]

'*Among a people generally corrupt, liberty cannot long exist.*' Edmund Burke (1729–1797)

'Will there be a fee?' the old woman asked as she got up to go. The Member of Parliament looked up in horror. He had fought several housing battles for her in the past and had just agreed to help her again.

'Whatever for?' he exclaimed.

'For the letter. You read in the papers . . .'

'Of course not. I am shocked that you should think such a thing!'

Afterwards the Member of Parliament told me how upset he had felt. 'I was so ashamed that the media attention on the

11

misbehaviour of just two MPs should have so tarnished the reputation of us all. I wanted to weep. Everything I stand for is being destroyed. There she was, a pensioner on a very low income, convinced that she now had to pay her MP to get justice. One wonders how many others think as she did.'

Democracy in Britain is in a dangerous state. Faith in politicians and in our democratic process has sunk to the lowest point in living memory, in the wake of a series of widely publicised allegations of sleaze and corruption, affecting every level of political life. Every new revelation carries with it the expectation that many more are waiting to be exposed, and the certain knowledge that many others never will be. The most shocking thing of all perhaps has not been the scandals themselves, but the obvious failure of senior politicians to understand the damage to the image of public office.

A recent poll shows that many people now think that most MPs are corrupt, willing to 'make a lot of money by using public office improperly', and will 'tell lies if they feel the truth will hurt them politically'.[3] As the gap narrows between the main parties, it is likely that personal values will become more important in winning votes than slight differences in public policies.

Some argue that Parliament has always been corrupt, but is less so today than at many other times in the 700 years since Edward I summoned the first Parliament in 1295. While this is undoubtedly true, there is much evidence to suggest that there has been a revolution in culture and attitudes within the 'Club' since the end of the Second World War. There is a generation of elder statesmen in Parliament today who entered public life after military service. They had fought and nearly died together and came into politics to help rebuild a nation ravaged by war. They have had difficulties coming to terms with the new super-breed of young, anti-social, ambitious, affluent and strongly opinionated MPs that have flooded into the House since the late 1970s.

Despite this it is also true that the British Parliament is still one of the least corrupt institutions in Europe and the rest of the world. As a nation we expect the highest standards of those in government and regard our 'Mother of all parliaments' with respect and affection. Hence the sense of outrage and indignation when it appears that politicians have been careless with the reputation of such a priceless heritage.

Much of the public anger so far has been directed at one party with three out of four saying that 'the Conservatives these days give the impression of being sleazy and disreputable'. This compares with only 16 per cent saying the same of Labour.[4] Half the voters say that the Conservatives are worse than MPs from other parties, and that as a result they are less inclined to vote for them than before. Perhaps more seriously for the future of democracy, almost all the remainder feel that all the parties are just as disreputable as each other.

It seems to many that there is one law for voters and another for those in power. There is ample evidence that when MPs are in trouble, they tend to close ranks with other members of the establishment to protect the accused from public scrutiny, with every appearance of deliberately obstructing justice. But what is it about the 'Club' that has turned so many respected men and women of integrity, calibre and vision into people unwilling to speak out against abuse of power, afraid to vote for what they know is right, covering up for colleagues they know have done wrong, and hurling insults at people they agree with?

I have been confronted many times by this important question through my work as a doctor in the voluntary sector. Over the years I have had many dealings with Ministers, back-benchers and Peers; I have corresponded personally with several hundred of them and addressed Members of both Houses on several occasions. In contrast to their deteriorating media image, I have always been struck by their dedication to duty, their sense of public service, and the common traditions of decency and honour that transcend all party interests.

Yet with every passing week this personal experience has seemed further removed from the negative public perception, fed by investigative and tabloid journalism and 'sensationalised' broadcasts.

The purpose of this book has been to attempt to reconcile these two conflicting views, not as a journalist, nor as a politician, but as a fellow professional seeking to understand the truth behind the headlines, as someone who comes from a strong family tradition of political neutrality.

If politicians score the lowest trust ratings in society as a whole, together with journalists, then doctors score the highest. Perhaps in part this explains why so many politicians have felt free to talk, revealing their burdens of office, conflicts of conscience and confusion about codes of practice. Researching this book has been a fascinating but disturbing process, and sometimes the full impact of interviews has only hit me later, on transcribing the tape recordings before committing their contents to a bank vault.

The law on libel means that some stories can never be told, or revealed only in part, because those who know the truth are unwilling to testify in court. I regret that, but it has been necessary to protect vulnerable sources and to honour promises of confidentiality. Writing this book has also been made exceedingly difficult because of a stack of writs by a number of well-known individuals. Make no mistake. The truth about Westminster is a complex kaleidoscope of interleaving events and personalities; a mix of the very best and the very worst in human nature and of everything in between.

It is far too easy to lay most of the blame on one party, the Conservatives. Corruption by definition involves the abuse of power and so is always most likely to be obvious among those with most power over the longest period. Therefore it is to be expected that most of the recent examples of the abuse of power will refer to Conservatives in office. We must not be so naive as to think that changing a Prime Minister, a Cabinet, or even an entire government will eradicate the problem. The Conservatives may well have shown themselves thoroughly disgraced in the eyes of some after more than sixteen years in national office, but the Labour Party faces great difficulties of its own and deeply-rooted financial corruption has been serious for a long time in Labour-controlled local government. Therefore I have no doubt that recent Westminster history will repeat itself under a Labour administration, albeit in different ways, unless the underlying problems are addressed.

My thesis is that while very few MPs are overtly corrupt, the political process is itself corrupting and needs urgent reform. However, new codes of practice, or even a constitutional revolution, will not be enough to restore confidence in those who lead our nation. Only sweeping changes in people and their values will cause the radical changes this country needs.

My purpose is not to condemn or point the finger at those who have fallen, are falling or are struggling to survive, but to understand and to point a way forward. Those who have never had to face the severe rigours of public life should, I believe, be slow to judge. The pressures on these men and women are enormous, particularly from the media. There has never been an age in human history in which those in such positions have been so aggressively exposed before millions of others.

There is no human on this earth today who is perfect in

private or in public, and all are prone to mistakes. If we want perfect leaders, then we will have no leaders left at all. Nevertheless, there are certain reasonable expectations which appear to have been systematically ignored by more than just a minority. While one cannot legislate for integrity, steps can be taken to encourage the highest values. It is not enough to 'keep to the rules' if the rules themselves need changing.

It is my belief that anger and dismay at the current crisis will cause a new generation of men and women to enter public life, driven by a vision of a different kind of world and a different kind of Parliament. They will bring a new sense of self-sacrificing purpose, compassion, calling and destiny. I see signs of it already: an awakening of political conscience as we prepare for a new millennium. It could capture the heart of the nation.

Patrick Dixon
August 1996

1

MPs Available for Hire

'This country has always been in a frightful mess. Parliament has always been held as a place of no repute.' Lord Weatherill *(1920–)*

The Prime Minister was visibly sweating under the studio lights as the sound technician adjusted the clip-on microphone for the third time, making way for a last-minute fluster by Make-up in the closing seconds of the commercial break. Another scandal, another row, another inquiry, another report, another long week in politics, but in every interview there is the same nagging problem. It affects opposition and government alike; it dominates and overshadows every interview; it undermines every public statement and fuels speculation out of every spoken word. The issue is this: 'Will I come across well? Do I look like I'm telling the truth? Will people believe me?'

Recent polls show clearly the nature of the credibility crisis which threatens to wreck our democracy. In 1993, a MORI survey found that only one in ten people thought government Ministers could be trusted. There are very few polls which produce such a decisive result. It is hard to imagine a more serious situation than 90 per cent expressing mistrust. It could be said that the Cabinet and junior Ministers have been condemned as unworthy of office by almost the entire nation.

But what of the rest of Parliament including the opposition? A mere one in seven generally trusted Members of Parliament to tell the truth. In contrast, doctors and teachers were trusted by more than eight out of ten.[5] In 1994 most people thought that the majority of MPs were making 'a lot of money by using public office improperly'.[6]

Three-quarters of those polled agreed that 'the ethical and moral standards of British politicians have been declining in recent years'. Only one in four said that 'most MPs have a high moral code', while nine out of ten said that 'most MPs will tell lies if they feel the truth will hurt them politically'.[7] A year later 78 per cent said that 'most candidates for Parliament make promises they have no intention of keeping'.[8]

As we will see, 'economy with the truth' is deeply embedded in the psyche of Westminster and is the root of many of the problems we will address, for what is open can be judged and the electorate can then exercise the power of the ballot box. Secrecy means power in politics.

So then, politicians on television are usually assumed to be dishonest by viewers and probably by those who interview them. But the most important question of all is this: what happens to a democracy where every electoral pledge is suspect, every claim is discounted and every 'fact' disputed? The result is that the democratic process itself begins to die. This is the sad reality of politics in Britain today, and the saddest thing of all is that the last people to see it are often politicians themselves.

This crisis of confidence affects not only how politicians are regarded, but also the way people feel about the whole political process. British democracy may have been a model for the world, but the majority of the British people now think that the model is failing. In an eighteen-nation Gallup Poll, the British scored sixth from the bottom in a league of satisfaction ratings for the way democracy works. This was lower than Thailand, Taiwan and Chile, and higher only than India, Venezuela, Hungary, Mexico and China.[9]

In the light of these things, it is hardly surprising that pressures are growing for reform. In 1995, a MORI 'State of the Nation' survey found 78 per cent in favour of a Bill of Rights and 81 per cent wanted a Freedom of Information Act. Two-thirds said that rules for MPs' conduct should become part of criminal law, 78 per cent wanted allegations of 'serious misconduct' against Ministers to be investigated by the police or an independent commissioner, while only 11 per cent were happy for the Prime Minister to continue to be the final judge.

These polls show that people are fed up and angry at the 'nauseating' way in which there seems to be one law for ordinary people but no law for MPs, because they sit in judgement on themselves: the 'distrusted', 'dishonest' and despised judging the disgraced, with few if any punishments ever given.

Three-quarters of respondents wanted to improve the way we are governed (up from 63 per cent four years previously and 49 per cent in 1973). Only 43 per cent still believed Parliament works fairly well, the same as the number satisfied with their local MP. Four out of five wanted a written constitution 'providing clear legal rules which government Ministers and civil servants are forced to operate'.[10]

Fair assessment or a jaundiced view? Few alive today have more experience of the 'Gentleman's Club' that is the House of Commons than Bernard Weatherill. Made a Peer in 1992 after thirteen years as Deputy Speaker and Speaker of the House of Commons, five years as Chief Whip, in the

Commons for twenty-eight years, he has clarity as well as charm. His views are vitally important because he represents a ground swell of opinion within Parliament.

I asked Lord Weatherill whether he thought we were facing a crisis. He agreed that there were problems but declared that they were nothing new, and that things were not as bad as they seemed. He thinks the problem in Britain today is that we spend far too much time 'denigrating our achievements'.

'Please believe me. This country has always been in a frightful mess. Parliament has always been held as a place of no repute.' He quoted William Wilberforce in 1801: 'I dare not marry – the future is too uncertain,' and described how William Pitt in 1803 saw 'nothing around but ruin and despair', while in 1849 Disraeli at the Ministry of Commerce came to the conclusion that there was 'no hope'.

'In the end politicians had made such a mess of it that they said the only chap that could sort it out was the great Duke of Wellington, no less. He was made Prime Minister and he also failed. As he lay on his death bed in 1852, he said: "I am glad I am going so I shall not see the consolation of ruin that is gathering around us." '[11]

However, even if we accept Lord Weatherill's argument that things have always been bad, it does not help settle the nation's wholesale distrust of politicians today. Sleaze does indeed have a long history and the past does affect the current crisis.

A short history of sleaze

In previous centuries corruption was an accepted part of public life: dubious practices by today's standards were considered normal and necessary. For example it was common practice to buy support, as happened quite widely under

Henry Pelham, Prime Minister from 1743 to 1754. Even today the government Chief Whip is called the Patronage Secretary. Although the nature of rewards has changed, many of the principles remain, as we will see.

Parliament was a protected enclave of the wealthy élite until the Reform Bill of 1832, which significantly expanded the small numbers eligible to vote. However, you still had to be a man who owned property to qualify. If we accept that the advent of true democracy in a country like South Africa has only dawned with a universal voting system for all adults regardless of status, colour, sex or creed, then we have to say that true democracy only became a reality in Britain as recently as 1928, less than seventy years ago. It was only in that year that all women were able to vote at the same age as men (twenty-one).

Political scandals in the twentieth century are nothing new, although they have certainly become more frequent. Between 1911 and 1913, a huge scandal hit the government over irregular share dealings. Lloyd George, then the Chancellor of the Exchequer, and a second government Minister bought shares in the American Marconi company, knowing that the British government had just placed a huge order with the Marconi company in Britain. The government Chief Whip also bought shares on behalf of the Liberal Party.

The shares doubled in value when they went on sale to the public shortly afterwards. At first the Ministers tried to cover up what had happened. When they were found out they resorted to claiming that they had done nothing wrong. The Commons Select Committee split along party lines and the press were uninterested; Lloyd George became Prime Minister, while the other became Lord Chief Justice and Viceroy of India.

After the First World War there were many worries over how wartime contracts had been awarded. The coalition government had also been selling honours to raise political funds. Ministers then lied to Parliament by denying honours were for sale. The last straw for King George V was when he discovered that a peerage had been granted to a man convicted of fraud which he declared was 'little less than an insult to the Crown and the House of Lords'.

Maundy Gregory was accused of brokering patronage over an estimated 26 peerages, 130 baronetcies and 481 knighthoods paid for between 1916 and 1922. Immediately following this, the Royal Commission on Honours was set up, with all political honours vetted by three Privy Councillors as happens today. Lloyd George was also linked to a love affair conducted by him in Downing Street at a time when such behaviour was far less acceptable in society generally than today.

In 1941, Bob Boothby was forced to resign by Churchill, over a conflict of interest involving a campaign to release Czech gold. In 1948, the Labour junior Board of Trade Minister John Belcher left the government after an investigation by the Lynskey tribunal.[12] He had accepted gifts from a number of businessmen which it was feared had affected the issuing of government licences and permits. In 1962, Tam Galbraith was wrongly accused of involvement in the Vassall sex and espionage scandal. He resigned, was later cleared and then given a senior government position.[13]

In 1963, the Secretary of State for War, John Profumo, was linked with a sex and spies scandal after a much publicised affair with Christine Keeler. The problem was that she was also very friendly with Captain Ivanov, a Security Officer at the Russian Embassy, and this was at the height of the Cold War. Profumo tried to bluff his way through it, doing enormous damage to the government at the time.[14]

Apart from these few incidents, there was little sleaze reported from the time of Lloyd George until the Poulson scandal in the early 1970s.[15] John Poulson had paid civil servants, local councillors, council officials, nationalised industry and NHS employees, and Members of Parliament various amounts in cash and in gifts in a bid to secure contracts. A number of people were jailed as a result. The Home Secretary Reginauld Maudling was also criticised. The Royal Commission into Standards in Public Life followed (the Salmon Commission) with new rules for local government.

In 1973, the then Prime Minister Sir Edward Heath refused to believe reports from MI5 that the War Minister Viscount Lambton was having sex with two prostitutes at once. MI5 arranged for the *News of the World* to take pictures and the Minister resigned. The following day the Prime Minister asked the remaining Ministers if they had anything to tell him. It emerged that Earl Jellicoe had also been seeing one of the girls and he too stepped down from office.[16]

Despite these experiences while he was in office, Sir Edward Heath, as the most senior Member of the House of Commons, has a rosy view of Westminster. 'I have been an elected Member of Parliament for forty-five years, and I have rarely encountered cases of wrong-doing by my colleagues on either side of the House. Most of those I have served with have been men and women of integrity and honesty and that continues to be so today.'[17]

If that is the case, then it should be a relatively easy matter to deal with national mistrust of politicians through greater openness and transparency, so that nobility can be revealed and respect restored. Unfortunately the petty dishonesty seen in day-to-day political posturing tends to undermine this. A prime example is where an opposition MP attacks the government for policies which he or she knows would not be reversed if they were in power.

There have been other significant changes over the last few decades which are very relevant to the way scandals have been handled, as we will see in the rest of this book. There has been a growth in the role and power of the Cabinet, also huge growth of government expenditure, and increasing domination of government by successive Prime Ministers, particularly where, more recently, there have been large majorities. This control of the government executive by one person has been made possible by frequent Cabinet shuffles and sackings.

The ability of Parliament to scrutinise the executive has been weakened, reducing government back-benchers and opposition MPs to mere spectators, and frustrations have grown. Meanwhile the House of Lords has remained relatively stable as a Conservative-dominated but almost powerless 'improving Chamber', occupied by a number of free thinkers who are constantly seeking to modify or delay hasty and ill-thought-out legislation.

This concentration of power in the hands of a few over a long period is unhealthy. If those few are entirely benevolent and utterly beyond reproach then the result could be a benign dictatorship of sorts. But what if those with such unprecedented political powers are fallible, frail and all too human?

New generation of MPs fights back

More recent recruits to parliament are in no doubt that Westminster is in disgrace. Simon Hughes became a Member of Parliament in 1983 and has been on the Liberal Democrat front bench ever since. He told me: 'It is not trite to say that the parliamentary process is hugely discredited in this country.' It worries him greatly. 'All we do should be geared to restoring a belief in the political process.'[18]

Jerry Hayes was first elected at the same time as Simon Hughes. Now a Parliamentary Private Secretary he admits: 'Most people do regard us as corrupt. They assume we've got our fingers in the till and they also assume we've got our leg over our secretary.' However, 'The truth is depressingly mundane. The majority of MPs work very hard for their constituencies and work as best they can.'

Teresa Gorman is a passionate, strong-minded Tory backbencher who entered the House of Commons in 1987. She is highly critical of the way in which Members of Parliament conduct themselves and says the place is run like a boys' school. 'That is why women are treated as an anomaly. The whole antique structure needs shaking out. That can only be done by a party that wants to modernise.'[19]

Ken Livingstone also has a gloomy view. He claims the appalling public image of MPs is well deserved: 'Every government since 1951 has squandered opportunities, has deceived people. I don't think people would be terribly worried about who's screwing whom if they felt confident and secure about the economy.'[20]

David Amess, Tory back-bencher since 1983, is angry about sleaze, blaming 'the huge vanity of all Members of Parliament'. He thinks the media have had a huge effect. '[MPs] are stupid to think that the more publicity they get, the more they talk to the radio, television and newspapers, the more they will be loved. If they only kept their mouths shut, none of this nonsense would have started in the first place. It all started with the televising of Parliament: one of the stupidest things my colleagues could have done.' The media 'latch on to someone, build up a relationship, bang they're created, bang they're destroyed and move on to the next person'.[21]

So, Parliament has had its sordid and glorious moments in the past, yet the common view is that there has been a recent deterioration in standards and behaviour, bringing Westminster into disrepute. While the new generation of MPs is far from happy with what it feels it has inherited, the old school sees things rather differently. For them the finger should be pointed mainly at newer MPs who have lower standards. As we will see, the changes in culture and standards have certainly been dramatic.

Corrupted by money

It is widely held that the most damaging allegations involve money rather than private sexual morality or supposed lack of it. We need to look first at some of the urgent concerns that led to the setting up of the Nolan Inquiry in the autumn of 1994: payments for special treatment or extra attention, hidden directorships, lucrative lobbying consultancies, Cabinet members going onto the boards of the corporations they have privatised, and MPs or Peers finding other (controversial) ways of enhancing their incomes.

While many MPs have a far more relaxed approach to these matters than twenty years ago, the public still hold remarkably strict and consistent views. A Gallup survey in November 1994 asked what the public thought MPs should and should not do.[22] Around half of those responding felt that MPs should not even allow someone else to buy them a meal – which seems to me to be rather Draconian. However, the message could not be clearer: the country expects the highest standards of integrity and is strongly against any extra perks or benefits.

It is possible that any softening of attitudes has been hardened by the stream of 'sleazy' news items about politicians. Some of the responses below are so puritanical that they could almost be described as a backlash in an otherwise very liberal society.

	% who think this is wrong
Payment for asking questions in Parliament	95%
A free holiday abroad	92%
Money/gifts in connection with parliamentary duties	89%
Payment for advice about parliamentary matters	85%
Free tickets to Wimbledon/other sporting events	69%
Free lunch at restaurant	47%
Bottles of wine or whisky at Christmas	45%

So, the public are clear about what they expect from those they elect, but what has happened in practice? There is always a danger in focusing on mistakes made by some, because the reputation of all becomes tarnished. However, as we will see, the unwritten rules of the 'Club' have changed over the years, creating an atmosphere which positively encourages abuse of privilege at every level. It would be a serious error therefore to write off all that follows as the aberrations of a few, failing to recognise the underlying malaise.

MPs for hire

For some years there were persistent rumours that companies were paying MPs to ask questions in order to gain a commercial advantage.

On 10 July 1994 the *Sunday Times* published a sensational front page article claiming that David Tredinnick and Graham Riddick had each accepted £1,000 for tabling a parliamentary question and that a third Member, Bill Walker, 'agreed to table a question in return for £1,000 before telephoning back and requesting the cheque be made out to his favourite charity'.

The newspaper added, 'The revelations confirm parliamentary rumours that some MPs are prepared to "sell" their services.' Many were concerned about the allegations but also at the subterfuge of *Sunday Times* reporters, posing as businessmen offering money for parliamentary activity.

All MPs and Lords have the right to ask any Minister any questions they like, usually in writing, and these are passed to officials to compose a reply that the Minister signs. Replies on sensitive subjects are often evasive half-truths, but they are better than nothing and often have commercial value.

The Thatcher regime created a market in almost every part of the government, ranging from running hospitals to cleaning streets and building motorways. Billions of pounds every year were now up for grabs to the most competitive bidder, but details of competitors' bids were often secret, and so was much of the tendering process. Written answers from Ministers were often invaluable in winning big contracts.

On 12 July the Speaker of the House of Commons announced a formal inquiry and what follows is based on the official report.[23] The Speaker quoted from a 1991–2 committee: 'Members who hold consultancy and similar positions must ensure that they do not use their position as Members improperly,' and added: 'A financial inducement to take a particular course of action may constitute a bribe and thus be an offence against the law of Parliament.' However such financial inducements are not an offence under criminal law, so long as the payment or benefits relate only to parliamentary activity.

The Speaker also reminded MPs that established practice was that 'the offering to a Member of either House of a bribe to influence him in his conduct as a Member, or of a fee or reward in connection with the promotion of . . . any . . . matter or thing submitted or intended to be submitted to the House . . . has been treated as breach of privilege'.

The committee decided that 'the offer of payment to table a question . . . is not of the same character as the offer of payment for a Member's vote, and does not seem . . . to fall into the definition of bribery . . . nevertheless, such an offer if made and accepted . . . is certainly dishonourable and damaging to the standing and reputation of Parliament'.

But what had actually happened? The committee began by asking for all the tape recordings made secretly by the *Sunday Times* together with all notes made at the time and other records. They also interviewed all those involved.

The *Sunday Times* said that they had been informed some time ago by a businessman that he had paid four named MPs to ask questions on his behalf, and that the 'going rate' was £1,000. The *Sunday Times* had been unable to check out the story or print it without compromising the anonymity of their source and so had decided to carry out a limited experiment of their own, approaching just twenty MPs picked 'at random' with a similar offer, ten each from the two main parties. However they did exclude paid Members of the government and Members who had no declared outside interests.[24]

The official transcripts of the tapes are a fascinating insight into attitudes. Let us take for example the conversation at Westminster on 7 July between David Tredinnick and Jonathan Calvert from the *Sunday Times*.

Calvert said: 'I don't know if it is the sort of work you do or maybe . . .'

'It's hardly work,' replied Tredinnick.

'I mean I will pay for it.'

'I think, I mean, I'm not sure that I'm . . .'

'It's worth about £1,000 to me, partly because I can, you

know, negotiate with them and really, I mean, I don't want to put in a lot of money and find at the end of the day that I've wasted my money really.'

'Okay. Well – I'm just going to check on the . . . [inaudible] . . . I don't see any reason why I shouldn't do it.'

And a little later Calvert says: 'I can pay you here and now. I've already made out the cheque in case you wanted it.'

'That's very kind of you. I will put the question down . . . [inaudible].'

Later that day, Calvert rang to confirm. 'You tabled the question this evening?'

'Yes.'

'Fine. Brilliant.'

'So you'll get an answer on Tuesday.'

'Right, okay.'

And a little later: 'I'll send you the £1,000 in the post now then.'

'That's very kind of you.'

Sir John Gorst's response was quite different. He expressed distaste at the idea of receiving cash just for asking a question, for although (as he rightly said) it was legal to enter into such an arrangement, he felt that it was contrary to the spirit of Parliament. Sir John Gorst indicated to Jonathan Calvert that he was only interested in entering into a long-term consultancy arrangement. To be fair to Mr Tredinnick, he explained to the Committee of Privileges that he regarded the payment offered to him by Jonathan Calvert as constituting 'some form of retainer' for a consultancy arrangement.

Jonathan Calvert began: '. . . this sort of consultancy work. Is it the sort of thing you do?'

'Yes, I could do it, certainly,' replied Sir John Gorst. 'Though my preference is for doing things that are on a longer-term basis rather than just a sort of one-off particular question. My speciality, if you can call it that, has been more in giving advice than necessarily implementing it, but obviously I can see that what you want is a bit of information.'

'Yes, a straightforward piece of information, really. It seems that the only way I can get it is by asking a written question in Parliament. I would be willing to pay for this.'

'Let's leave the question of that aside for the moment, because obviously the nature of one's position in Parliament is that it's legal, but it doesn't look very nice if you simply ask questions because you have been paid to do so.'

Jonathan Calvert then raised the issue of money again. 'Look, I mean, I've sat down and worked out what it's worth to me, and I'm investing quite a lot of money. I mean, it is worth about £1,000 to me to get this information. If I got it from a market research company . . .'

Sir John Gorst replied: 'Let me put it this way. If you were interested in a sort of longer-term relationship, public relations/public affairs advice, that would be more my field. I'm quite prepared to ask the question, and forgetting any question of a retainer or anything like that, simply in order to establish what the information is about this. And then, if at some subsequent stage you felt there was something we could make an arrangement about, we could discuss it on that basis – simply to establish the facts, to get an answer to a question. I think that would not be, in my view, a breach of the spirit of the parliamentary – one's position relative to Parliament.'

MP Bill Walker was also approached, and agreed that £1,000 should be sent to a named charity. He never intended to accept any personal financial reward for asking parliamentary questions. Indeed, he agreed to seek the information which Mr Calvert wanted before any suggestion of payment was made by Mr Calvert. Graham Riddick asked for a cheque payable to him to be sent to his own home.

On one occasion Jonathan Calvert asked him, 'Who were you going to talk to? The Members' Interests people?'

'Yes. I don't see any problem,' Graham Riddick replied.

'There's no problem at all?'

'No.'

'Well I mean, how much . . .?'

'I'm quite happy to go ahead.'

'How much information will you have to give when . . .?'

'What I will say is something like this. I would put: "July 1994 – Consultancy project carried out for Mr Jonathan Calvert".'

A minute or so later Jonathan Calvert again mentioned payment. 'What do you want me to do about paying you the £1,000? Would you like me to put the cheque in with the résumé or would you rather do it after the question has been raised or . . .?'

'I don't really mind. I mean, why don't you send that, why don't you just send it to me? To my home address?'

'Yes, okay.'

'You can send it there.'

The committee decided that Graham Riddick's action 'fell short of the standards the House is entitled to expect of its Members'. They pointed out that 'Mr Riddick had concluded before it was exposed that the transaction was not a proper one, that he had returned the cheque at the earliest opportunity, and that he had acknowledged his fault and apologised to the House.' Nevertheless they recommended that the MP be suspended from Parliament for two weeks with loss of two weeks' salary.

The committee noted that David Tredinnick was under great work pressure at the time, and that he had been influenced by the belief that the approach had come via a senior and respected colleague, 'but we do not think these factors are sufficient to outweigh an action which was in itself a serious error of judgement, and which must be taken together with an apparent intention to register a one-off consultancy on the basis that the transaction would be "confidential between the two of us".' The committee recommended that David Tredinnick be formally reprimanded, and suspended without pay for twenty sitting days.

They concluded that Bill Walker had never 'intended a personal financial reward by tabling parliamentary questions. . . . However, although in Mr Walker's mind there was no direct link between his tabling of parliamentary questions and the suggestion of a payment to charity, the manner in which this was raised made it virtually obligatory on Mr Calvert to make such a substantial donation to charity.

'It must be wrong for a Member to link payment to a charity or any other body however worthy, more especially one for which he has any direct responsibility, with asking a parliamentary question or tabling a Motion or an Amendment or making a speech. In our view such conduct diminishes the standing of parliament and, if it became prevalent, could lead members of the public to think that such a contribution would give them an advantage in dealing with their MP.

'We conclude that Mr Walker acted unwisely . . . (which to his credit he acknowledges) and specifically that he committed an error of judgement in suggesting a donation to charity in these circumstances.' However, no action was recommended. The committee also criticised the *Sunday Times* for clandestine methods. Of course John Gorst's response, being entirely exemplary, attracted no criticism whatever.

My own view is that these events were not isolated examples. It is hard to believe that out of sheer luck, hunch and intuition these reporters were able with twenty calls to locate the only two MPs out of 651 who were willing to ask questions in similar financial arrangements.

The inquiry almost became a farce, delayed by a bitter row about whether proceedings should be held in public or in secret. The Labour Members insisted on openness and walked out, while the Tories said that public hearings would only make witnesses nervous, and wanted all evidence to be published with the verdict.[25] Tony Benn then began publishing his own records and was thrown out.[26]

These committees are not like a court. They offer no legal protection for defendants or witnesses and the chairman does not have the power of a judge to rule certain questions out of order. Witnesses are able to make highly damaging, libellous and sensational allegations under the protection of parliamentary privilege, without any threat of being sued or even of cross-examination.

For these reasons it was even more important that hearings were in private at the time and only published with the verdict, preventing a media circus. Incidentally, the Labour protest was surely a prime example of political mischief; the sort of thing that brings politicians into disrepute. Labour MPs gave the impression that the Conservatives were trying to keep the evidence secret. That was highly misleading and factually incorrect. The only issue in debate was whether the evidence should be published day by day in the press, or whether verbatim transcripts would all be published with the verdict.

The Conservatives were in favour of late publication in line with previous custom.[27]

The row dominated media reporting of Parliament with Labour MPs making flamboyant gestures of protest, gaining enormous political capital in the process. Having read the detailed transcripts of oral evidence and written submissions, I cannot see how the term 'secret' could possibly be applied to the process. Unfortunately these sorts of emotive comments and distortions are all too common from those of all parties. The result is that many media interviews degenerate into near farce with accusation and counter-accusation, but with little serious discussion of the real issues about which most MPs are in agreement.

Graham Riddick told me afterwards that he had been deeply disappointed at how the whole investigation by the committee had worked, in a process described by one journalist as 'an insult to the judicial instincts of kangaroos'. 'I had genuinely believed that I would get a fair trial,' he said. He was particularly grieved that he was prevented from challenging the journalists from the *Sunday Times* when they gave evidence – not allowed even to be present or to read transcripts. He wished that he had been allowed to have proper legal representation, and pointed out that he only saw all the evidence used against him on the day of the verdict.[28] Similar concerns have been raised over the Scott Inquiry, although much of those proceedings was held in public. Nevertheless, the alternative is expensive and lengthy court hearings which would have constitutional implications.

Despite Graham Riddick's concerns, he made it clear that he was not 'whingeing' and accepted the verdict, although he felt it was harsh. He had apologised to the House soon after the incident, despite the fact that he never actually accepted any money for the questions he placed. His constituency has been very supportive.

The tapes of the *Sunday Times* calls are to me a damning indictment of the state of Westminster. I do not accept that the response of Riddick and Tredinnick was a 'freak incident', as many other MPs have tried to claim, but was partly a result of the way the whole 'Club' had been operating.

As if sensing the dangers of guilt by association, there was a loud chorus of moral outrage and indignation from many of the remaining 649 MPs, directed at Riddick and Tredinnick. Yet there seems to have been more than a trace of collective hypocrisy in this since, as we will see, many of these MPs were themselves accepting money for consultancies and some of the moral issues were similar.

I asked Lord Weatherill for his own verdict as a member of the Upper House. He was severely critical of the two MPs: 'I don't think they should stay,' he said bluntly. 'Their political careers are finished.'[29] However not everyone sees things in such black and white terms. Lord Archer felt that the practice of accepting money for questions was 'a very grey area'. I asked if the MPs should resign. 'Now this has come out in the open, it is what the constituencies will demand. They will get rid of them.' Lord Archer said that the practice was not confined to the Commons. 'I am told Members of the Lords do it as well which always surprises me, because I can't imagine what anyone thinks they are going to get from asking a junior Minister something in the House of Lords. It seems to me a complete waste of time.'[30]

Nevertheless, as we will see, the whole lobbying industry has been built on a heavily promoted idea that influence and access can be bought. This may be a myth, but society tends to inflate the image of public office, and it is widely believed that individual MPs and Peers do have some power.

But how common among MPs was the practice of asking questions for money, or of receiving payment for short-term consultancy projects which included the asking of parliamentary questions to order? Robert Key has been a Tory MP for over twelve years with recent spells in government. He feels the two MPs are an exception. 'Every time I am offered a free lunch I ask why. I was shocked by the conduct of Tredinnick and Riddick. A couple of clots! In my view the *Sunday Times* carefully targeted them – two out of 649 others who would not even have considered it, and anyway in the end they didn't even take any money. It was just a temporary error of judgement.' However he considers that being a paid consultant is acceptable: 'I do feel that money for questions is entirely different from consultancy. I never agreed to be a consultant to ask questions – only to give expertise.'[31]

Nevertheless, in practice these distinctions are hopelessly blurred. After all, what is the definition of a consultancy? Is it just that the arrangement must last more than a week? It is almost impossible to make an absolute distinction on the basis of logic. Graham Riddick seems to display some uncertainty and confusion in the tapes, as does David Tredinnick, for understandable reasons.

Simon Hughes blamed lack of guidelines. 'There are rules for the conduct of Ministers but there are no rules for the conduct of MPs. When I got elected, I discovered that in a way this was the most wonderful job in the world, because my contract was a blank sheet of paper. We needed a place where MPs could go to take advice on an impartial basis as to whether something was right or wrong.'[32]

Tony Benn sees greed at the root of it all, threatening democracy itself. 'Unless the whole philosophy of putting profit before service, and the culture of secrecy, are challenged and completely rejected in public life, the whole fabric, both of democracy and society, could be undermined. One very early statement of what is expected of us is contained in the Prayers for Parliament read by the Chaplain of the House of Commons at the beginning of each day's sitting, one of which reminds us of the moral aspects of this matter by calling upon all members to lay aside ". . . all private interests, prejudices, and partial affections . . ." '[33]

Those words could hardly be clearer, but where do you draw the line between the gift of a book by an author, a friendly lunch, tickets for the theatre, a weekend away for two, free use of a car for a year, a house in the country or an income for life?

Alistair Burt, Minister of Social Security, agrees that it can be hard to decide. 'One person may be innocent and one person may not be, because it all depends on price. I don't have a problem in being taken out to lunch by virtually anyone, because no one, I believe, can seriously think that I would alter the course of policy just because someone has taken me out to lunch.

'Now I suspect that as you go further up the scale this either retains or loses credibility at a certain stage. I believe, for instance, that if someone offers to buy you a house in the country, or gives you a few thousand a year, then the inference would be the other way. Nobody would do that for you unless they were getting something for it. Between those two extremes somewhere the line crosses, and I think that is the difficulty. There are people who earn very little in life for whom £5,000 a year is a lot of money.' He pointed out that for most people in the House of Commons it would be utter madness to risk the whole of their political career and considerable future earnings for the sake of such a sum.

'The problem is that some of the people looking at it are outside the system and don't know, but the danger for those inside (and how standards slip) is that it can be terribly easy to take for granted certain things where other people might say, "Hold on a minute. Why did you do so and so?" It forces you to think, "How would outsiders see this relationship?" That is difficult to judge. It's very, very personal.'[34]

But standards in public life are surely far too important to be left in a way which is 'difficult to judge' or 'very, very personal'. Far clearer codes of practice were needed which reflected public opinion more closely. In any event, one thing is absolutely clear to me: once payments are accepted in cash or in kind, an obligation is created that is likely to weaken independence and objectivity. Such obligations are in direct conflict with public duty, which by definition requires an even-handed approach.

All such obligations therefore are likely to one degree or another to be corrupting in nature, since the end result could be the abuse of power in favour of a few, rather than its use for the public good. While a meal in a restaurant is hardly likely to undermine the integrity of a politician, other more substantial benefits could do so, given the inherent weakness in human character.

Unfortunately, these problems are far more widespread in Westminster than isolated examples of cash for questions. Buying and selling of MPs' time has taken place on a breathtaking scale, and was the real reason behind the cash-for-questions episode. As we will see, almost every recent 'scandal' in politics has its ancestry in other less serious but generally accepted behaviour patterns. There has been no moral slide, but more a gradual step-by-step erosion of common values.

2

Buying and Selling MPs on a Large Scale

'Those who have once been intoxicated with power, and have derived any kind of emolument from it, even though for but one year, can never willingly abandon it.' Edmund Burke (1729–1797)

'Politics is supposed to be the second oldest profession. I have come to realise that it bears a very close resemblance to the first.' Ronald Reagan (1911–)

Cash for questions is shocking enough to most members of the public, but unfortunately the rot has been deeper. It was only a tiny problem on the surface of a vast, rapidly growing system of unofficial payments to MPs. In 1995, Lord Nolan found that 30 per cent of all MPs were being paid for consultancies (advice and lobbying) related to their parliamentary role.[35] These were jobs they were only qualified to do because they had seats at Westminster, a direct perk of being elected.

The only purpose of these arrangements was to buy or sell information about Westminster or to gain influence. Very few of these 200 or so MPs would have been able to obtain these

40

commercial roles unless they were or had been MPs. This was the real root of the cash-for-questions affair. Most of the MPs involved were Conservatives, and if you exclude Ministers who are not allowed to accept money, it probably means that in 1995 the majority of Conservative back-benchers were 'spoken for' by one commercial lobby or another. Many MPs had several such interests, worth some tens of thousands of pounds in some cases. Paid consultancies were often attached to large corporations, but whole businesses were set up simply to sell access to senior politicians.

The British people are utterly opposed to MPs offering time on a commercial basis for lobbying, consultancies or even retaining previous long-standing business arrangements. In 1995, it was found that a mere 3–4 per cent agreed that MPs with long-established business interests should be allowed to continue as MPs, or that MPs should be able to speak on matters where they had a financial interest.[36]

So how do lobbying organisations work? One such 'lobbying company' was set up by Ian Greer, who began in politics as the Conservative Party's youngest agent, working for Cabinet Minister Peter Walker. He remained a Conservative agent for thirteen years after which he has enjoyed close links with senior Conservative politicians. In 1969 he began lobbying as a business. Ian Greer Associates (IGA) now has a turnover of £3.5 million and employs forty-five staff.[37] His clients include British Airways, Cadbury Schweppes and Prime Minister Bhutto.[38] Today it is just one of many companies cashing in on the lobbying industry.

A sign of Ian Greer's status and acceptability is that in 1992 he held a reception at the National Gallery to celebrate ten years in the business. It was attended by the Prime Minister John Major, Norman Lamont, former Chancellor of the Exchequer, John Wakeham, former Leader of the House of Commons, and the Environment Secretary John Gummer. Ian Greer's credentials are second to none. He first knew John Major when he was just a back-bencher, has dined with him at Chequers, and has been to several parties in Downing Street. However, Ian has also developed powerful contacts within the Labour Party.[39]

He has made it clear that one or two MPs have not declared the payments he gave them. However, he said he thought accusations of sleaze were exaggerated. 'I'm not really sure much goes on. There's a lot of suggestions . . . in the media that much goes on. I'm not aware of anything.'[40]

Ian Greer has never made any secret of paying MPs but says it was never directly to ask questions. He has never employed an MP as a consultant. Payments were given as 'commissions' if an MP introduced a client to him. This is entirely lawful and permitted by Parliament. Ian Greer was the architect of new self-regulation introduced by lobbying companies in 1994 which prohibited members from acting as consultants. He has argued since 1985 for a statutory code of conduct.[41] He wrote then: 'Unless action is taken swiftly to legitimise and regularise the activities of the lobbyist at Westminster, the suspicion and mistrust which is being built up by the unskilled operators will do irreparable damage to an important part of our constitutional process.'[42]

Roy Hattersley, formerly on the Labour front bench, has been one of the strongest critics of lobbying. He felt that 'MPs for hire demean democracy. If Lord Nolan and his committee do not propose that Parliament bans lobbyists and the recruitment of MPs to lobby on behalf of private interests, they will have failed to deal with the most pressing problem of standards in public life.'[43] He described 'squalid little events in which integrity and reputations are sold for a few hundred pounds'. But he was embarrassed himself when the *Evening Standard* reminded him that he had once been paid as a consultant for two months by the US computer giant IBM while he was an MP in the early 1970s. 'Was it two months?' he asked. 'It was twenty years ago and I don't remember exactly. I gave it up very quickly as I did not approve of a number of things the company was involved in. It didn't work for me and I don't see why it should work for anyone else . . . I'm sounding very pious. I don't want to. I'm sounding like John the Baptist.'[44]

Another lobbying company to hit the headlines was Decision Makers, partly because one of the directors was no less than Dame Angela Rumbold, Vice-Chairman of the Conservative Party. On Friday 28 October 1994, at the height of media frenzy over Mohammed Al-Fayed's allegations against senior party figures, she suddenly resigned from Decision Makers.

Earlier in the week there had been a report in the *Evening Standard* alleging that Decision Makers had played a key role in the location of the Channel Tunnel Rail Link station. The decision to choose Ebbsfleet had been announced six weeks earlier.[45]

Massive commercial interests were tied up in the final decision which lay between a tiny, almost unknown place in Kent, and densely populated Stratford in East London. One of the biggest potential winners was Blue Circle cement company, which owned the land where the Ebbsfleet station might be built. The site was once Europe's largest cement works but without a new development the land was almost worthless.[46]

It was Blue Circle, rather than local community associations, that hired Decision Makers to try and persuade the government to use their land. The decision was said to be worth around one billion pounds and would lead to building 40,000 new homes as well as the station.[47]

The timing of Dame Angela's resignation was highly

significant, as she confirmed during the Nolan Committee hearings. The *Evening Standard* had obtained a leaked document allegedly written by Decision Makers for Blue Circle. Marked confidential, the contents were 'astonishing'. The editor of the *Evening Standard* told the Nolan Committee that he had been shocked 'to see the extent of the claims' about meetings with senior Ministers and even the Prime Minister himself. The question was whether the contents of the document were true.

Lord Nolan heard evidence on 18 January 1995 from Maureen Tomison, Chairman of Decision Makers, from Dame Angela Rumbold, and from Stewart Steven, editor of the *Evening Standard*. This was part of his in-depth inquiry into various legitimate parliamentary activities in the context of his later report on integrity in public life. Their evidence reveals the inside story when it comes to lobbying power, or the public perception of it. What follows is extracted from the transcripts of the hearings.

As Maureen Tomison of Decision Makers confirmed, Dame Angela Rumbold had not been engaged in directly lobbying MPs or Ministers and she had acted with the utmost probity. Her role had been to provide political and governmental experience, not to exercise influence. The Decision Makers campaign had been huge. She explained that they had first campaigned over the route of the rail link.

'During our campaign for the route, we met 360 all-party Members of Parliament, including all the relevant Ministers and Shadow Ministers, with tremendous support from John Prescott and Joan Ruddock, the Labour transport team. We also wrote to every Member of Parliament three times, and I topped and tailed to each one of them with the specific paragraph about each one.

'It was a huge job but this massive weight of informed discussion eventually succeeded in overturning government thinking. In October 1991 our route was adopted and at that stage most politicians had been convinced of the merits also of locating the intermediate station at Dartford.

'At this stage Dame Angela Rumbold was still a government Minister and therefore had not worked for Decision Makers and I had not even met Blue Circle. Blue Circle asked us as late as March 1993 to work with them to conclude our task and locate the intermediate station at Ebbsfleet on the Dartford Gravesham borders. This was for a small fee and there was no success bonus. To our minds the major part of the lobbying had already been done.'

She went on to explain: 'At the height of the media controversy about sleaze, the *Evening Standard* published a report on 24 October 1994 based on a leaked document, dated 20 May 1993, and this had been written for our client only – and bear in mind our client understood what was going on.' She said that 'totally inaccurate conclusions [had been drawn] about a certain meeting which had led to a Kafkaesque experience in which the reputation of Dame Angela and my company was threatened by a whole series of unrelated accusations'.

Diana Warwick (part of the Committee) asked: 'Did you distinguish in seeking to influence [ministerial] decisions between official meetings, unofficial meetings, hospitality and so on?'

Maureen Tomison replied: 'Yes of course. There is a huge difference between formal meetings and informal meetings. I am in the House of Commons a very large percentage of the time but I do not simply bang into a Minister and say I would like a station; that is not how it happens. I would go to a meeting with a Minister and explain the arguments about the station.

'As far as entertaining is concerned, one of the great problems is that because lobbyists do not have a registration or a real entity – they are not recognised – you actually have got a difficulty in meeting people and one of the better places to meet people is actually over lunch . . .'

'How did you actually approach Ministers to obtain those meetings? . . .'

'I phoned up the Minister's Private Office, I think in almost every instance, explained . . . what it was all about, then I would send them a note which they would show to the Minister, asking for a meeting . . .' She added later: 'Everybody knew that Dame Angela worked for us; they knew that she did not ask questions; she did not intervene in debate; she did not lobby on their behalf . . .'

'Given your experience and you may have many friends in Parliament and among Ministers, is it not a little ingenuous to say that somebody in the sort of influential position that Dame Angela was, would not be providing a considerable service? If she was doing what you yourself are capable of doing so eminently, obviously, why was she on your books?'

'Well I do not have the monopoly of wisdom . . . I have never been a Member of Parliament. I have not taken a Bill through Parliament.'

Maureen Tomison went on to explain that Dame Angela Rumbold was on her books in order to provide valuable advice and expertise.

Diana Warwick later turned the questions to the fairness of lobbying. 'One of the arguments [against lobbying] is that lobbying provides privileged access for those who can afford to pay and therefore disadvantages those who cannot. What are your views on this?'

'I do not think there is any doubt that in an ideal world everybody should have their own lobbyist.'

Lord Nolan asked whether having an MP on her board was a 'very good selling point for the organisation'.

'Well it would certainly be much more useful than if I were to say I have got a plumber or an electrician on my board.' She also added, regarding her own personal contacts as Chairman of Decision Makers: 'It is obviously important to know a Minister or Member of Parliament. What the Minister or the MP at the end of the day is concerned about is, here is this woman, I knew her at university, can I really be bothered seeing her, is she going to waste my time?'

Lord Thompson asked about the allegations in the *Evening Standard*: '. . . Allegedly on the basis of this leaked document, that there was a dinner with the Prime Minister, there was a reception at number 11 Downing Street as part of the campaign that Miss Tomison organised. What I want to know is, is that true or not, or is that a false statement by the *Evening Standard*?

'There are opportunities and there were opportunities to attend a dinner with some 400 other people at which the Prime Minister was present. My client took that opportunity but I am not sure that that client took any opportunity to discuss his particular case with the Prime Minister. . . .'

'And the reception at number 11 Downing Street?'

'There was a reception at Downing Street which we were not able to offer the client access to. The client, I believe, paid for that in the way that they would have paid for it and in the same way as we paid for the meeting in Brussels.'

Lord Thompson remarked: 'I do, I must say, draw a distinction between the public home of a Minister (as a venue for sponsored reception) and a meeting in Brussels or a hotel in London organised by any political party.' It was pointed out that Hansard contained a statement that no such reception had taken place on the night in question.

Dame Angela Rumbold told Lord Nolan's committee later that morning that she had first earned £8,000 a year from Decision Makers and that this had risen to £12,000 a year.

She was asked by Professor Anthony King if she still held the view that 'it is all right for a Member of Parliament to be paid to work for a general lobbying firm'.

'Of course I do,' Dame Angela replied.

'You do?'

'Yes, absolutely.'

'There is no problem about that at all?'

'Absolutely no problem at all, provided there is a code of conduct, provided it is clearly demonstrated to everyone who wishes to know exactly what that role entails.'

Professor King asked her about the alleged meetings she had attended as part of her role with Blue Circle or with other clients.

'You spoke of lunches and various meetings outside the House of Commons, and so on. I mean, who on these occasions would you have been seeing?'

'Well, I might have been talking to people who were clients of Maureen. I might have been talking to Maureen herself in the evening, when it was possible for both of us to meet, so we did have a number of meetings like that, both in . . .'

'Specifically not Ministers and fellow MPs?' asked Professor King.

'No. I think only on a couple of occasions did I have an evening meal with someone who happened to be a Minister at the time present.' Dame Angela pointed out that in any event as Deputy Chairman of the Conservative Party she had no access to ministerial papers or to the decision-making process in government and her party role had 'no bearing whatsoever on my role as Member of Parliament'. She had been 'seven years a Minister' but was not in office while lobbying.

Professor Anthony King made it clear that she was 'in no sense on trial. You followed the rules. . . . What we want to do, however, is see whether your experience, precisely because you've played by the rules, throws some light on what those rules should be.'

He asked later: 'Is there not a problem about public perception, and although everything you say [about the adequacy of current rules] may well be true, is there not a problem that people may find it odd that somebody should be paid to be a Member of Parliament, should be a senior figure in a political party, yet, at the same time, working for an organisation whose express and stated function is to lobby the institution of which he or she is a member?'

Dame Angela replied that the 'mystery that surrounds this particular area' was something she hoped the Committee would sort out.

Lord Nolan took her back to her resignation from Decision Makers. 'You resigned because you had been put in an impossible position, you felt, and had become, in effect, an embarrassment to the company, quite unjustly because you were behaving perfectly, but because there was an apparent conflict of interest in the eyes of the public. Is that right?'

'I felt . . . that it was extremely important from the company's point of view not to have further embarrassment . . .'

Dame Angela's evidence was then followed by that of Stewart Steven from the *Evening Standard*, whose article had precipitated her resignation. He gave a copy of the leaked document to the Committee and began reading from it.

'On page three: "Ministerial Meetings, No 10 Downing Street" is the portentous heading. "The Prime Minister had already been brief (sic) on the proposed East Thames Corridor Project in an informal and private presentation by the campaign team." Then it says: "The Prime Minister showed a keen interest in the project and would like more information." I found that incredible.

'As a matter of fact I have to say that the following day we approached No 10 Downing Street for an on-the-record statement, which they were not prepared to give us before publication. It wasn't clear if the meeting had happened, but the Prime Minister was aware of the lobbying: he was aware of the issue. Quite what had gone on between the Prime Minister and the lobbying firm I think is a bit murky. All I can say is that here it specifically states that he had been briefed by this lobbying team at No 10 Downing Street and that he had shown a keen interest.

'The document is remarkable. It is remarkable because it seems to suggest – of course we are dealing here with a PR company so one has to remember there are obviously elements of hype which could be involved as well – that indeed they are deep into the government of this country so that when they say in this document, as they do on page three, "The following lists details of the key meetings and briefings of senior Ministers and officials" there is indeed a long list. Later it goes on to say that Dame Angela as Deputy Chairman of the Party has been able to keep the Party fully appraised of Blue Circle's plans of the East Thames Corridor. She told you today that, of course, she did not involve herself with the constituency. It also says here: "Dame Angela has recently visited the project site and met local authority leaders." It then goes on to say that, timetable, there was a dinner with the Parliamentary Labour Party: "28 May. A dinner with the Prime Minister." It does not mention here that 400 other people were allowed to be present too. "18 June. Evening for the Ministers at Hampton Court. 28 June. Reception at No 11 Downing Street." If there is any hype at all I do wish to emphasise that that hype is not *Evening Standard* hype, it is the hype by Decision Makers.'[48]

Lord Thompson asked what conclusions he had drawn at the end of the investigation.

'We drew two conclusions from it. First of all we did feel that, when MPs get involved in this sort of thing, at the very least their activities are likely to be misrepresented. It is possible, I suppose, that the people who have the greatest reason to complain about the activities of Decision Makers is Blue Circle who received the document called "The Campaign Update" which may be a load of "tosh". Maybe these meetings did not take place at all. Maybe this influence which Decision Makers tell the directors of Blue Circle they have, they do not have at all. That of course we do not know. . . . There is a subsidiary issue, which is whether we are sure that the government service is sufficiently immune to the activities of lobbyists or not.'

And later he added: 'The facts in this case are the document. This is a document, 20 May 1993, headed "Strictly Private and Confidential, Update on activities carried out by Decision Makers on behalf of Blue Circle Properties Ltd". Once we had proved that this was a genuine document, that it was not a forgery . . . it seems to me that it would have been intolerable not to have printed it . . . In retrospect, looking at the document and hearing Maureen Tomison say at this table today, "When this document says that we arranged a meeting with the Prime Minister, actually 400 people were present and we are not even sure whether our lobbyist actually managed to address the Prime Minister," all I can say is that didn't appear from the document.'

So what are we to make of all this? It is clear from Maureen Tomison's comments that she is utterly convinced that lobbying can succeed in 'overturning government thinking', indeed that Decision Makers had been able to do just that, providing no doubt an excellent return on the money spent on lobbying by Blue Circle.

Many senior politicians have told me that people are fools

to think that lobbying plays a real part in altering ministerial decisions. They say that the effect is very marginal, if it exists at all. Indeed I have even heard that argument used by people involved in lobbying, particularly when they have been criticised for attempting to pervert the democratic process.

However, you can't have it both ways. Either aggressive commercial lobbying is a real threat to impartial decisions, with the most well-funded lobby able to 'buy' influence and the hope of a favourable decision, or the whole lobbying industry is a con-trick designed to deceive, selling non-existent power. The very name 'Decision Makers' seems to me to imply what the company is trying to sell: a decision made or altered as a direct result of their action. The truth about the degree of actual influence may lie somewhere between the two extremes above, depending on the issue, the Minister, the civil servants involved, and the quality of government contacts.

Nevertheless, Blue Circle may have been delighted to know that the Vice-Chairman of the Conservative Party was herself going to become personally involved as a result of their payments, providing them with expert support and advice. Decision Makers certainly delivered an effective campaign, if their own briefing document is to be believed. Members of the company and representatives of Dartford and Gravesham Borough Councils had personal meetings with a series of government Ministers, including John MacGregor who was then Secretary of State for Transport, and even with the Prime Minister.[49] These meetings were said to have happened informally over lunch, dinner, or at social events such as an evening with Ministers at Hampton Court.[50]

This was a powerful operation with the highest possible access. Ministers are extremely busy people. Formal meetings can be very hard to arrange, and informal contacts are therefore of greater importance to those buying services from lobbying companies.

My view is that Dame Angela's involvement was fraught with danger from the start and liable to public misunderstanding, particularly in the current climate, following months of sleaze allegations against senior politicians.

She kept to the rules and her involvement with Decision Makers was entirely legitimate, but one could argue that in the light of possible public reaction, her involvement in such a high-profile campaign was unwise.

Ronald Dworkin, Professor of Jurisprudence at Oxford University said recently: 'A conflict of interest is a *situation*, not a particular piece of wrong-doing. The difference is very important, because avoiding conflicts of interest means avoiding relationships and connections that might raise questions of improper motives.'[51]

Sir George Young plays down the significance of lobbying. I asked him in that case whether MPs involved in lobbying were deliberately misrepresenting the access they had for commercial gain. Sir George pondered for a moment. 'When a Minister is confronted by an MP who is arguing something, if he knows he's paid to say it, it is just discounted. If the guy comes along and says something because he believes in it, he knows about it or it touches his constituency, you sit up and listen.'[52]

My own experience in the voluntary sector is that most MPs are delighted to help, advise or support any cause that they believe in, as part of their public service. On many occasions I have found their help invaluable, particularly in drawing the attention of a Minister to important issues. Lobbying is thus an essential part of any healthy democracy, and is clearly most effective when a case is presented passionately, with deep conviction, by an MP acting out of a sense of public duty, rather than as a job for a fee.

The controversy arises only over paid lobbying arrangements where one suspects an MP is doing more in support and advice than he or she would if no money were involved. Some MPs vigorously deny that they behave in this way. They say that they only do for a consultancy what they would have done anyway even if unpaid. But if that is the case, why do firms waste all this money paying them retainers?

David Alton is in no doubt that lobbying can alter voting in Parliament and gives the new Sunday Trading laws as an example. (The year) '1994 saw the greatest victory yet of vested interests in Parliament. I think that individual Members of Parliament and political parties were bought lock, stock and barrel by the powerful Sunday Trading lobbies. The succession of dinners; champagne receptions at political conferences; contacting constituency parties; hiring of surplus party political figures at the end of the last election; the direct financing of funds of political parties, [all] created an umbilical link between their interests and those of politicians in this place. They bought Parliament.'

I asked him how much he thought the Sunday Trading lobby had spent. 'Probably tens of millions over the years. Huge sums of money have been poured into the coffers of political parties. By comparison, those who fought against that were like a bow and arrow against an armada with nuclear weapons.'

Of course MPs change their minds for many reasons, and it would be wrong to conclude that just because such a change has taken place after intensive lobbying, that the lobbying necessarily had anything to do with it. In any case it is no shame to change your mind after being presented with another view. However it is sobering to reflect that the sole purpose of both the pro- and the anti-Sunday Trading lobbies was to do precisely that: change the way MPs voted. If there was no effect then presumably every penny of the millions spent was entirely wasted.

So, accepting money to assist companies is a widespread practice among MPs, established over years and deeply rooted in the psyche of the House of Commons. The practice has been fully sanctioned by Parliament, the only restriction being that such paid consultancies have had to be publicly disclosed by the MPs concerned in the Register of Members' Interests. This explains the bizarre and nauseating displays of righteous indignation by MPs when Lord Nolan's inquiry suggested that such behaviour should cease. Many MPs argued in reply that there is a huge difference between offering professional advice on a commercial basis to help people understand how Parliament works, or to interpret political trends, and advising on particular legislation, campaigning on amendments and otherwise assisting in a representational role – including asking questions.

However, as we have seen, on the strictest definition it could be said that all commercial arrangements which affect actions taken or not taken by MPs are merely forms of bribery. In Canada, Article 119 of the Criminal Code states: '[One who] corruptly accepts or obtains, agrees to accept, or attempts to obtain any money, valuable consideration, office, place or employment for himself or another person in respect of anything done or omitted, or to be done or omitted by him in his official capacity is guilty of an indictable offence and liable to imprisonment for a term not exceeding 14 years.'[53] Should such a general principle not be applied to MPs at Westminster?

After the Poulson scandals, the Commission headed by Lord Salmon recommended that 'Parliament should consider bringing corruption, bribery and attempted bribery of Parliament within the ambit of Criminal Law'. In 1976, James Callaghan, then Prime Minister and now a Peer, agreed that 'a Member who accepts a bribe in return for some action which is proceeding in Parliament cannot be the subject of criminal proceedings'. Although Mr Justice Buckley cast some doubt on this in 1992 when dealing with false allegations against Harry Greenway, all legal opinion concurs that this matter is uncertain, to say the least.

Interests in making money

In the 1970s and 1980s so many MPs were being paid by so many different businesses that undue financial influence seemed inevitable. As a result a Register was set up, which was supposed to be a full list of all financial links which might compromise an MP's impartiality. The Register is maintained by a small team on the first floor of Westminster, overseen by a Registrar, and it has always been incomplete.

MPs are required to declare nine types of interest: for example directorships of companies, remunerated employments, trades, professions and vocations, financial sponsorships, and the names of clients when they are making representations to Ministers or civil servants.

Every MP is sent a form to complete after a new election, and thereafter a reminder is sent every year with a fresh form to register changes. The Register was a big step forward but it does not tell the whole story. There are often delays, deliberate omissions and accidental oversights in registration.

Until 1996 the Register did not say if an interest was worth £500 a year or £500,000, which made it very difficult to interpret the significance of an entry. There was great resistance from Conservatives to list the amounts because it was seen as an embarrassing 'invasion of privacy'. Perhaps they would have changed their minds earlier if they had thought that large sums of money were finding their way into the back pockets of Labour MPs from trade unions. There is also no requirement to register directorships where there is no payment at present – an important gap as we will see.

Simon Hughes has always wanted far more information to be disclosed.[54] 'I think you should require that everyone standing for election states whether they have had any other interests, expressly how much they were paid for them, and what their commitments were. The Register should show the money received, not just the jobs done.' He felt that unpaid positions should also be listed, 'because every other claim on your loyalty ought to be something your electorate know about'.

I asked Lord Ennals what he thought about MPs' disclosure and whether the Lords should have to do the same. Lord Ennals represented Labour in Parliament for almost three decades, half of which was in the Commons with many posts in government.[55] 'I think the amount ought to be given absolutely. Far more information needs to be known.' But what about copies of contracts being made available for inspection, or even tax returns? 'Never thought of it. I'm more inclined to say "yes". I think if they are going to elect a Member of Parliament, they should know what he is. How much time is he going to give to it if he is a member of ten companies?'

'And the Lords?' I asked.

'I would have no objection to it. Not nearly so important because none of us is paid apart from our expense allowance. Therefore it is expected that people will have outside interests. The second reason is that we have no constituents.'

There is plenty of evidence that commercial lobbying has infiltrated the House of Lords too. A Channel Four *Dispatches* programme in November 1995 claimed that unnamed Peers were accepting up to £2,000 a time to host receptions for companies in the House of Lords rooms, which are available to Peers free of charge.

Lord Ennals is however against a professional class of full-time politicians, who do no other work. 'I'm not saying there are no circumstances in which people should have no other work. There is something I would find disappointing about a House of Commons where they were all professionals. There are too many of them as it is. I think it ought to be a group of people, men and women, broadly representative of people. And it's a good thing to have a farmer, doctors and nurses.'[56]

Ken Livingstone would take disclosure as far as tax returns. 'I think everything should be revealed down to the last penny, including contracts. I'm happy to have my tax returns published. They tend to be much more revealing. First time I stood for Parliament I challenged the other candidates to all open our bank accounts.'[57]

One big gap in the Register's usefulness is the omission of unpaid directorships. These are relevant. Clearly unpaid directorships may also involve some sense of obligation or there would be no point in being a director. A sense of obligation is by definition capable of creating a conflict of interest.

Paul Halloran and Mark Hollingsworth made a comprehensive study of the lists of directors of different companies at Companies House and compared them with the lists registered by MPs.[58] They found a large number of directorships had not been registered in the House of Commons, presumably because every single one of them was completely unremunerated and therefore there was no requirement whatsoever to register them at Westminster.

There is one exception to this: it is perfectly in order for MPs to register the directorship of a holding company as a remunerated position, without having to register the names of all the subsidiary companies. However this is another important and confusing gap. The purpose of a Register of Members' Interests is to ensure that everyone is aware of areas of potential conflict of interest. The name of a holding company may not indicate very well that – say – a subsidiary company is involved in arms manufacture or television production.

I have found two examples recently where non-registered directorships (presumably unpaid) have been later registered as paid directorships. This is important and hardly surprising. Take the example of a new company which cannot afford to pay its founding directors for the first year or two. After profits start to grow, income begins to flow.

In such a case one could argue strongly that there was a strong commercial interest in the company from the start, even if no payments were made in early years, and there is no requirement to register. The answer is simple: MPs should indicate all directorships, whether of holding companies or subsidiaries, remunerated or not. An increasing number of MPs are already beginning to do this on a voluntary basis, presumably because they recognise that the public want to know, and should know.

In conclusion, we have seen that almost a third of all MPs are being paid by commercial interests to advise or represent them at Westminster, and that it is not unknown for straight offers of cash to motivate an MP into selective action. However, as we will see when we look at party funding, perhaps another third or more are also vulnerable to union 'string pulling' through individual sponsorship arrangements. Therefore the truth is that by the end of 1995, most MPs were being paid or sponsored by organisations with an interest in what their MPs were doing politically, in arrangements frowned on by the majority of the electorate. This is part of the culture of Westminster. In addition some hundred Peers may be involved in similar activity.

On 6 November 1995 history was made when MPs voted

decisively to change their ways, with a ban on all commercial lobbying arrangements from 31 March 1996.

The Register of Members' Interests published on 31 March 1996 was the first under the new rules for disclosure of amounts earned from parliamentary consultancies and other categories of income. The list runs to no fewer than 148 pages of A4 in small print, and lists relevant earnings in various bands. In the text below, 'received £xx–£yy' means that this is the band in which the exact amount lies.

Examples of items declared are as follows.[59]

Doug Henderson received £15,001–£20,000 from the Joseph Rowntree Reform Trust Ltd for 'research support' as well as more than 25% of his election expenses at the 1992 General Election from GMB Union. He also received £5,001–£10,000 as Consultant to Machine Tool Technologies Association.

Another example is John Greenaway, who received money as Parliamentary Advisor to the Institute of Insurance Brokers (£10,001–£15,000), to Yorkshire Tyne Tees Television plc (£10,001–£15,000) and to General Healthcare Ltd (£5,001–£10,000).

Quentin Davies received £20,001–£25,000 as advisor to NatWest Securities and £10,001–£15,000 as Parliamentary Consultant to the Chartered Institute of Taxation. Nigel Forman received £20,001–£25,000 as Political Consultant to Saloman Brothers International Ltd (investment bankers). John Butterfill received £10,001–£15,000 as Parliamentary Advisor to British Insurance and Investment Brokers Association (BIIBA) and £10,001–£15,000 as Parliamentary Advisor to British Venture Capital Association (BVCA). Jack Aspinwall received for Parliamentary and Public Affairs Consultancy £15,001–£20,000 from BAA plc, £5,001–£10,000 from British Gas plc and £5,001–£10,000 from Rentokil plc.

One difficulty is deciding what is and is not related to a parliamentary role. Some MPs have taken the view that many of their sources of outside earnings are entirely unrelated to their parliamentary role, and so have not declared the amounts. In practice it must be hard to determine whether one has obtained a consultancy purely on the basis of non-parliamentary expertise. Nevertheless, the new rules on disclosure have brought far greater openness, with many MPs declaring more detail than is required.

We now need to turn to the question of pay and allowances. What is the truth about MPs' pay? Are MPs being paid too much anyway (particularly in the light of other earnings), the right amount, or scandalously little? Are the rumours true that some MPs fiddle their expenses? And what is the truth about allowance claims by Peers?

3

MP Fiddles and Some Reluctant Lords

'My MP would simply tell me to claim to the maximum limit, and so I would make up the trips. It was total fiction.' MP's secretary, 1995

'A proportion of those who attend [the Lords and claim expenses] every day play little or no part in our proceedings.' Member of the House of Lords, 1995

We have looked at some of the ways that many MPs have earned 'a bit on the side' by exploiting the fact that they are at Westminster, and how this laid them open to accusations of impropriety, but have they needed to do so because their basic pay was too low? Many people have suggested that MPs should be paid twice as much, and in return agree to forego any outside earnings.

The most Draconian suggestions include an absolute ban on any extra earnings, while allowing MPs to continue whatever links they wish on an informal and voluntary basis, as part of their public service. However, others have said that in that case, the highest-calibre leaders in society would be unwilling to make the necessary financial sacrifices to enter politics, and Westminster would be emptied of successful achievers.

The history of MPs' pay

Payment of MPs has been very low until quite recently. In 1322 the Shires and Boroughs paid their knight representatives four shillings a day and citizens two shillings a day, throughout Parliament.[60] Local rates had tended to vary – from two Aldermen representing the City of London, who were paid ten shillings a day in 1296, to 500 mackerel paid in 1463 by the Borough of Weymouth to its own representative.[61]

Direct sponsorship of MPs by their own electors had ceased by the end of the seventeenth century. Their finances improved in the eighteenth and nineteenth centuries: being an MP became a quick way to get rich from 'sinecure offices' and pensions. Many MPs paid large amounts for a seat at Westminster, or sought a patron who had a few seats to give away.

In 1911 Lloyd George campaigned for a regular salary for all MPs, and called the existing system 'indirect, surreptitious and corrupt'.[62] However he seemed to have few scruples about selling peerages as we have seen.

Salaried MPs had been suggested in 1780, 1830, 1838, 1870, 1888, 1892, 1893, 1895 and 1903 but MPs remained unpaid until 1911 when they were granted an allowance of £400 a year from public funds. This change came just two years after the trade union support of MPs had been declared illegal. Lloyd George declared that it was 'not a remuneration, it is not a recompense, it is not even a salary. It is just an allowance, and I think the minimum allowance, to enable men to come here, men who would render incalculable service to the State . . . but who cannot be here because their means do not allow it.'[63]

The £400 was increased at irregular intervals until 1970,[64] when William Whitelaw, then Leader of the House, announced an independent review body. There have been attempts to link MPs' pay with other groups, most notably senior civil servants.[65] In 1975, MPs' pay was £5,750, and £14,510 in 1982, about equivalent to a junior doctor one year after qualifying. Annual increases lifted this to £34,085 by 1996, somewhat less than a junior hospital consultant.[66] In July 1996 huge increases were approved by Parliament; but what was the situation up until that controversial vote?

MPs received a number of benefits in addition to salary: free inland telephone calls from the House; use of rooms for secretary and administration; free postage; free copies of Hansard and certain other official publications. They also received very generous mileage rates – for example 72.2p a mile for the first 20,000 miles using a car with an engine larger than 2.3 litres. After 20,000 miles the rate was still good – at 36.1p.[67] Such generous rates were clearly subject to tax. No journey details were required except where claims exceeded 20,000 miles a year. In addition they had travel warrants for rail, sea or air tickets between home, constituency or Westminster. Fifteen free return tickets were also available for spouses and children under eighteen.

They had an office costs allowance of £42,754 a year which was supposed to cover secretarial assistance, general office expenses and researchers. Some spend far more than this. For example Simon Hughes told me that he used up to £16,000 of his own personal income to pay for additional staff and equipment.[68] However, others spent far less, transferring the rest into their own family account by paying wives or other relatives as staff members.[69] Of course, many relatives provide valuable service, but since there were no standard rates, an MP could choose to pay more to a relative than they would to someone else doing the same work, or to pay a spouse for no work at all.

Those MPs with Inner London constituencies could claim a supplement of £1,289,[70] while those outside London claimed up to £11,268 (April 1995) for the costs of staying overnight when away from home on parliamentary business. There was also a 'winding up' allowance of £14,251 for someone ceasing to be an MP, to cover secretarial and other costs in closing down the office, and a 'resettlement' grant which varies between half to a full year's salary depending on the length of service.[71]

Clearly the value of the total remuneration package varied, but let us take the example of an MP 200 miles from London, with a 2.4 litre car and a second home totally paid for by the job on June 1996 rates.

Annual allowance:		£34,085
Mileage of 15,000 a year @ 72p per mile:		£10,800
Overnight allowances:		£11,661
Total revenue:	approximately	£56,500
Less costs:		
London flat:	£11,661	
Car costs:	£5,000	
Total costs:	approximately	£16,500
Net disposable income (before tax):		£40,000

Obviously the cost of a London flat will vary according to size and location, while those who have been MPs for years may have small or non-existent second mortgages, and large capital gains from a second property in London when they leave Parliament.

We can argue about whether the package was really worth £34,085 or more than £40,000 but either way the income was low considering the almost complete disruption of 'normal' family life, the lack of job security in many cases, and six-figure earnings in the private sector or many of the professions.

John Butcher thinks that low pay has damaged Parliament: 'No middle manager earning £40,000 with good prospects would want to be an MP under current arrangements . . . It's ridiculous that junior Ministers end up commanding civil servants who earn more than their bosses.'[72]

Government Minister Alistair Burt was sympathetic to the idea of a higher salary but with deductions on a sliding scale, taking into account outside earnings directly related to an MP's role. 'Then no one will be able to say an MP is being bought. At the moment that's a danger.' He felt it was a different matter if someone was carrying on with an established vocation. 'You shouldn't come into it for the money but money shouldn't be a problem if you want to do the job.'[73]

This, then, was the background for a momentous decision, taken by MPs on 10 July 1996, to award themselves a 26 per cent pay rise, based on the figure recommended by the Senior Salaries Review Body the previous month. The Commons approved this by 279 votes to 154. Basic MP pay rose by £9,000 to £43,000, while Ministers were awarded a total increase of £17,000, taking their pay from £69,651 to £86,991 immediately, with a further rise to £103,000 promised after the next election. The Prime Minister's salary increased from £84,217 to £101,557 immediately, with a further rise to £143,000 after the election. The opposition leader's salary increased from £65,992 to £83,332, rising to £98,000 after the election.

The leaders of all three main parties had urged restraint, and it was unclear whether they would accept the increases. Most Labour MPs ignored the plea, with twelve out of eighteen of the shadow cabinet voting in favour of the rises. Most of the influential members of the Conservative 1922 Committee also voted in favour. As part of the package, excessive rates for car expenses were abolished, with the top level of 74.1p per mile being reduced to 47.2p.

While a strong case could be made that MPs deserved a pay rise substantially higher than inflation. I would suggest that it might have been achieved in a more sensitive and creative way, perhaps by relating to the amount of time in the House, age, experience and responsibility. We will look at this further in a later chapter outlining proposals for reform.

How MPs fiddle their expenses

The audit of MPs' expenses is sloppy and open to fraud, and some are taking advantage of this. The amounts involved can be large, with over-claiming of mileage at very generous rates, or lying about the size of a car engine, or claiming for a rail ticket as well as car travel for the same journeys, or inventing taxi journeys (receipts are not required), or paying wives for work not done. Lord Nolan described 'fiddling of expenses' as 'a crime, whether it is done by a Member of Parliament or anybody else', so how widespread is it?

At least six cases of suspected abuse are uncovered every year by the Commons Fees Office, of which an average of two are referred to the Whips' Office for action. However, no MP has ever been publicly disciplined and these may only be a tiny fraction of the true number. It is disturbing that such matters are always kept secret even if discovered, despite the fact that if the truth were known; such MPs would face banner headlines, national disgrace and political oblivion.[74]

In November 1995, it was reported that the Inland Revenue had uncovered twenty cases in the previous year where MPs had fiddled their tax returns, by not declaring they had received a company car when claiming car expenses against generous mileage allowances.

One Labour MP said, 'The rules are so lax it is difficult not to abuse them. In fact I am the only Labour MP I know who actually does the mileage.' Two MPs and three current or former Commons secretaries have alleged that they know three other MPs who have been claiming for bogus journeys. One secretary confessed: 'My MP would simply tell me to claim to the maximum limit, and so I would make up the trips. It was total fiction.' But such fiction was worth up to £1,300 every month in claims. A Labour MP said he knew a colleague who was travelling to London by rail while pretending to do a return trip by car during the week.[75]

Another secretary described one year how her MP had diverted the entire surplus on his £40,380 office allowances to his wife, even though she did no work. The amount was considerable, since the only actual costs were £20,000 for staff and some extras for stationery and other office costs – say £15,000 'profit'.[76]

Do Peers also work the expenses system?

I spoke to a prominent Conservative Peer who was deeply troubled but extremely anxious not to be identified. He described to me how some six weeks previously, a Commons researcher had come to him in great distress. While he was researching an unrelated matter it had come to his attention that ten well-known members of the House of Lords had apparently been claiming daily attendance fees worth thousands of pounds for periods when they were not at the House. The researcher had been shocked because of the seniority of some of the people concerned and the high regard in which they were held.

The Peer added: 'We could be talking about people claiming up to £100,000 over ten years – that makes £1,000 cash for asking questions look like peanuts.' One of the named individuals was a well-known Conservative. My own investigations show no evidence of fraudulent attendance claims, although, as we will see, it is possible that a minority may be clocking up high attendance claims quite legitimately with brief appearances on a large number of days.

Not long after I met this Peer, on 18 April 1995 the *Daily Telegraph* ran a whole page feature on the dramatic growth in expense claims by Lords – up by 20 per cent in real terms from £4.01 million in 1988–9 to £6.27 million in 1993–4. The chief reason for the rise was the increase in attendance which had climbed from 316 to 378 as an average daily rate. But where are they all? If you go into the Chamber at most points in the debating day, you will be lucky to find more than a tenth of that number, although some Peers will be in committees.

Every day that a Peer enters the Chamber is a day when allowances can be claimed. Taking part in a committee counts as well. The rates are as follows: day subsistence of £32, overnight subsistence of £71.50 (which is supposed to cover things like a second home in London), and £31 for secretarial support. In addition travel is paid – first-class rail if available, 44.4p a mile for the first 20,000 miles of private car use, and then 20.4p a mile. Peers are also allowed free telephone calls.

In 1993–4, more than forty Peers claimed in excess of £20,000 each, and a total of 201 Peers claimed more than £13,000, compared to half that number the previous year when there were fewer sitting days. This is a remarkable difference.

Lord McIntosh of Haringey, Opposition Deputy Speaker, said that some come 'because they need the money. There are maybe half a dozen Labour Peers and presumably a lot more in other parties who come in to the Chamber for a short time, and rarely speak or vote. I can think of one former Minister who's never seen here after 3.30pm.' Another prominent Peer told me: 'I am distressed by those Lords who collect their money every day and don't do anything. I know myself who doesn't go – and I'm there (almost) every day.'[77] On the other side of the equation, of the 861 Peers who turned up in 1993–4, 110 claimed no expenses at all.

The problem is how to measure in an objective way what individual Peers do. Leaving aside for a moment the important work of Select Committee members and Law Lords, there are two basic functions carried out in the Chamber itself: making speeches and voting.

It is particularly revealing to look at the number of speeches made by the Peers who attend most often. Of the 118 Peers who attended at least 90 per cent of sitting days, eight Conservatives, one Liberal Democrat and two cross-benchers (independents) did not utter a word. However one Minister commented: 'It seems bogus to say that a Peer should speak for the sake of it. Some are back-room figures. Anyway the Lords would be an absolute nightmare if everyone spoke every year.'

Lady Young, Chairman of the Association of Conservative Peers, said that the idea that 'lots of Peers are getting enormous sums of money for doing nothing' was ridiculous. 'Those who take the House seriously just about cover their expenses.'[78] And that of course is the paradox. While one may ask whether some Peers are justifying the daily cost of their attendance, the expenses are hardly adequate for a Peer with few other sources of income, who wishes to play an active part. It may be fine for a retired person, but not for someone younger who is choosing to give up other remunerated work to attend.

However, there are other less obvious advantages to being a Peer. Lord Layton said: 'Let's be honest about it. Most people come up to London to do other things as well as attend the Lords.' The forty-seven-year-old hereditary Peer is a financier based in West Sussex. 'I make a few phone calls, use the fax machine and it's a great place for contacts. I haven't spoken much but I make my views felt elsewhere, in the

Bishops' Bar. I'm not very happy about getting up and speaking in public.' One Peer did not utter a single word in the House during two parliamentary sessions in 1994–5 yet attended on 127 days.[79]

Peers have to put in an appearance to qualify, or sit on a House of Lords committee. Their attendance is ticked off on a list and, according to the Accounts Office, is verified later against expense forms.[80] However, no receipts are required from those making claims. So, for example, there is every opportunity for a Peer to pocket every penny of the secretarial fees including money for postage, office equipment, books and periodicals, or to put in for the full £71.50 for overnight accommodation even if staying with friends.

Few people know more about Westminster than Lord Whitelaw, in many ways the 'Father of the House'. Lord President of the Council, Leader of the House of Commons, then Leader of the House of Lords, he has a view of Parliament which is unique. I went to see him in his office at the House of Lords where he is surrounded by warm memories of his forty years in public life. He welcomed me with great courtesy, slouched back into the seat at his large desk and pondered the past with affection.

As part of our discussions I asked him whether he thought the criticisms were unfair.[81] 'In a small way [it is] justified,' he replied. 'Lords put in a claim form but it is checked. The one that is most checkable is the messengers. If you get the money you have to attend in a session. It doesn't say you have to stay for a period in time. It is totally free will to take part; you can't be made to take part.'

I asked if he felt the system was being abused.

'You can argue that someone who never voted and never spoke – well, you could argue even then that he took an interest, he wouldn't come into the place otherwise and that he therefore is then discussing with his friends what is going on and trying to influence things. That is at its extreme, and I think the numbers would be very small. I think it is probably a perfectly sensible way of doing it and it is very carefully watched.'[82]

It must be remembered that not only do some Peers claim none of the expenses to which they are entitled, but a further one in three claimed less than he or she is due. For example, one former Prime Minister claims nothing at all, while James Callaghan always claims less than the going rate. (The majority of non-claimers are hereditary Peers who attend only occasionally, and who combine coming to the Lords to vote with other reasons to travel to London.)

However, around eight out of ten Peers do claim for every-thing they are entitled to, and often for more than the total of £134.50 of basic allowances per day because of their costs of travel. This is perfectly reasonable. After all, as we have seen, the allowances are hardly generous for a working Peer with few other sources of remuneration. The issue though is whether the system is fair to those who work the hardest.

The average daily claim per Peer can be worked out as follows: the total bill in 1993–4 was £6.27 million which, divided by the total number of days that Peers attended, gives an average figure of £122 per Peer per day (142 days).

Infrequent voters

Lord Whitelaw's comments about voting patterns prompted me to look at this further. It is interesting to see who 'crawls out of the woodwork' when the division bells ring, announcing that a vote is taking place.

These bells ring throughout the Westminster precincts, giving six minutes for Peers to find their way into the voting Lobbies from wherever they are. Divisions can happen in the Lords several times a day from the early afternoon until late evening. On some days the House sits without voting at all, while on others there may be a string of votes on minor amendments at relatively short intervals. Although there is usually advance warning that a vote will take place, the exact timing may be uncertain since it depends on how many people wish to speak in a debate and for how long.

Voting is only part of a Peer's total contribution to the life of Westminster, but you could argue that in a democracy there is nothing more important than casting a vote, and that someone who attends the House regularly as a Peer but *never* votes may perhaps be neglecting a primary duty. Some Peers may dislike making speeches, but all can pass through a voting Lobby, assuming of course that they are actually at Westminster rather than having left after being ticked off on an attendance list.

The differences in voting patterns are quite startling between Peers who attend on a similar number of days and raise questions, although many low voting 'scores' can be explained by meetings elsewhere in the House, or by ministerial business or other public duties as Peers.

I have heard the view expressed that voting 'is a waste of time' in the Lords. But if that is the case, then perhaps making speeches in the Chamber is also a waste of time, and much of the role of Peers is reduced to irrelevancy. What is the point in being in Westminster, expressing a strongly held view in the Chamber and then walking out as if the final result did not matter at all? Of course there may be some motions that seem less important, or where majorities are so huge that an extra vote seems irrelevant, but voting is surely central to parliamentary life – or should be.

I decided to look at the most recent parliamentary year for which complete attendance and voting records were available, which was 1993–4 (ending in October 1994). Over the twelve-month period, the House of Lords sat for 142 days and voted 135 times. The first step was to obtain official attendance records for every Peer. This in itself makes interesting reading. However, there are no cumulative voting records to compare against this list.

The House of Lords Information Office was able to supply a complete list of all divisions. The next step was to find all the dates in Hansard transcripts of the year's proceedings (the length of an encyclopedia) and to begin analysing a total of 25,862 individual votes by over 870 Peers. A detailed picture then emerged of how many times each Peer voted, in proportion to the number of days they attended. The first thing to note is that the average number of votes is 191, while the average attendance is twice this number. The key is not the actual number of votes cast, but the frequency as a proportion of the number of days each Peer is said to have been 'in the House'.

Analysis of 135 divisions with 25,862 individual votes

Voting frequency (averages) per number of days registered as present in the House of Lords.

Number of Peers voting once or more per day they attend	48
Number of Peers voting at least once every 3 days	567
Number of Peers voting only once every 10 days or less	68
Number of Peers voting only once every 20 days or less	18
Number of Peers voting only once every 30 days or less	8
Number of Peers voting only once every 50 days or less	4

As we have seen, some Peers do have heavy duties within the House or within government and may find it hard to get into the Chamber to vote, but all are allowed to do so, including the Lord Chancellor, or whoever as Deputy Speaker stands in his place.[83] Some Peers are very frequent voters. For example, Viscount Gochen attended 139 times and voted in 129 out of 135 possible divisions. Lord Graham of Edmonton attended every day (142 times) and cast 129 votes – a remarkable achievement since he was also a part of six different Select Committees.

As each vote was analysed, it became clear that some Peers choose to come in especially on days when there are going to be a number of important votes. They finish with totals of more than one vote per day. Take Lord Jeffreys, for example, who turned up on only 15 days but managed to vote 37 times; or Baroness Cumberledge who attended 111 times and voted in 117 divisions; or Baroness Chalker who attended 88 times and voted 94 times, or Lord Chesham who clocked up 62 votes in 50 days. In contrast, some other Lords vote very infrequently.

Jobs for former Ministers

Any discussion of pay, allowances or expenses would be incomplete without turning to the vexed issue of ministerial pay, and jobs in the private sector after a time in office. As we have already seen, government Ministers have to give up all other earnings. Prior to July 1996 a Parliamentary Under-Secretary could receive as little as £14,000 extra for all the added effort and responsibility after taking the reduction in MPs' salary into account. In practice, an MP's income can still actually fall as he or she is promoted, despite the recent increase in ministerial pay.

The weight of ministerial office falls unequally on a few, yet all cabinet Ministers receive the same, apart from the Prime Minister. For example, Ministers serving Northern Ireland have been plunged into a security nightmare from the moment of appointment, continuing for years after ending their time in office. They and their families have been seen as prime terrorist targets, needing round-the-clock protection. This has posed terrible strains on personal privacy, on marriages and on children.[84] Yet there has not been any additional income to compensate for these intrusions, which continued during the cease-fire period, albeit to a lesser extent.

There can be a benefit to Ministers on resignation or after being sacked. You could be set up for life afterwards. A survey published by Labour Research found that former Cabinet Ministers who served under Margaret Thatcher and John Major held a total of 125 directorships and 30 consultancies. Out of 40 ex-Cabinet Ministers still alive, 31 had jobs in business.[85]

Several former Ministers had far larger incomes in the private sector than when they were in government. Yet this is by no means a universal picture. Many former Ministers return to the back benches with no extra means of support other than as an MP with other associated income.

Lord Ennals was particularly disgusted with the way Ministers have gone from government into companies they dealt with in government. 'The most awful type of example is those who have been involved in privatising while in government. Before you know where you are, they are getting sums of money out of being on the boards of the industries they have privatised.' Surely it is legitimate for the public to be concerned at any area of policy making where it is possible that a Minister might benefit in the future from decisions he or she makes today? It is a fact that if these industries had not been privatised, certain job opportunities might not have been realised for former Ministers. Here then was another potential conflict of interest.

Many in Parliament fear that an 'over-reaction' could result in ex-Ministers facing curbs which are too severe. Lord Whitelaw told me: 'I think it's not fair to say that retiring Cabinet Ministers shouldn't take other things on. I don't think that makes any sense whatsoever. You can't have a whole lot of people who've done very well as Cabinet Ministers and at the age of sixty or sixty-five, all still wanting to have jobs and yet unable to. That's absurd and quite a lot of them won't have any money anyway.'[86]

So far we have looked at the damaging effects of lobbying and consultancies, the problem of private interests, jobs for ex-Ministers, official remuneration and ways of boosting expenses. We have seen overwhelming evidence that the number of MPs and Lords whose integrity may be compromised by these matters has been significant and growing. We have seen how money can buy influence and how many in Westminster have been only too willing to sell what they have.

We have also seen the gulf between what the public expects of those in Parliament and the far lower standards that many MPs and Peers are willing to accept for themselves, especially in financial matters. This then is the background to the far more serious problems addressed by the remainder of this book.

We now need to turn to another important matter. Money may buy influence, but there is a far more effective way to swing an important vote: the abuse of patronage.

4

The Power of Patronage

'Some people can be bought off with an MBE, others with a knighthood.' Former Conservative Party Agent 1995

'Politics are . . . nothing more than a means of rising in the world.' Samuel Johnson (1709–1784)

'The object of power is power.' George Orwell (1903–1950)

'I work for a government I despise for ends I think are criminal.' John Maynard Keynes (1883–1946)

Patronage is a powerful system which allows favours to be given to 'friends' as rewards for support or loyalty, or offered in advance to buy their co-operation in the future. It creates an élite where the only route to power lies in finding favour with 'the powers that be'. Patronage destroys a society based on merit and rots the democratic process. Patronage gives power to patrons and takes it away from everyone else. Patronage thrives on secrecy because the process is so shameful that even its greatest enthusiasts are loath to have to justify each decision.

Every extension of the power of patronage is a step further towards centralisation of authority, a step nearer to a totalitarian regime. The ultimate patronage state was Communist Russia, where every job, every home, every place at university, every privilege was handed out at the whim of party officials. Patronage belongs in British history to a medieval age where kings bestowed favours, estates and titles as a means of control.

However, patronage shows no signs of dying. A colleague of mine was recently offered a possible place in the House of Lords, if only she would reverse her previous decision and agree to support a government policy by heading up an important project. She refused because she fundamentally disagreed with the proposals. She told a very senior figure within the Department: 'You need to realise that there are some things that cannot be bought.'[87]

This shameful episode is an example of patronage at its very worst, just another form of bribery, used for the sole purpose of undermining integrity. The individual is concerned that her blunt refusal may affect her future career and for this reason has kept quite about what happened. She is scared that her identification may lead to retribution from the Department concerned.

How many others have been targeted in this way through shabby offers and then silenced with fear? I have since discovered several cases where people seem to have altered their positions on matters of public policy and then been rewarded with an honour or a government post or some other favour. It is impossible to prove a link and so the individuals must remain nameless, but they know who they are.

We see unhealthy patronage not only in the honours system which we will return to, but also in the appointments to quangos, non-elected bodies that are taking over more and more of the roles of local government. Tony Wright presented his extensive research on the abuse of patronage in a written submission to the Nolan Committee in January 1995.[88] This is a summary of some of his points.

The growth of quango patronage

The growth of quango power has been staggering. There are now 5,521 executive quangos responsible for almost a third of all government spending centrally. Examples are the Health Education Authority which until recently had an annual budget in excess of £16 million, or the Forestry Commission, or the Arts Council. They are not properly accountable to the public, and some appear to have fallen far short of acceptable standards.

By 1989, these quangos had mushroomed to the point where Ministers had the authority to give away 51,000 public appointments, with 10,000 new appointments or re-appointments every year.[89] Executive and NHS bodies account for 4,000 each, advisory bodies 10,000 and tribunals 22,000. These appointments were a crucial engine for driving through new policies during the revolutionary Thatcher years, by selecting people with strong views which matched where she wanted these quangos to go.

Departments keep their own shortlists of candidates. However, major appointments have often been made of people outside such lists. Advertising and executive search has hardly played a part in the process. From April 1992 to December 1993, only thirty public appointments were advertised out of several thousand – excluding the health service. During the same period 'head hunting' agencies were used to fill sixteen other posts, at a cost of £341,224, of which £27,000 was for one post alone.[90]

There is another list of 5,000 names maintained by the Public Appointments Unit (PAU), with a secondary list of

20,000 more, and others have been encouraged to nominate themselves, but this is almost a complete waste of time. The 1992 edition of Public Bodies records only 84 appointments from these sources. In any event the PAU is hugely biased towards those in the South East and the over-fifties. Those in the South East form only 31 per cent of the population, yet account for 57 per cent of the list.[91] This speaks loudly of an élite.

One key change has been a programme to increase the number of women appointed. In the first two years after the initiative was launched in 1991, the percentage of women in public bodies increased from 23 per cent to 28 per cent.

The Prime Minister has great power over many appointments. The 'Questions of Procedures for Ministers'[92] states that the Prime Minister should always be consulted over all quango appointments with possible political significance. In 1992, the Prime Minister was directly involved in 137 senior quango appointments.[93] The patronage exercised by a Prime Minister has always been far-reaching. In 1977, James Callaghan was asked to list all the appointments which were his to make. The incomplete list filled four columns of Hansard.

The Chief Whip is also a key influence on who gets what job. Indeed, his former title was Patronage Secretary. The 'Guide on Public Appointments Procedures' states that the Chief Whip's Office should be notified in advance of all significant appointments and 'the list of candidates held by the Chief Whip's Office should be consulted before Ministers make or recommend appointments to significant Committees, Commissions and other public bodies, in case there are other names the Chief Whip would wish to be considered with other candidates'.

As we will see in a later chapter on whipping, parliamentary voting discipline depends on sanctions and rewards.

Keeping the Whips happy is vital to survive in politics. Without their support an MP's career is all but finished and influence becomes negligible.

The appointment process can be interesting. The Chairman of one quango wrote recently that he was appointed 'as a consequence of sharing a cab with a stranger'. He thinks that such a method can work rather well. 'Another quango Chairman was appointed following a pheasant shoot at which a Secretary of State was a fellow gun. The subsequent Chairman of a Water Authority bumped into a Cabinet Minister while birding on a Greek island. It is a splendidly capricious and British way of doing things. I am advised that the success rate is about the same as when head-hunters are engaged. And look at the thousands of guineas you save.'[94]

One former Tory politician said that she could not remember 'knowingly appointing a Labour sympathiser' to a single one of hundreds of quango appointments that were hers to decide.[95] Such a boast would have been worthy of the party machine in Romania, China or any other communist regime.

Baroness Robson had to retire from a Regional Health Authority 'for family reasons' and described to the House of Lords how a replacement was found: 'I was asked if I had any suggestions to make about who should be my successor. I went to see the Secretary of State to recommend a man he might approve. I expected to be questioned about why I was putting that person forward. When I saw the Secretary of State he asked me whether I knew what the man's political opinions were. I said, "No, I am afraid that I have not asked him." The Secretary of State said, "But you do realise that almost every MP in your region is a Tory MP and we do have to make sure that there is compatibility." '[96]

The National Health Service reforms have also seen the removal of many elected representatives on Health Boards and their replacement by ministerial appointees. One survey found that out of 185 trust chairmen, sixty-two had 'clear links' with the Conservative Party, and three-quarters had a background in private business.[97]

The Labour Research Department did a survey of all 482 NHS Trusts in the UK and found 121, one in four, had someone associated with the Conservative Party among the non-executive members. Many spouses of Conservative MPs were on trust boards. For example, the West Midlands Health Authority was chaired recently by the former Chairman of the Federation of University Conservative Associations, and he in turn was succeeded by the President of the Chester Conservative Association. Quango appointees with views out of line with Conservative policy have been systematically replaced.

The Observer found that 40 per cent of the heads of the largest thirty-eight quangos had Conservative Party links. 'A picture reminiscent of the rotten boroughs of the eighteenth century.'[98] The *Financial Times* concluded from its own survey of the ten largest Health Service quangos and the thirty largest non-health quangos that 'if there is a new élite running British public services . . . it appears the best qual-ifications to join are to be a businessman with Conservative leanings'.[99]

The BBC programme *Here and Now* analysed 20,000 members of 1,500 quangos and found that unsuccessful Conservative candidates from the 1992 election were ten times more likely to be appointed to a quango than Labour candidates. Thirty-three quango jobs were given to failed Conservative candidates after the 1992 election including the former Ministers Christopher Chope, Michael Fallon and Francis Maude.[100] Twenty-four Conservative MPs and Peers had spouses who had been given quango jobs.[101] More worryingly, perhaps, the directors of companies which gave money to the Conservative Party were three times as likely to have jobs on quangos than those which did not. With the Gallup Poll of October 1994 showing 61 per cent agreeing that the Conservatives gave the impression of being 'very sleazy and disreputable', such patronage has continued to damage public confidence.[102]

I asked Lord Whitelaw if he thought patronage became imbalanced when one party had been in power for a long period. On balance he disagrees: 'I don't think that is as true as is thought, [but] I think one or two things have happened which in my judgement should have been avoided.'[103]

Of course, many would point out that patronage is nothing new and is not a party political issue. Labour governments in the past also used their patronage to appoint friends and allies. In the 1978–9 parliamentary year, twelve out of twenty chairmen of the largest public bodies were Labour supporters, with members of the General Council of the Trades Union Congress being well represented.[104]

So how are these posts to be filled, if not by ministerial favouritism? There are only a few options. One is 'random selection' or statistical representation. This is the basis of jury selection, and is hardly likely to be suitable. Quotas are a variation on this. Then there is 'inheritance', which still survives in the House of Lords and the monarchy, but is unlikely to survive the turn of the century as a means of selecting who governs. Another option is 'free competition', which includes election. Competition has been the basis for civil servant recruitment since the reforms of the last century. Elections are a variation of it. There is also 'patronage'.

Clearly patronage exists to some degree or other at every level of society – for example where someone chooses to employ a friend or a member of the family in a small business. Society as we know it would probably collapse if all such low-level patronage was banned. Relationships are always likely to count as much if not more than a piece of paper listing achievements. But what we are seeing is a wholesale domination of public life by an extreme form of patronage which is an abuse of privilege and power.

Tony Wright commented in his submission to the Nolan Committee: 'In Britain the patronage powers are vast, the constraints minimal and the dangers enormous.' Patronage by the State has been a fact of life for centuries. In the age of Walpole, patronage was a lubricant. Decades later, in a memorandum to Gladstone in 1854, Charles Trevelyan wrote: 'Patronage in all its varied forms is the great abuse and scandal of the present age.' Totally incompetent people were being given great responsibility.

Just over a century later, in 1963, Peter Richards wrote: 'Perhaps the greatest danger for the future is the possibility that one party will exercise uninterrupted power for too long a period. Temptations would grow as security bred careless-ness.'[105] In the early 1980s, it was the Right Wing of the Conservative Party who led the fiercest attacks on the system, seeing the growth of quangos as a needless extension of state bureaucracy.

It would be tempting for Labour to try to substitute one kind of patronage for another, having seen the scale of what is possible. The Conservatives could become the natural champions of quango reform – indeed, this may be a small but hidden additional motive behind accepting some of Lord Nolan's reforms on quangos.

What a stroke of genius it would be for the Tories to strip local authorities of massive powers, give them to non-elected quango staff, appointed on a political whim, and after packing out quangos with your own supporters, reform the system so that from that moment on, even if the next election is won by the opposition, they are left with existing quango staff whom they cannot shift, and a new appointments system which is scrupulously committed to fairness. It could take twenty years or more to eradicate a dominant Tory culture.

However, the public view is clear. Eight out of ten say that there should be a political balance in quangos.[106] The only way to restore imbalances on quango boards in the short term would be to recruit selectively on a strict quota basis. This would require a strong will by a large-majority Labour government.

Political honours for good behaviour

As we have seen, another much despised area of patronage has been the political Honours List. The granting of honours to people as a political reward has a long history. After Lloyd George allowed party fund-raising through honours sales, a Political Honours Scrutiny Committee was set up. However, it has no real power and works in secret. It failed to influence or prevent the infamous 'Lavender List' when Harold Wilson resigned (said to have been handwritten in great haste by his secretary on a piece of lavender writing paper), or rumours of honours to Conservative Party donors by Margaret Thatcher and John Major.

Should not the whole process of patronage be based on merit, as with the appointment of civil servants? What happened to equal opportunities? In 1968, the Fulton Report had declared that civil service selection 'should be, and be seen to be, independent of any form of patronage', so should not the same apply to rewards for public service? The honours system has become a mockery because it is increasingly obvious that one way to get an honour is to give money to fund the party in power, or to have the right opinions.

In September 1992, a survey was published showing that 'heads of big firms have a 50 per cent greater chance of being honoured if their companies donate to Tory Party funds'.[107]

The Minority Report of the House of Commons Home Affairs Committee printed further statistical evidence of honours for money. The Report goes on to say: 'Asked if there was any connection between donations to the Conservative Party and allocation of honours to industrialists, Sir Norman Fowler told the committee, "As far as honours for political services are concerned, they are scrutinised by an independent committee of Privy Councillors. Since 1979 we have also been in a position where any honours added by 10 Downing Street are also scrutinised. All political honours must be certificated to the effect that no payment or expectation of payment to any party or political fund is directly or indirectly associated with the recommendation." '

The report continued: 'It is apparent that Sir Norman's confidence in the system is not shared by all members of the Political Honours Committee.' Lord Carr of Hadley, a member of the Committee and a former Conservative Minister, was asked on BBC Radio's *Analysis* programme whether it was just a coincidence that industrialists giving money were honoured. He replied, 'Yes, er, and yet it can't be as simple as that, can it?' Lord Shackleton, a former Chairman of the Committee, told *The Observer* last year that secret donations to the Conservative Party front organisations could enable honours to escape scrutiny. He is quoted as saying, 'There is an obvious gap here. It is highly likely that these secret donations are by-passing the scrutiny system and that honours are being effectively bought.'

The report concludes: 'We believe that, whatever the truth, there is a widespread perception among both recipients and the public at large that there is a connection between financial contributions to Conservative Party funds and the award of honours. Our attention has been drawn, for example, to a report in the *Sunday Times* which quoted an unnamed company secretary, whose Chairman was knighted after his company donated £160,000, as saying, "It was made perfectly clear beforehand that if he did this [give a contribution] he would get a knighthood." '

Political service, as distinct from donations, has always long been linked with honours. A study in 1992 concluded that Tory MPs elected that year would have 'a 72 per cent chance of becoming a front-bencher or a knight' if they stayed in the Commons for a reasonable length of time.[108] Thirty years previously a similar analysis found that 'an honour was almost inevitable for those Conservative backbenchers who stayed in Parliament long enough'.[109]

On 2 December 1994, a Parliamentary Written Answer revealed that 115 Conservative MPs had received knighthoods since 1979.

A former Tory agent with fifteen years of experience in local constituencies told me how revolted she was by the abuse of patronage to control people. 'They *are* corrupt. The root of it all is the honours system. It's the way they keep constituency Chairmen, Treasurers, Area Officers in line. Every Chairman I've ever known has ended up with a knighthood. Constituency agents could nominate people for honours. I never did because I didn't believe in the honours system. Patronage is a very powerful tool in the hands of the Prime Minister and it needs to be stopped.'

She also said that she had seen the same system abused in whipping rebel MPs. 'I've seen the hierarchy over Whips. The constituency Chairmen will have been threatened if they don't deselect [rebel MPs]. Some people can be bought off with an MBE, others with a knighthood.'[110] Tony Wright commented in his paper: 'This kind of patronage matters. It goes a long way to explain why the House of Commons has become so supine, depleted in vigour and independence (recent events notwithstanding).'[111]

There is another new development which has further

damaged the independent spirit of Parliament and increased Cabinet control, and that is the expansion of the so-called 'payroll' vote. It is well known that government Ministers have to vote with the Party and cannot rebel without being forced to resign. Clearly one way to increase the power of a Prime Minister is to duplicate government posts until a majority is guaranteed without whipping, 'buying' obedience from frustrated, powerless back-benchers.

In order to prevent such a dictatorship developing, the House of Commons Disqualification Act (1975) limits the number of paid office holders in the Commons. However, there is a back door way in which this limit has been systematically abused. Many new 'unpaid posts' have been made, such as assistant Whips and additional Parliamentary Private Secretaries, all with minimal responsibilities. These are also governed by blind obedience in voting. In 1900, the total MP 'payroll' was forty-two, but it has grown alarmingly to more than 130. By 1995, between a third and a half of all Conservative Party MPs had been sworn to complete loyalty in this way. We will return to the power of 'payroll voting' in a later chapter on the abuse of the whipping system. As we have already seen, many of these MPs have also been involved in commercial consultancies. The combined effect of 'payroll' and consultancy pressures is hard to determine, but is undoubtedly significant in the public mind.

In conclusion then, honours and office holding have been twin weapons in destroying the life of the Commons, until it has become little more than a collection of 'yes men' whose votes have been 'bought', together with a number of 'eccentric' radicals, dangerous ex-Ministers and a minority opposition.

Opposition Party MPs are also open to the influence of patronage. It is quite wrong to assume that Whips in an opposition Party have nothing to offer in the way of rewards.

Over several decades Labour MPs have also been knocked into line by the lure of such things as future Cabinet posts, involvement on Select Committees, and political honours. Ken Livingstone has felt this acutely. Having run the Greater London Council before its abolition in the mid-1980s, he has huge experience of many issues in local government, yet has never once in eight years been nominated by his own party to sit on a single Select Committee.[112]

I have met many people who aggressively defend patronage in all these forms because they say it makes for strong government and political stability. But the price of patronage is a serious lack of accountability and nothing less than the wholesale prostitution of the democratic process. The result is a culture in Westminster that punishes integrity and moral conviction.

Instead of rewarding those with the courage to vote for what they believe is right, the system has told people to vote against their political conscience for things they do not believe will help the country. 'It is right to vote for what you believe is wrong and wrong to vote for what you believe is right – let the party tell you what your vote should be.' This is the basis of whipping, as we will see in a later chapter.

The ultimate role model for a 'rising star' MP is a morally feeble politician, who looks good and sounds convincing, never makes trouble, and always votes as he or she is told. A whole generation of MPs has been encouraged to sell their souls for hope of a title or ministerial office. Now one begins to understand why the level of debate in Select Committees and in the Chamber is often so poor. Those of the greatest calibre in the majority party may well be among the third of those on the payroll. Their lips are sealed except for words of adulation and flattery, or for trotting out the party line.

This is the reason why resignation speeches of Ministers

are often such bloody affairs: years of frustrated, pent-up, suppressed truthfulness come flooding out. The results are often deeply shocking, because the opinions expressed are so vastly different from what has been said from every public platform or in every media interview over previous years in office. Whatever happened to integrity?

It can be argued that collective responsibility is essential in any board, business or government. But where does loyalty end and honesty begin? It is hardly surprising then that the public say they hardly believe a word of the statements that Ministers make. Even if the facts they give are true, what often comes across is a sickening lack of sincerity written all over their embarrassed faces, although some are quite good at acting.

A further result of patronage abuse has been a loss of morale and direction among the majority who are not in office. Meanwhile the real debates have moved out of the deserted Chamber and into the media, which together with the judiciary have developed an aggressive questioning role.

I asked Tory rebel Teresa Gorman what she thought of the honours system and patronage in Westminster. As leader of a rebel group that nearly brought down the government, she has seen abuse at first hand. 'It is extremely corrupting,' she declared without hesitation. 'Many businessmen for example know that the government's policies are antipathetic to business but when you ask them to do something about it they shy away. They know it will affect their chance of getting a knighthood sometime in the future – or they believe it will.

'The system of giving out honours distorts our public life generally. Colleagues [MPs] see them as the ultimate reward for just being good, minding your own business and never saying anything out of place.'

She is critical of the way 'obedient political clones with no real experience of life get promoted while those with spirit and a track record of achievement are often crushed or ignored. The lack of business experience among politicians is very evident. People get [ministerial] jobs having never managed anything in their lives. They are putty in the hands of civil servants. People with strong personalities do not do very well in either party. Dennis Skinner is an excellent politician, a man of the people, but he has never held office in the Labour Party. You watch people suddenly become desperate for office and begin to conform. The black sheep coming back into the family. Office follows. Parliament works on coteries: you have to be part of a group, a network in which people help their chums along. Women are mainly excluded from the system. People get promoted on the old boy system, rather than on know-how or ability. You have to be a team player.

'First, you get to be a Parliamentary Private Secretary, a bag carrier for a Minister, modelled on the public school fagging system. Grown men humble themselves in this demeaning exercise. Other rewards follow. Maybe they get to be in the Whips Office, or [get given] a junior Minister's post. Merit hardly comes into it.'[113]

So, while a number of those in Westminster have already compromised their integrity by accepting dubious payments, others have been bought through the offer of jobs in government, or in quangos, or by the lure of honours. The combined attractions of money and patronage have created a culture which is unhelpful at best and corrupting at worst. We will see these influences recurring time and again throughout the remainder of this book, and they are the key to understanding the otherwise inexplicable behaviour of many parliamentarians when under pressure.

We will look further at patronage in particular when we

examine the process of whipping, but first, in the light of the possible link between political donations and honours, we need to examine closely the whole question of how political parties raise their money.

5

The Truth about Party Funding

'In politics a man must learn to rise above principle.'
Anonymous MP

'I would rather be an opportunist and float, than go to the bottom with my principles around my neck.' Stanley Baldwin (1867–1947)

'The Tory Party is in so much debt that it could be insolvent by the turn of the century.' David Porter MP (1948–)

'I've no idea about party finances.' Government Minister, 1995

The funding of political parties in Britain is in urgent need of reform. Fund-raising is a vital part of politics, for without funds a party ceases to exist. Money means advertising, promotions, leaflets, campaigns and an effective media office. Traditionally most Conservative funds have come from business and wealthy donors, while Labour has been underpinned by unions and the other parties have struggled to survive on individual donations. However, the picture is changing and so are the influences, for with money comes obligation which has been seen most clearly in the historic domination of the Labour Party by trade union pressures.

Crisis for Conservatives

The national Conservative Party is desperate for cash, heavily in debt and is in a very precarious state, judging by recent balance sheets. Very few people realise that if bank loans had been called in during 1995, the Tory Party could have been forced into immediate bankruptcy, going bust owing millions of pounds, even after the sale of buildings and all other assets. Yet the most striking thing I have found has been complacency or ignorance among MPs I have talked to – with one or two exceptions.

A former Tory agent told me: 'You never knew where the money was going. In one constituency I refused to send any money for our quota. A way they bribe you is the golden, silver or bronze award. Gold is three times your quota. Then you're invited for a bash in Number 10.'[114]

A Tory back-bencher, who feared for his future if identified, told me: 'When I was first elected in 1983 I got no help from Central Office. I had no financial backers. I was just brought in on the coat tail of Margaret Thatcher. We spent £1,239 and we had everything. So where all this money goes centrally I don't know. I'm supposed to be a key marginal. I think [when it comes to the threat of bankruptcy] we will just have to take the consequences.'

David Porter is another Tory back-bencher who is in no doubt about the seriousness of the situation, but he sees a way out. 'If Labour gets in there will be state aid. The Conservative Party is in so much debt that it could be insolvent by the turn of the century with a receiver called in. A new party would then be formed with a different name – certainly *not* the Conservative and Unionist Party.'[115]

The greatest problems have been created by lack of openness which has opened the Party to speculation and criticism. What are the facts? For decades the entire financial position of the Party has been shrouded by oppressive secrecy. There have been no balance sheets, no published records of income and expenditure or of pension fund details.

With an annual turnover in excess of £10 million a year, party officials have had no legal requirement whatever to allow public scrutiny of the accounts. All companies are required to provide audited accounts and regulations are also very strict for charities above a certain size, but parties are exempt.

Under increasing pressure from party members and the media, the Party finally agreed to publish a balance sheet towards the end of 1993, but there was still no information about previous years. At the time the Conservative reforming Charter Movement strongly objected to the culture of secrecy. It was worried particularly by rumours of substantial foreign donations, even if they were entirely legitimate, from individuals or organisations. 'The Party should not be funded from abroad. It should not be financed by those who have no vote in the UK elections. It should not be funded in a furtive way. It should not be financed by excessively large donations or loans from those who are not prepared to be publicly identified. It should not be financed without proper accounts to its members for its income, expenditure and its reserves for debts.'[116]

It was inconsistent, they said, for the Conservative government to oblige unions to reveal to members how their money was used, without allowing members of their own party equal access to such information.[117]

Just three weeks before, in April 1993, the *Guardian* had run the headline: 'Conservatives given £7 million by foreign donors,' quoting as their source 'a former Party fund-raiser'.

Major General Sir Brian Wyldbore-Smith had been the Party's Director of Fund-raising from 1980 to 1992. He said that huge amounts had come from abroad, from individuals or companies quite legitimately, rather than from governments, which would not have been allowed. 'These people have an interest in the success of the Conservatives.' Overseas funding was said to have provided two-thirds of the £11 million spent on the 1992 election campaign, over and above the normal year-on-year expenditure.[118]

Sir Brian said that the £7 million was around 20 per cent of the total party income in the pre-election year, if local association turnover was included. Constituency organisations had raised £14 million and the Central Office £21 million (including the overseas amounts). The Party was reported to have overseas bank accounts in Jersey and accounts with British Overseas Banks Nominees.[119]

I have studied in detail the only three years' accounts made available to me by Central Office. In the year ending in March 1994 the income came to just over £14 million, although the report says virtually nothing about where it all came from.[120] The expenditure in a non-election year was around £12 million, the surplus £2 million, 'So what is all the fuss about?'

The reason for concern is that on 31 March 1993, the total liabilities of the Party, including an overdraft and other loans of £18 million, came to £22 million. Listed under current assets for the year ending in 1994 is one item labelled 'cash deposits' valued at no less than £2.7 million. This relates to short-term loans from local associations to try to keep Central Office relatively solvent.[121]

The interest on the bank overdraft and other debts came to around £1 million a year. The bank overdraft alone (£15.3 million) was far greater than the entire annual income of the Party (£11.5 million).[122] If the bank had become nervous and insisted on repayment of the overdraft in March 1993, the Party would have gone bust, owing a staggering total of £13 million, a breathtaking sum, even after the sale of property together with every last computer, desk, filing cabinet and dictating machine.

By the end of the following year the figures for insolvency would have been £9.8 million, but over £1.3 million of the apparent improvement was because the valuation of property owned by the Party had been increased.[123]

What kind of non-commercial organisation could possibly operate in that way? This is a vitally important question. As someone with many years' experience of working in the voluntary sector I have seen many times the nervousness of donors when asked to give. They want evidence of proper financial control, sound management, efficiency, professionalism – and above all else they want to see a balance sheet based on audited accounts.

In the case of the Conservative Party there is no doubt in my mind that if proper accounts had been published year by year, many corporate donors could have been scared off, or insisted on stricter financial controls, as they would have done with donations to any other 'good cause'. In that sense a political party has far more in common with a charity than a business. After all it has no product to sell (unless there is overt corruption), and relies on voluntary support from people who believe the mission is worthwhile, and that the organisation is well run. For these reasons it is obvious that a decision to keep the state of the accounts secret could well have been influenced by fear over what might happen to income or senior jobs if the truth were known.

It is hard to conceive of a situation where a household name charity of many years' standing, with an income exceeding £10 million a year, could allow itself to spend so much more than its income for so long without radical changes at the top being demanded by supporters. What bank would normally lend a charity a sum exceeding its entire annual income on overdraft with so little collateral security? If interest rates rose, then 15 per cent or more of all donations could be spent simply maintaining the loan, but what about repaying it?

It could be argued that such a massive loan involved a significant risk, especially in the light of a falling party membership and an ever-fickle electorate. A rumour of imminent financial collapse could have triggered a major crisis with constituency parties wanting their own loans repaid and donors scared off.

The year ending on 31 March 1995 showed some improvement, with another surplus of income over income and expenditure. But this was a year when hard savings were needed to build up a reserve for the next election. The balance sheet remained very worrying.[124]

The overdraft was still £11.4 million, and would have been £17.2 million without other short-term loans. The only security given to the bank according to Martin Saunders, Finance Director, was leasehold property, estimated as being worth £6 million. In other words, almost £6 million of the bank overdraft remained unsecured.[125]

In strict accountancy terms, on 31 March 1995 the Conservative Party was absolutely insolvent, depending entirely on the whim of senior executives in the Royal Bank of Scotland for its day-to-day existence. At any moment the bank could decide to call in the loan, making the Party spectacularly bankrupt.

If such a decision had been made by the bank in March 1995 then the bank's shareholders would have taken a loss of almost £6 million, and constituency associations would have been fighting tooth and nail to get their own money back. Many other angry individuals and companies would have been arguing their case with the official receiver over amounts owed to them of a further £1.8 million for goods and services not paid for. This would have been an appalling national scandal, one of the worst political disgraces in the last two hundred years.

One Minister told me: 'I wouldn't want to be a shareholder in a bank that lent so much money to the Party.' The remark was made 'off the cuff' in a light-hearted way – after all, £6 million difference in the balance sheet of a large bank is hardly a major crisis for shareholders. Nevertheless he was recognising that the bank was taking a real risk.

Such a potential disaster remains a spectre in the future, but not a reality just yet, thanks to the goodwill of the Royal Bank of Scotland which continues to enable the Party to pay their bills on time with millions of borrowed money.

The dark day may never come. It may be that the Party will manage the near impossible. It may somehow manage to pay for the next election (perhaps £10 million extra expenditure), and still repay all the loans in a reasonable time. However it remains a risk and the Party remains financially vulnerable. It all depends on donors remaining convinced that a Labour government means disaster for Britain. But as Tony Blair's New Labour continues to identify with traditional Conservative values, that assumption of donor loyalty can no longer be taken for granted.

There is another concern. The size of the overdraft facility is critically dependent on the property valuation. Clearly there are limits to how much the bank will risk without security. It is therefore strange to read in the accounts that the valuation was carried out not by a wholly independent company, but by the directors of the Party themselves, in 'consultation with the professional property advisors of the Conservative Central Office'.[126]

In other words the Party carried out its *own* valuation of its own properties. But what if those valuations were too optimistic? The entire future of the Conservative Party could hang on such a question. One might therefore have expected a fully independent process of valuation. Perhaps in reality the valuation was more robustly independent than stated in the accounts, but if so, then why not say so? Are such things considered unimportant?

Martin Saunders told me: 'I've got to save money. Formal evaluations cost money. We're not bound by law on this one [unlike companies]. We as directors have to take our own view as to the accuracy of the accounts. It's an internal evaluation [of property] by the directors. We do talk to an external firm but I cannot say more.'

'But the figure is very important for the bank.'

'What we say to our bankers is between us and our bankers.'

I asked him why the accounts had been so secret in the past.

'I came in 1992,' he replied. 'My brief was to bring up to date all the accounting and reporting systems. There's not an awful lot of stuff there which is highly secret, to be honest. The trouble is we have had three successive years with £5 million deficits, and it's been a lot of effort to sort it all out.'

One obvious and legal alternative to Conservative Central Office for worried donors would be to fund a cluster of marginal constituencies (so long as the official ceiling on each candidate's campaign costs is not exceeded), or to create a separate organisation to buy advertising hoardings and other components of a national campaign. Who wants to see their entire donation swallowed up in paying off huge costs run up over the previous five to ten years? Companies give money to help win the next election, not to pay for a victory years ago.

There has already been some resistance by party members to funding head office, because of a squeeze on local party funds as an elderly membership has declined. Young Conservative activists are a tiny group who will be unable to sustain the Party's future on current trends. Almost half the members of Conservative associations are over sixty-six, only 5 per cent are under thirty-five and the average age is sixty-two.[127]

There is no Central Office record of Conservative Party membership but it has been estimated as around 750,000, down from 1.5 million in 1981, and 2.7 million in the 1960s. Labour's own membership fell from a peak of a million in the 1950s to just 265,000 in 1988, but was 372,000 by June 1996.[128] There has been no new ideology to inspire and fill the void left by the debunking of capitalist and socialist myths.

This redundant energy and passion for idealism in politics has been channelled into new 'causes' such as animal welfare movements, or environmental agencies like Greenpeace. Greenpeace alone has more than 350,000 UK members, and Friends of the Earth 200,000. Even assuming some people belong to both, these two 'single issue' groups alone have more members than the Labour Party and Liberal Democrats combined. But single issue groups can never be a proper substitute for an overall vision for the future of society, and can produce unbalanced responses from government if they become too powerful. They also direct funds away from traditional parties.

As local party funds have been tighter, and as worries have grown about the running of Central Office, constituency quota income from local groups to Central Office has been falling from 20 per cent of total national income in the 1970s to around 5 per cent today. This is a fixed amount paid in proportion to a constituency size. In the year 1992–3, the yield was £1 million contribution towards the £14 million needed for the Party to survive. But one year later it had dropped by a further £250,000,[129] although there has been a rise since.[130] Individual members give more each in real terms than they did twenty years ago which has compensated for some of the decline in membership numbers.[131]

Local associations have been so pressed for cash that many MPs have been paying up to £11,000 a year from their own parliamentary allowances to their local offices.[132] As we have seen, each MP received £41,308 in 1995 for research and secretarial services, which was an increase of 42 per cent on the 1992 figure. Conservative MPs alone now have £15 million between them to spend on these areas.[133] Although these amounts are in theory for expenses incurred 'wholly, necessarily and exclusively for parliamentary duties', in practice it is often hard to separate local office activity to help re-elect an MP from work to serve constituents.

Many local associations 'charge' an MP for secretarial work and office space. Some MPs donate their own personal income to local parties, in addition to diverting their expense allowances. This is a clear breach of the Maxwell-Fyfe rules introduced in the late 1940s to protect candidates from demands for cash which would otherwise prevent poor people from standing for Parliament.[134]

One Tory MP in 1993–4 gave so generously from his own pocket that he was paying for half the entire annual budget of his local party. Another London MP gave £6,000 towards the salary of his party agent, and a similar amount for 'office and equipment and for publicity for advice centres'. A detailed survey revealed that almost forty Tory constituencies had received financial support via their MPs. The total value of these subsidies probably exceeded £250,000, mostly from official allowances.[135]

Despite these emergency measures to keep local parties in existence, many constituencies are reaching a point where they cannot afford even a part-time agent, making re-election more difficult. The picture then is of a party structure in serious decline, hardly a healthy state for paying off massive debts. (See note at end of this chapter.) If the Prime Minister had carried through a recent threat of a snap election over Europe, he would have been very foolish. Not only were the opinion polls stacked against him, but he could have pushed the Party into practical insolvency.

Where does the money really come from?

Some £14 million a year is a lot for the Tory Central Office to find, and much more will be needed – ideally around £20 million a year over the next few years to pay off debts and pay for the next election (or two). If less than £1 million comes from local associations, what then? Complete secrecy over the sources of most party funds has bred damaging rumours. That kind of money does not just fall out of the sky. It has been said that enormous sums come from companies in Britain, but there is little evidence of this.

In September 1989, the Labour Shadow Leader Frank Dobson published Labour's annual survey of political donations by companies. The report revealed that 275 of the country's top 1,500 companies had given almost £3.5 million to the Tory Party or its supporters in 1988.[137] However, what disturbed him was that 'last year we managed to ferret out details of donations of just over £4 million to the Tories and their front organisations but the accounts circulated at the Tory Party conference showed an income of over £15 million. The Tory Constituency Associations contributed £1.2 million – so the rest, amounting to almost £10 million, came from secret, undisclosed sources.'[138]

The survey found that only £3,800 of the £3.4 million donated by companies went to parties other than the Conservatives. None had gone to Labour.[139]

An important question is whether the Conservative Party might be receiving in good faith, quite unwittingly, large sums of money through indirect routes from foreign governments. Foreign governments are an obvious potential source of vast wealth, particularly oil-rich but insecure countries in the Middle East. They may feel they need a government in power that would not hesitate to go to war again in the Gulf. Donations to political parties by foreign governments are against the rules but I believe it is possible for foreign governments to circumvent these rules.

For example, there is a blurred distinction in some Arab nations between the wealth of a Royal Family, and the wealth of the State. In a country with a ruling monarchy, how can you tell the difference between a personal donation and a government gift? The answer is that it is near impossible. It is hard to stop such a government from providing substantial party income, whether via a number of intermediary companies operating in various parts of the world including Britain, or through other less well-known individuals. In this way very substantial amounts could be donated by a foreign government, and accepted in all innocence, without anyone in the Conservative Party having the faintest idea what was happening.

The potential for indirect funding of the Conservative Party by foreign powers is ever present and probably impossible to detect or prevent under current practice, despite all the efforts to do so by past, current and future party officials.

And so the rumours have continued. I doubt if they will ever go away so long as the Conservative Party allows not only single donations of unlimited size, but also donations from any individual or company anywhere in the world, and a guarantee of absolute confidentiality.

Eric Chalker was on the Conservative Board of Finance as well as being a Joint Honorary Treasurer between 1989 and

1993. He told the Home Affairs Committee of the House of Commons that he had been very disturbed by the lack of openness and accountability.

'There is no higher body with financial responsibility within the party on which a place can be secured by direct election . . . Yet members of the Board are consistently denied more than the barest minimum of financial information.

'When I first joined the Board, its members did not even receive the annual income and expenditure account that Central Office had published, with great reluctance, since 1984. There is still no formal presentation of these figures to the Board and their approval of them is not required. . . .I was elected to the Board with a specific mandate to pursue the quest for more information than had previously been available. As a consequence I regularly sought details of Conservative Office expenditure. I regularly sought examination of their budgets and I regularly sought some discussion of what was clearly (to me, at least) an impending financial crisis. It was all virtually to no avail. The paid employees and the vested interests obdurately stood their ground and democratic accountability was non-existent.

'Board members were actually *entitled* to some of the information I sought, by virtue of the Board's constitution, but this made no difference to the actual availability (including, initially, even the existence of the constitution itself). Board members – despite having been elected – are effectively there as guests of the unelected Chairman, in whose hands the power lies.'

The Select Committee Report goes on to say: 'Of his four years on the Board, Mr Chalker says, "Over £67 million of expenditure was recorded by Conservative Central Office in that time, but nobody had to account for one penny of it to the Conservative Board of Finance nor to any other elected body." More than £43 million in donations was received by the Conservative Party during Mr Chalker's four years on the Board of Finance. He says, "while members . . . receive a partial breakdown of donations by UK region, value and number, more complete information is kept from Board members. In 1991, press reports started to appear of some very specific, very large individual donations to the party, including some from abroad; this caused me grave concern and, as a consequence, I asked the then Chairman of the Board (an appointed Officer) for information that I believed would reassure me and the constituency associations that I represented, namely the following: Was there any limit to the amount of financial support that the (appointed) Treasurers were willing to accept from any one source? Was he aware of any potential donor who had been turned away, or of any offered donation that had been declined? Was there any established policy that would have prevented the acceptance of a particular donation, or would have subjected an offered donation to special scrutiny?

"No answers were forthcoming."[140]

I decided to find out for myself the level of knowledge about Tory finances among senior members of the government. I went to see a Minister who is widely respected for his integrity and his measured approach to sensitive issues. I have known him for some time and regard him very highly. There are few people in politics today whom I would trust more. I asked him first whether he was aware of the size of the Tory Party debt. He replied: 'I don't know to what extent it is underpinned by assets.'

I had to spell out to him the uncomfortable truth: that the assets still left a net liability of around £10 million. I asked him what sort of bank he thought would lend such a large sum without any security. He commented: 'The bank may have made a commercial decision as they make assumptions about what is in their best interests, or they may be satisfied – although how can they tell? – that the risk is very low.' He then added almost in the same breath, 'I've no idea at all about party finances.'

I expressed to him considerable surprise that he had needed to ask *me* about the size of Tory Party assets versus liabilities. I pointed out how odd it seemed to me that the figures seemed not to be being taken seriously, even by people as senior as him.

He then said: 'I suspect that the Conservative Party has had an overdraft for some time, bigger now.'

'Suspect?' I asked.

'Well, it is in fact the case that I don't take much interest in the financial position of Central Office.'

'Even though it has an overdraft of £15 million?'

'It makes no impact on me as a Minister. It makes no impact on me as a local MP. Central Office does not play a large part in my life so. . . .'

'So what do they do with £14 million income a year?' I was curious.

'They run the party conference and they service the Party, and they service the political bit, the political side of govern-ment is served by it. As I understand it, income and expen-diture are no longer in imbalance.'

'Yes, but in a non-election year!'

'Yes, but the income goes up, I suspect. But I'm afraid I don't regard this as a very important issue.'

I asked him if it would be more important to him if he thought the Party could become bankrupt.

'But what is the organisation that goes bankrupt?' he replied.

'Central Office . . .'

'But what is that? I'm not quite sure what is the vehicle.'

'The national association – doesn't that worry you?'

'I don't think it would go bankrupt. I think there are competent people managing the Party, Chairman, Vice-Chairman. I don't worry about the Central Office's financial position. Perhaps I should but I actually don't.'

I asked him whether he had any concerns about where income came from, about secrecy and the possibility of single donations of several million pounds hidden in larger totals.

'My understanding is that Central Office are now much more cautious about accepting money from anyone. In a sense it's good that Ministers don't know, because our decisions shouldn't be contaminated by how the Party's funded and it isn't, because we've got no idea at all who is funding the Party. I haven't the slightest idea who has contributed.' He seemed unaware of the lists of publicly available information about corporate donations.

He continued: 'I think one just has to rely on the good sense and good judgement of Central Office, when they decide where to ask for money and who to accept it from. The key thing is that it shouldn't contaminate the decision-making process in government. I genuinely don't believe it does.'[141]

However, Peter Lilley was far more worried as a Cabinet Minister about the debt problem of the Tories. He told me he was very concerned about it, 'especially trying to fight an election on a £10 million overdraft'.[142]

I also asked Lord Whitelaw about funding. He was Tory Chairman from 1974 to 1976. I wanted to know what he thought about secrecy and why he had never at that time published any accounts. He admitted to me that debt was nothing new. 'There was certainly a major overdraft when I was Chairman. We had two general elections in a year. But I got enough money to fight the election.'

'But why have the accounts been so secret for so long?'

'I think the answer to that is that we don't see why we should give the details of all the people who happen to give money, nor do I think there is a very good reason why you should.'

I pointed out that the first issue was where the money went after it was donated – accepting for the sake of the argument that donor anonymity would be preserved.

'Then you will go a long way towards it after all.'

'But why have we only just got audited accounts? Why the secrecy over how the money is spent?'

Lord Whitelaw explained: 'A lot of money goes from the centre to the constituencies – of course I accept there is a lot of money spent at the centre on advertising and the rest. That's where it goes.' (I doubt if many constituencies would agree with him.) 'I suppose the answer is the same in all parties. The trade unions on their side still have the money from their own arrangements and give their money to the Labour Party. It's not very different.'

I explained that the absence of audited accounts seemed strange to me.

'I don't think it's strange because it is a perfectly fair answer for both the Conservative and Labour Parties, that there have been over the years various ways of obtaining money whereby donations from individuals and from firms. . . .'

'But I'm talking expenditure here. That's why the Charities Commission requires charities to have audited accounts, to prevent someone from putting £250,000 into their own pockets. Why did it take so long?'

'Well I suppose it was because it was a private affair among people who were working together and that was the reason it was done.'

I remarked that it was extraordinary that the very first set of accounts should show such a massive debt. I wasn't surprised the Party had been reluctant to make the accounts public.

'It just never was [made public],' he replied.

I asked how he was sure there were not large donations being made to the Party by foreign governments indirectly.

'A rather silly comment, but I don't think anyone imagined that it had ever happened – ever.'

I reminded Lord Whitelaw about the former Tory fundraiser who said £7 million had come from abroad in a single year.

'I don't think it ever occurred to us that this would happen, because it had always been the same. But it has been built up in all the parties in the same way. A great many things in life just go on. One doesn't even know. The accounts were there, one knew roughly, but that's about all.'

So who would have known in his day?

'The Treasurers. I had three of them.'

'And it would rely entirely on their personal integrity?'

'Yes.'[143]

I also raised Tory financing with Lord Archer with his experience of helping run Central Office in the past, as part of a wide-ranging interview.

'I think that anybody has the right to give money to anything they like as respectable as the Conservative Party or the Labour Party, without having it disclosed. I don't see why you should disclose. I don't have to, to give to the Red Cross, or to Save the Children. I don't see why I should have to say how much I give to the Conservative Party.'

'But what about overseas funding?'

'It's all the same. If they want a Conservative government, if they want a Labour government, it's up to them if they want to give money to it.'

'And from a foreign government? There is a restriction . . . .'

'You're quite right. I don't remember that arising when I was in Central Office. I mean, it may have done but I wasn't in the Treasurer's Department and as I am sure you have found out already that is a very secret Department. Even the Chairman and Deputy Chairman are not in it. I can see no harm if people want to support the Party.'

He agreed however that there should be a restriction on accepting money directly from foreign governments. But how would he be able to tell if – say – the Saudi Royal Family were putting in £10 million?

'At least!' he exclaimed with laughter. 'Sixteen million pounds down! Well yes, I can see what you're getting at and the purists would obviously say that's disgraceful and shouldn't happen. I've never been faced with that dilemma. That's interesting. No, obviously, no government should be helping another.'[144]

I asked a Tory back-bencher what he thought of state funding for parties. A sensible idea surely?

'Disastrous. I've never heard such a stupid idea in all my life, that the State should pay for political parties. Let's be quite clear about this. Once you get the State doing that you are institutionalising political parties. I do not think existing parties should be here for ever. It is wrong to buttress support on something that happened before. It's up to polit-ical parties to raise money and if they do it corruptly then the full force of law should be brought down on the party.'[145]

Finally I went to visit the Conservative Central Office itself. It is an impressive building, surrounded by security cameras just a few hundred yards from Parliament. After being ushered through metal detectors and guards, I was led upstairs to meet the then Chairman, Jeremy Hanley. He was larger than life, warm, effusive, friendly and accommodating – and to my surprise happy to see me on my own, unlike the escort requirements of Cabinet Ministers.

What was his explanation for the past secrecy over accounts?

'It's not odd that an organisation like ours should not publish its accounts, because there is no legal requirement to do so.'

But was there further delay because of the embarrassing size of the overdraft?

'Quite the reverse. We published our accounts when our liabilities were at the highest. In any case, the vast majority of the supporters of the Conservative Party give to their local Conservative Association. All those accounts are published every year.'

'So why not Central Office?'

'If you're asking about history, don't ask me. The fact is that we do publish accounts now. I am looking forward to publishing my accounts this year so it seems sterile to ask, "Why didn't you publish accounts before then?" There is a very big difference between the funding of the Conservative Party and the funding of the Labour Party. The Labour Party is funded by trade unions. They have between £5 million and £6 million a year which has to be paid on an annual basis. Therefore they get a very "flat" income. Whereas the majority of our donors give at the time of an election. Between elections we live on a deficit. If we spend more in an election campaign than we raise, then there is a deficit to carry forward.' He agreed that it was very hard to pay off debt and build up a 'war chest' at the same time.

I asked Jeremy Hanley about the sources of funding and secrecy over donors. He pointed out that Labour also have two companies through which anonymous donations can be made. I asked him whether he had thought about giving more information about donation numbers and values, while still keeping them anonymous.

'But whose interests am I whetting by giving this information?'

'Suppose it's me . . . I am a potential donor.'

'They can come and ask me,' he replied.

'I am asking.'

'But I don't believe you are a bona fide potential donor. I respect the anonymity of our donors. I publish our accounts voluntarily. They are audited. We also adhere fully to the code that was published in the Select Committee Report last year. In other words we don't accept money from foreign sovereigns, foreign governments or foreign heads of state. We don't accept money from illegal sources.'

'. . . but there is a fuzzy edge?'

'By the way, the income from foreign sources is a tiny proportion of the total raised in a year.'

'But isn't there a possibility that government money from – say – an Arab state could find its way into the Conservative Party through a back door without you even realising it?'

'Hang on just a second. The Treasurers themselves have this Chinese wall between the government and the Treasurer's Office. That is why the Labour Party set up these two front organisations by their own admission. Government Ministers don't know anything about the amount individuals give to the Party. As you know, as far as the honours system is concerned you have independent scrutiny.'

I pressed him further.

'If we knew that [a donation had come from foreign governments] we would return it. If we knew that it was illegal, we would return it. But what you're saying is an impossibility. You're saying that if we've been given money by a person, we would have to know who they are, satisfy ourselves so far as such a thing is possible that the money is completely bona fide . . .' He pointed out that it would be impossible anyway to prevent laundering of illegitimate foreign funds through UK subsidiary companies.

'What I've done,' he continued, 'is to examine every penny of the money raised since I became Chairman of the

Party. I have said that I will not accept a single penny except where I am satisfied that we have adhered to the Code of Conduct. And that I've stuck to.'

'So if I was a foreign donor, who decides whether my money is accepted?'

'The Treasurers are chaired by Lord Hambro. There are three, four, maybe five Treasurers in all. They will investigate an individual. So long as that individual is to their satisfaction, they will then come to me and ask if I am satisfied, and I will then ask additional questions.'

'Would it help to have some kind of independent body to help check?'

Jeremy Hanley replied: 'Will you consider that perhaps most of the stories are rubbish stories. Would you just consider for a moment that there are people with honour, financial honour? As a chartered accountant, that means more to me than anything. I have actually rejected donors because I am not satisfied . . . There is a slippery slope which is so easy to follow. There is one principle which I think is vital: there is a right of individuals, a right which is ever eroded by our press, which seems to enjoy destroying every institution we have in our country. When it comes to political donations, I see no reason on earth why I shouldn't have an element of privacy if I choose over the money that I've earned. There's no reason why anybody can't publish the fact that they have made a donation. Companies of course have no choice but to publish their donations.'[146]

Unfortunately for the Conservative Party, while they continue their absolute commitment to donor secrecy, three-quarters of the population in Britain say that the identities of all major donors should be revealed.[147]

Of course, one immediate way to deal with many of the concerns about the sources of overseas funding would be to ban all donations other than those with an obvious origin in the UK, excepting perhaps those with British voting rights resident abroad. It is worrying to think that a powerful alliance of foreign sources might try to interfere with a British election by funding one British party against another.

In summary it is clear to me that the Conservatives have chosen to sacrifice the reputation of the Party for financial gain. Thus the Party has continued to survive, bolstered in the past by secrecy over its precarious financial state, and by the continued acceptance of millions of pounds of income from secret albeit entirely lawful sources outside Britain.

The trouble is that overspending has been allowed for so long, and on such a grand scale, that refusal of future funding from overseas could precipitate total bankruptcy. Listing large donors by name could also have the same effect, because so many might be severely embarrassed if the extent of their political generosity were revealed. Therefore we are very unlikely to see any policy changes in the near future, and the Party's reputation for secrecy is likely to continue.

The Labour Party

The Labour Party also faces severe problems of its own. Any party reliant on trade unions for income is going to be vulnerable following the catastrophic decline in union membership throughout the 1980s and early 1990s. And with union funding comes a feeling of union ownership and obligations, which are increasingly embarrassing to 'New Labour'.

Their income is around half that of the Tories in a non-election year and the amount they have available for media campaigns is usually far less. So ironically, one effect of the Tory cash crisis might be to level the playing field. The Labour Party has also traditionally been at a disadvantage in much of the so-called 'Tory' press, although with a possible slight compensation in broadcast media such as the BBC.

That is now changing, with many Tory editors taking a very anti-Tory line, especially over sleaze.

The Labour Party has been criticised for the same kind of concealment of donor identities as seen with the Tories. On 23 February 1995, the Register of Members' Interests showed that both Tony Blair and Gordon Brown had received funding from a shadowy organisation called the Industrial Research Trust, headed by Lord Gregson. The money is said to come mainly from unions, although the identity of donors is kept secret even from Tony Blair.[148] When Tony Blair was elected as party leader, his personal campaign budget was almost twice that of any other candidate. He showed no inclination to reveal where around £80,000 had suddenly come from.

As one of the longest-serving Labour politicians in the country, Lord Healey is unhappy about the funding of the Party by unions. 'The Labour Party has got a problem but is prepared to face it and would welcome, certainly Blair would, welcome a chance to break with the union financial connection.'

'Is that a problem?' I asked.

'Oh yes,' he replied. 'Without union money in many cases we could not run election campaigns. The unions do expect a return for it. I was a union-sponsored MP. In my case I got a £200 contribution to my expenses at general elections. The cash dependence on the unions of the Labour Party is a problem.'

So is he against all voluntary funding?

'I wouldn't object to that, providing it is all registered. What is quite unacceptable I feel with the Tory Party is that the source of their funds is never disclosed.'[149] But Labour also has a Foundation which launders anonymous funds. Indeed, a new one has been created called Common Campaigns Ltd, with directors Lord Haskel and Lord Clinton-Davis.[150]

Lord Healey admitted the existence of such trusts. He described how the Cadbury Foundation gave money openly to the Parliamentary Labour Party, so that members of the Shadow Cabinet would have research assistants. The identity of the people who give to the Cadbury Foundation is never disclosed. But donations from the Foundation are declared. 'They funded one shared research post for me when I was Shadow Chancellor.'

Ken Livingstone says that candidates from all parties routinely break the strict funding rules in by-elections, where there is a strict legal limit on the amount that can be spent on campaigning in a constituency.

'Rules are systematically broken . . . in by-elections. All the main political parties spend much more than the legal limit. But because they all do it and everyone knows it, no one. does anything about it. But once you get to a general election. . . . the first problem is raising even the money allowed. You get occasional errors when people spend more than they should have done.'

I asked what support he got from unions himself.

'At the general election, TGWU will give £2–3,000 towards my election. After that they will give me £600 towards my general office costs. Now some unions do cough up £10–12,000 but I've never heard of anyone getting more. I was once approached by the NCU and they were talking about £12,000 for a researcher, primarily looking into NCU areas of interest and policy. If you are being sponsored for that sort of sum, then they expect you would really be doing some work for that.'[151] This therefore is identical in many ways to pressures on an individual MP who receives corporate funding.

Tensions can easily develop between a sponsoring union and an MP. In 1971, it was alleged that a trade union threatened to withdraw cash support from pro-European MPs. The

Privileges Committee declared that it was wrong to 'take or threaten action which is . . . calculated to affect a Member's course of action in Parliament'.

In the 1974–5 session of Parliament the Yorkshire Area Council of the National Union of Mineworkers seemed to be threatening to withdraw sponsorship from MPs opposed in debates to union policy. Once again, concerns were expressed about the abuse of influence. If unions are seeking extra support for their policies through sponsorship then this would appear to be a breach of the spirit of the Committee of Privileges' recommendations set out in the 1946–7 parliamentary session: 'It would certainly be improper for a Member to enter into any arrangement fettering his complete independence as a Member of Parliament, by undertaking to press some particular point of view on behalf of an outside interest, whether for reward or not.'[152]

However union sponsorship is a normal part of life for most Labour MPs. In 1995, the unions sponsored 165 out of 272, which is 61 per cent.[153] They would argue that, because the money is used for expenses not personal income, it is very different from commercial sponsorship. Nevertheless, since most if not all MPs are keen to be re-elected, it could be argued that they have a strong interest in any sponsorship helping them to do just that.

So, funding of both the main parties is unsatisfactory. The Tories have massive debts and are being as secretive as ever about how they will survive in the future, unable to shrug off unpleasant rumours about donations and honours, or illegal overseas gifts. This culture of secrecy is important because, as we will see, it has affected how many other issues have been handled. The 'way of doing things' in any political party is an influence on the kind of people drawn to it as volunteers, campaigners and candidates.

The Labour Party is still union-dominated and will continue to be so for as long as the unions continue to provide most of their income. The need for reform is obvious. State funding would be attractive to many Labour MPs and could be the salvation of the Tories, although it would not save them from bankruptcy since it could mean other income dries up, leaving them with unmanageable debts.

By August 1996 it appeared party finances had improved, with reports that the overdraft had been cleared – but only by borrowing £8.5 million from elsewhere. What is more, this was the situation at the start of an election campaign, when reserves needed to be highest.[136]

6

Sex, Money and Power

'The life of Members of Parliament is liable to place them in the path of great sexual temptation.' Lord Healey (1917–)

'There is only one step from the sublime to the ridiculous.' Napoleon I (1769–1821)

Some say that what politicians do in private is entirely their own affair, and media 'muck-raking' should cease. It is certainly a fact that prolific media reporting of sexual antics or other matters can quickly destroy a career. The allegations do not need to be true, but simply widely aired.

From 1992 until 1995 fifteen members of the Conservative government resigned, including six Parliamentary Private Secretaries, either shortly after or shortly before certain stories appeared in the press. There have been further resignations since.

Private indiscretions of public figures do matter. Sex scandals in particular may not relate directly to what an MP or Peer does in Parliament, but they do undermine respect for those in public life. Personal problems are nothing new however, and are not so fatal to political careers in the longer term.[154]

There is one particular individual whose sexual antics became the laughing stock of the nation, and who is widely blamed for bringing Westminster into disrepute. David Mellor was seen as a rising star in the Conservative Party, having been MP in Putney since 1979, junior Minister for Energy, then in the Home Office, Foreign Office and Department of Health, then Chief Secretary to the Treasury, and finally the Cabinet Member responsible for National Heritage. Indeed he was a continuous member of the government for more than ten years.

But David Mellor lived dangerously, taking huge risks in his private life and with the reputation of his entire government. The first tabloid 'scandal' in July 1992 was over a passionate affair with a little-known actress called Antonia de Sancha. However, the biggest and most damaging headlines were not about betraying his wife, but about lurid, detailed accounts of his sexual antics.

At first he was stoutly protected by indignant comments from Downing Street about the intrusive press. He earned some sympathy when it was discovered that his phone calls to Antonia had been bugged, within the law, by her landlord who had wired an extension to the phone which trailed outside into the garden so that a journalist could listen in. This intrusion into privacy was justified as in the 'public interest' after David Mellor was heard saying that he was so 'seriously knackered' by his sexual antics that it was affecting his concentration as a Minister.

His enemies said that he had shown grave errors of judgement and that he could no longer be entrusted with high office. Others felt that his main crime was bringing his political profession into disfavour. The biggest worry was what other media time-bombs might still lie hidden in the rest of his private life. However, to the consternation of his critics, the Prime Minister John Major stood firm in support of David

Mellor and he continued as a Cabinet Minister for some weeks.[155]

The timing of the revelations was critically important. Before the stories broke, David Mellor had been about to introduce new government measures to restrain press invasions of privacy. Not long before he had warned the press that they were 'drinking in the Last-Chance Saloon'. The press therefore were delighted to destroy both the reputation of the person driving the measures forward, and the measures themselves, arguing that if they had become law, exposure of his sordid past would have been near impossible. He might have survived had it not been for the public mockery – he had already been nicknamed the 'Minister of Fun' because he was overseeing the leisure industry, but now such a nickname had an embarrassing double meaning.

It is hard to overstate the damage that was caused, compounded by the misguided loyalty of John Major, who appeared to be saying that David Mellor's sexual adventures were irrelevant and unimportant to the government. John Major once again lost touch with the public mood. Here Major was, a family man, leading a party 'of the family', who seemed to endorse adultery as a normal and perfectly acceptable role model for leaders of the nation. In contrast, public reaction was one of disgust and contempt.

A considerable number of other press stories were to follow about other alleged private indiscretions by those in government. It is probably true that just as many similar stories could have been told about Labour politicians, but the media hardly took the slightest interest. Those headlines would wait until the day the opposition MPs gained power, especially in the newly 'respectable', pro-family, cosy world of Tony Blair and New Labour.

Lord Healey has strong opinions about sexual activity at Westminster. He says that the life of MPs is liable to place them in the path of great sexual temptation:[156] 'Being a Member of Parliament is very disruptive of family life. My children and my wife suffered because I was never home. I hardly saw the children. If you represent a constituency a long way from London then you have the question [of where you live].' He had no choice but to base the family in London because of his high profile role within the Labour Party. 'In my case I just went up [to my constituency] for long weekends. But a lot of my friends lived in their constituencies but spent the whole week in London. And then the temptation is drink and women. Relationships form . . . I don't think there's anything new there.'

Perhaps too there is something intoxicating about power itself, or a reaction against having to live so constantly in the public eye that leads some MPs to take such huge sexual gambles. There has never been a generation that has experienced such media pressures. Since the 1960s, television has made familiar faces of many politicians, but human frailties and vulnerability remain.

Having a huge profile can trigger a reaction in the human psyche. It is a pressure to know that several million people know what you look like. As a well-known personality walks down the street it is easy for the person to feel self-conscious, and there is a sense in which privacy disappears. Something like a private meal in a restaurant can become a public spectacle.[157]

The desire to be normal, to be anonymous, to be like an ordinary human being, can become overwhelming. The clothes that you wear, the food and magazines you buy, the wine you like, the friends you keep, may all become gossip column fodder. Your children are followed and photographed, and your spouse's appearance is scrutinised and criticised.

A point can come when the human brain flips into a state

of denial, winding back the clock to the carefree days of obscurity. However, such a mental state is highly dangerous because in such an unreal world great risks can easily be taken on a whim or an impulse.

This desire to escape may be what lay behind the 'bizarre' actions of the *Four Weddings and a Funeral* actor Hugh Grant, who stopped his car in the middle of Los Angeles to pick up a prostitute, and later have sex in his car, parked on a public street. Why should a man who had everything risk all for so little? Why did he refuse to pay a little more to go to a room? Hugh Grant himself explained the mental process rather well: 'Last night I did something completely insane.'[158]

It has also been suggested that those men in particular with huge drive and ambition, by definition more likely to succeed in politics, may also have correspondingly larger than average sex drives. Whether the right explanation is temptations away from home, mental strain under media pressure, large sexual drive or other factors, it is clear to me that those who are 'high profile' are in a way set up by the media and public expectations for a fall.

Another factor may be the general agreement among many at Westminster that private sexual behaviour is irrelevant in terms of suitability for public office. Teresa Gorman told me: 'I don't think sexuality should be a resigning issue. Hypocrisy is worse than infidelity in public life.' She says we must be realistic and not have too high an expectation of MPs. 'We are not here because we are plaster saints; we are not here because we are intellectuals; we are not here because we are particularly moral human beings. We are here as a cross-section of humanity, the jury of the nation. No one expects a jury to have a perfect private life. Exposure in the media itself is punishment enough without loss of office. Exposure is absolutely devastating. The press are utterly ruthless and completely indifferent to the damage they do to our institutions.'

'But surely the country expects certain standards of its leaders?' I asked.

'History tells us that few great leaders have led exemplary private lives. We shouldn't expect too much in this respect from our politicians.'[159]

However, one could argue that any behaviour likely to bring public office into disrepute is unbecoming of those in office, and that those serving the nation in Westminster have a responsibility to safeguard their corporate reputation. There are other issues than mere sexual privacy. For example, the majority of people in Britain disapprove of adultery, perhaps because it usually involves cheating and betrayal of trust. Someone in a long-term adulterous relationship may well be an expert liar and deceiver, but is that the sort of person you want to lead a nation?

Then there are issues of double standards – for example, an MP campaigning vigorously against single parenting as a model for society who, it emerges, has had at least one 'love-child'. There are also issues of legality, for example if an MP were to become involved in under-age sex; and of judgement, say if a constituent were to be seduced; or of indiscretion. As someone is in private, so they may be in public.

John Redwood surprised many people in July 1995 by suddenly resigning from the Cabinet and standing in a leadership contest against the Prime Minister John Major. He caused more headlines when he said that one of his policies if elected would be to ask people to say in advance if there were things from their private lives that could cause embarrassment later if they were appointed as Ministers.

Peter Bottomley declared that all that would be left would be self-confessed 'flashers and church mice'.[160] In other words, the only people who would survive such a process would be the arrogant, brazen and 'guilty', and the timid, diminutive and harmless.

While most people would probably agree that financial scandal involving an MP is probably far more serious than various sexual relationships, there have been some of the former too.

In conclusion, then, there has been a barrage of bad publicity over sexually incontinent Conservative MPs and others who have apparently lacked discretion in other private matters. Labour MPs are no bunch of innocents, but immune from media attention just so long as they have had no power. But whoever is in government, one thing is clear: we cannot afford the indulgence of another five years like the last. Behaviour must change if we are to have any prospect of restoring a sense of dignity and respect in public life.

I want to turn now from personal morality or lack of it to one of the most corrupting practices in Parliament today: whipping.

7

Whipping – and the Death of Conscience

'Damn your principles – stick to your Party.' Benjamin
Disraeli (1804–1881)

'A speech may change my mind; but my vote, never.' Georges
Benjamin Clemenceau (1841–1929)

'A little rebellion now and then is a good thing.' Thomas
Jefferson (1743–1826)

*'I sometimes wonder if we can afford the luxury of adversarial
politics.'* Lord Weatherill (1920–)

Whipping has only one purpose: to bully MPs into voting for
things they don't agree with or don't believe in. Whipping
has involved blackmail, verbal intimidation, sexual harassment and physical aggression. This is quite different from
presenting the case for a government line. Whipping therefore destroys integrity by definition, and invites corruption.
Giving way to a severe whipping involves the death of conscience, sacrificed on the high altar of ambition. Whipping
encourages mob rule, the end of free speech in debate, and

the end of free voting. The term itself is unhelpful, and is related to the 'whippers-in' of dogs in fox hunting.

Without Whips, individual Members of Parliament would vote for each measure according to the strength of the argument, which would be presented clearly in debate. Every vote would be carried or lost on its own merits. This does happen once or twice in every Parliament, usually over ethical issues where a government is unable to form a view, for example over capital punishment, but it is very unusual. If free voting were more widely encouraged, MPs would still be accountable to their constituents for the way they voted, with the sanction of being thrown out of Parliament at the following election if the electors felt that they had been badly served.

Every week a list of parliamentary business is circulated by the Whips Office of each party, with some items underlined once, twice or three times, depending on how strongly the party is going to insist that the MP turns up and votes in support of the party line. Hence the term One-Line or Two-Line or Three-Line Whip. Three-Line Whips are a tyranny, forcing MPs to remain within fifteen minutes of the Chamber for long periods because the exact timing of a vote or 'division' is often very uncertain.

A small mercy is a co-operative arrangement between the Whips Offices allowing 'pairing' to take place. For example, one Conservative may be in hospital with cancer, but there is also a Labour MP who is at a family funeral. Both are given leave and their votes cancel each other out by mutual agreement.

Sometimes Whips refuse any pairing and there is then the utterly disgusting and disgraceful sight of the very sick and dying being carted by taxis, ambulances and then wheelchairs into the Chamber, exploited by their Whips for so-called 'death-bed votes'. Lord Howie of Troon, Labour Whip in the

1960s, said recently, 'I think we killed three Members,' who were severely ill, yet were called in to vote and died immediately afterwards of heart attacks in or near Westminster.[161]

Voting by proxy or by post or any other means is strictly not allowed under any circumstances, even for people who are medically certified as hours or days from death – a heartless and stupid rule in a technological age. These 'death-bed votes' may not be common, but they sum up the cut-throat lust for power in the House of Commons, and the mindless obsession at times with glorious tradition, even when it violates all reason, compassion and common sense.

I have talked to a number of MPs both past and present about the merits and abuses of the whipping system. The Whips have extensive powers of patronage. They can help ensure ministerial appointments, honours, trips abroad and coveted places on Select Committees. Then there are invitations to Buckingham Palace, or to receptions in Downing Street, or the promise of a prestigious or lucrative quango appointment, or of a safer seat. Their ultimate sanction is 'withdrawal of the Whip' which in effect means excommunication from the party, likely to be followed by deselection and losing a seat in Parliament.

Teresa Gorman has been severely whipped over European issues and despises the whole process. 'This place is a male public school, a boys' school. The Whips are the prefects. Their job is discipline. Their currency is tittle tattle. They have never had a Tory woman in the Whips Office. "Only to do the cleaning," they will tell you. Shocking. This place is steeped in the 1920s. The Labour Party does have women in the Whips Office and has done for some time. It's mostly simple blackmail. I was treated to sexual abuse. The idea that I was an unworthy person because of my sex. It was tried on by a couple of Members. In my case they were being very vulgar.'[162]

In her book *The Bastards* she describes further details of the conversation between these two fellow Conservative MPs across her as she sat in the Chamber that day.[163]

'A woman's place is in the home.'

'Yes. Flat on her back.'

'Do you think Teresa would be any good on her back? I wonder what kind of knickers she wears?'

Teresa Gorman says that what follows was unrepeatable and she exploded with rage: 'Why don't you go somewhere else and find someone else to talk dirty to if you feel like that?'

'I thought you would be enjoying it. I thought that's what you like about this place, plenty of men. Women should be barefoot and pregnant. They shouldn't be let in here in the first place.'

She then left the Chamber rapidly. 'It was the worst half-hour in my life.' There was no one she could turn to although she was very upset. In the United States women have been awarded very large sums for less.

Afterwards she told me: 'It was the passion of the moment. There were very strong feelings on both sides. I'm not making an excuse for them. The argument is that we were sent to Westminster as MPs because the Party was embracing a particular political doctrine and the electorate were voting for that. [But] in this issue what we were doing was so profound, we were handing over power invested in us to Brussels.'

Another MP remarked: 'You must realise that there are jokes in this place about "irritating little squits" like __ who allegedly are periodically pushed up against the wall. You mustn't believe them all.'

Intimidation extends beyond confrontations with Whips. 'During the Maastricht debates when it came to votes on two crucial occasions the whole of the Cabinet moved in and encircled certain colleagues who they knew were thinking of voting against and almost elbowed them through and into the Lobby. And the Prime Minister did that to ____. He put his arm on ____'s shoulder, him having just made a speech explaining to the world why he wasn't going to vote for the Party. He was then literally conducted by the Prime Minister and that's very seductive. He literally went up to [him], put his arm round him and steered him, chatting away.'

I spoke to another Tory MP who was greatly distressed by what had happened. He ushered me into a quiet room in the House of Commons and grabbed my dictaphone from the sofa to dictate a statement 'off the record'. This is a full transcript which describes a corrupt and disturbing process at the very heart of our democracy. There can be no more important thing an MP does than cast his or her vote, yet these votes are being systematically rigged through buying people on the 'payroll' or through honours or by threatening or blackmailing the rest.

'The experience I had of the Maastricht (European) business was that as this was the first rebellion of Parliament after the '92 election they were coming at it fresh themselves and so they didn't know how to handle it. They started off with a sort of Mr Nice and Mr Nasty approach, where one Whip would be nice and the other Whip would be nasty. I had personal experience of being verbally abused in a loud way in a corridor in full public view by one Whip and then by the same Whip later.'

'Did he assault you?'

'Well, he didn't actually hurt me but he came very close to me and sought to take hold of my lapels in the privacy of a. . . .'

'So it was you that you were talking about when you said that you'd seen . . .'

'No. This was my experience. Now there was another

occasion when I saw somebody actually being lifted up by his lapels. And I, um, that was all the Mr Nasty [approach] so there must have been a lot of that going on. The Mr Nice approach was "Come in and have a drink old boy," or "Let's go and have a cup of tea," and this would be a different Member.

'They then went a little further and asked a friend of each of us to approach us. This would be somebody who was not obviously a part of the government but may have been on the payroll, or may just have been an MP that they knew was friendly. And this MP would try a totally relaxed and gentle approach, a sort of personal plea. "Look come on, the Prime Minister needs us to do this. I've got reservations but let's go for it because otherwise we'll be in trouble. We've just won an election and so on, and the Prime Minister has brought back the best deal he can on Europe" – all that sort of line. And "This will be the final high, er, the last line in the sand, this is the high tide of federalism, don't need to worry, it won't go beyond this," and all that sort of approach.

'They then, as things got nearer the vote, they became more desperate. They started the tack of ringing up Association Chairmen. And the line there was, "Look you've got this MP, he's not got a very good reputation in the House, and quite frankly, we'd like to see him deselected. Can you not pull him in line?" Or, "Your MP is rocking the boat, grave damage to the Prime Minister personally. If you want your title or your invitation to Buckingham Palace, or to the party conference reception with the Prime Minister, you'd better do something about it." Well, in my own case that didn't work because my Chairman's views on Europe make mine seem positively federal, so he told them where to go; he had no interest in tea parties or in Buckingham Palace and he doesn't expect any title for his services to the Party, so they got nowhere with that.

'A lot of wives were then contacted, either by the Whips

Office or by somebody from Central Office or by the friend of the MP attacked, depending on how well they knew the family. And the line with the wives was, er, sometimes persuasive, like, you know, "You're not going to get . . . Your husband's not going to get the title. You won't get the title or won't get the trips abroad or won't get this or won't get that," or quite threatening: "We know something about him, in his private life" – that sort of threat, which is really quite, quite unpleasant all round. So they tailored each approach to suit the Member that they had in front of them.'

'You say things about their private life . . . what sort of things? Sexual indiscretion?'

'Yes. Yes. I gather they have a record of a lot of "goings on" that they keep somewhere in the Whips Office and they were threatening to use it. And it so happens that if they had a hold over a Member, and that was all the hold they had, they would use it and they did use it.'

'Do you know they had that kind of record or is it just your . . . .'

'No. I surmise that from what other colleagues have told me. I don't have a direct experience of that and I didn't have that threat held over me. They actually did say that they'd find it difficult to have a threat over me, so I was more of an interesting case in some ways, because my wife wasn't interested in the title or Buckingham Palace tea parties and, er, as I've just explained my Chairman wasn't interested either. My friend that was assigned to me was in no doubt that on a matter of principle I was prepared to go against it, so they didn't really have a lever on me, so they gave up. Then as the night came and then the day and then the evening and the vote at ten o'clock, as that got nearer the numbers were just not adding up and they were getting more frenetic. Going round they would try a combination of all these things simultaneously.

'The plan fell apart and they would just physically, er, get hold of people, verbally abuse them, or persuade them there's drinks – the Prime Minister probably never poured out so many bloody drinks – and the Prime Minister was available. Graham Bright, his PPS, stood in the Central Lobby, something he never normally did, and said "Would you like to see the Prime Minister? *Now*! Come and have a drink with the Prime Minister" – this sort of thing. The Prime Minister is *never* that available, even in an emergency, but this time he was. He must have just sat in his room all evening, and desperately counting off the numbers.

'And then as the vote was called and the divisions began I saw people physically blocking the entrance to the Lobby to stop some Members getting in. I saw one MP physically carried into the Lobby. He wasn't protesting to the point of forcing them off him physically, he was obviously in a terrible dilemma about what to do. He knew his conscience was telling him not to go in the government Lobby, and all the persuasion had failed and he stood there dithering. And then, as they lifted his arms up, so his feet were off the ground and carried him forward, he sort of allowed that to be the final clincher, and he was carried like a child into the Lobby.'

'Perhaps living with his conscience because of it?'

'Yes. Somebody else had decided for him. Yes, maybe.'

'He didn't walk through?'

'He didn't walk through. Yes, that's right [laughter], yes, carried through. And then there were all sorts of procedural votes, I forget which one it was now . . . But between the divisions, fifteen minutes between votes, he sat in the Chamber and Michael Heseltine put his arm around his shoulder and said, "Come on" as the bells were ringing and the Prime Minister came round and put his other arm around his other shoulder and the three of them walked into the government Lobby, so in a sense it was like his feet were off the ground.

Same sort of thing really. Prime Minister's arm round . . . [demonstrates].

'And I was in the Lobby against the government and several Labour MPs gathered round me and said, "There don't seem to be any other Tories in here," and I thought, my goodness me. No! ___ is in here somewhere," and I looked around, [but] I couldn't see him. I didn't know what had happened 'til afterwards.'

'Goodness,' I exclaimed. 'These are serious things. The Whips in a situation like that. I mean there's technical assault, and intimidation . . .'

'Yes. Yes, yes. Yes, that's correct.'

'Although obviously they're outside the jurisdiction of the normal courts.'

'They have to be, yes. If we have a Whip system, that sort of thing has to be recognised as part of the machinery of Whipping, and for Labour MPs, some of them expressed themselves aghast at it afterwards when it was in the papers – but that's sheer hypocrisy as well because some older Labour MPs told me that we had got away lightly compared to what happened to them when the last Labour government was in a minority for several months and had that pact with the Liberals. Labour had a majority actually of only three after the '74 election, and they carried on for months and then with Liberal's support. And of course that sort of physical handling was constant, almost every day. Some of the Labour Whips apparently used to block the doors by the cloakrooms to stop Labour MPs leaving, and lock some of the toilets to stop them voting – that kind of thing was reported to me by two or three older Labour MPs.' (laughter)

The tape was then stopped because he wanted to tell me things he did not trust to tape.

I asked the MP referred to about what happened to him in the debating Chamber. He told me that he had felt under tremendous pressure after he was warned in no uncertain terms that the Prime Minister was determined to resign if the vote was lost.

He negotiated an assurance from Michael Heseltine shortly before the vote that the final reading of the Maastricht Bill would be delayed until after the Danish referendum and was then persuaded to vote with the government. 'There's not a great deal I like about being an MP,' he said. He feels that he personally had a hand in saving the Prime Minister. 'That night was so crucial.' He agreed that the events in the Chamber happened as described, but rejected any suggestion of undue pressure. But was he just putting on a brave face after a severe whipping?

I asked Lord Weatherill for a contrasting view in the light of all the criticisms of whipping. After all, he had been a Whip himself from 1967 to 1979, was trained by Lord Whitelaw and was Chief Whip from 1974 to 1979. He is widely respected by Members of all parties. What was his justification for this way of conducting party business? Did he concede that the public image of whipping was damaging to Parliament?

He told me that he had joined the Tory Whips Office in 1967, during a period in opposition, and gave a very different picture of what whipping is about, based on his own experience of days when the Conservatives were in opposition. He described a whipping process that sounded positively cosy in comparison, both reasonable and tolerant, compared to the near fanatical aggression and thuggery we hear about today.

'I remember Willie Whitelaw shaking me to my roots by saying "Now you're in the Whips Office, bear it in mind that it is your duty to help the government effect the business that is in the best interests of our country, even though we fight our own party. We only oppose where we believe that policy is not in the best interests of our country. We are Her Majesty's Loyal Opposition." Every Whip looks after an area. For the last five years I was known as the s____'s Whip. They weren't at all. They were often the *best* Members. You had to spend an awful lot of time with them over their genuine concerns. They by and large were not interested in office. They stood by their guns and I respected that.

'In those days we had to try and persuade our party that the government was doing the right thing. These days I'm afraid the opposition says everything is wrong. Occasionally you get glimpses of [consensus] – the Falklands War, the Gulf War. There seems to be a feeling that if you are not passionately opposing them all the time, you're a weak opposition.

'We have a system of adversarial politics which arises from the shape of the Chamber. The place was bombed in the last war and there was a debate as to whether it should be rebuilt in the shape of a semicircle which was stopped by Winston Churchill in a speech: "We shape our buildings. Thereafter they shape us." I often wonder if we can afford the luxury of adversarial politics when nearly everyone knows what's wrong and there isn't all that much disagreement about what you do to put it right, outside the Chamber. The Select Committee system could be used to good effect. For example, use it to help design a fair tax system. There is a consensus here. A lot of it is fictitious: fighting for the sake of it.'

(The Select Committees are small all-party groups which meet regularly to discuss various government policies and to scrutinise the work of various Ministries. They have grown in number and authority over the last few years, and have profoundly altered the way Parliament works. Each Committee meets in a semicircle, in a civilised and courteous manner, and the whole emphasis is on seeking consensus rather than conflict.)

I returned to the subject of whipping. The culture of the Whips Office almost twenty years ago seemed many steps removed from the mid-1990s. Did Lord Weatherill accept that the whole process of bullying people to vote against their conscience could end up damaging personal integrity?

Lord Weatherill disagreed. 'Every Member of Parliament is elected on a party manifesto (which they are expected to support). In my day there was a Whips' meeting every day. The Chief Whip would go round the room: "We've got this debate coming up. What's the view of the Members?" They would be told: "This is not on.' I can't begin to tell you the number of times I said to [the Leader of the Party], "Margaret, I've got some rather bad news for you."

' "What's that?" she would reply.

' "May I give you some whisky? The Conservative Party disagrees with you on this. I'm afraid we shan't be able to carry them."

' "It's your duty. . . ." etc.

' "We've really done our best, now please listen. . . ."

'And she did. The role of Whips is absolutely vital. I don't blame John Major. I blame his Whips. The Chief Whip is a vital member of the Cabinet. He is in it but not of it. He is not bound by decisions of the Cabinet. He never participates in the Cabinet discussions unless he is asked to do so. After the Cabinet is mindful to take a course of action, the Prime Minister will turn to the Chief Whip and will ask, "Do you think we can get this through the House?"

'And he will probably say, "Prime Minister I will need to consult my Whips about this." And an exercise will take place where every Member will be asked by his Whip what he's thinking. And at the next Cabinet discussion the Prime Minister will ask and the Chief Whips will either say they can probably carry it or that he would be unable to carry the Party on it.'

Lord Weatherill insisted that the main job of Whips should be to consult, not dominate, but he did acknowledge that times had changed. He blamed personality conflicts and leadership battles for some of the bitterest whipping fights.

'It is not the function of the whips to persuade party members to dance to tune. That is for the Cabinet. In recent years I am horrified at some of the weapons alleged to have been used by them, but in my day, if you ask any of the anti-marketeers, we never ever brought any pressure on them. We respected their views. Mind you, it was slightly different because of our relationship, when we were taking them into Europe in '71 and '72. Because of the good relations we had with them, rebels always supported us on procedural motions so we could always get a closure and there was a residual loyalty there which I think today has been extinguished very largely because of personalities. There were people very passionately "pro" Margaret Thatcher and very passionately "anti" her successor and I'm afraid it's patently seen.

'The most important man in Parliament after the Prime Minister is the Opposition Chief Whip. There is a system hardly ever talked about which is "the usual channels", ie the Whips. They deal between each other. I ran the floor show with Walter Harrison. Walter and I had absolute total mutual trust.'

I asked Lord Weatherill about the disturbing allegations I had heard over the European votes, of intimidation, sexual harassment and blackmail.

'If that is so it is totally reprehensible,' he said. 'Dishonourable. I wouldn't go along with it at all.'[164]

If fear tactics fail to work and the promise of rewards also falls on deaf ears, then the Whips have one other tool left, which is 'trading'. Sometimes MPs are 'bought off' with an agreement to some minor point in a piece of legislation later in Parliament. In effect what is being said is this: 'If you vote for this (against all your principles because you think it is utterly wrong), then I will do what I can to get the Minister to change his mind on the other issue.'

David Porter knows what it is like to compromise in this way. He gave an example of a debate on fishing rights. He eventually voted with the government despite his own objections and great anxieties from fishermen in his constituency, after receiving a letter from the Minister congratulating him on his campaign for change and offering to concede some ground in the future.

'I was bought,' he said. 'There is a danger of devaluing my vote if I vote against the government too often. The whipping business is often just games. I sacrificed a principle for a longer-term gain to get us out of a common fisheries policy. I became an MP in 1987. There were no surprises. I knew what I was letting myself in for because I had been involved in the party machine locally for some years. I voted against Maastricht as a conscience issue. I see a real risk of inter-European war – not so much a Bosnia as a Chechnya. Twenty years from now we could see a Brussels army bombing the rebel district of East Anglia.'

He described his revulsion at the way the 'payroll' vote is controlled from the very top. We have already seen in the chapter on patronage how the creation of a large number of new government posts had drawn a third of all Conservative MPs into the payroll by the early 1990s.

'Payroll whipping is secret – Ministers, PPSs, etc. A memo goes round. Officially it might be a One-Line Whip but it is a hidden Three-Line Whip. If a payroller ever votes against, he resigns or is sacked. The payroll has grown hugely and now all junior Ministers have PPSs – which keeps another fifty back-benchers as bag carriers to Ministers.'[165]

As a former Minister for four years, and a PPS for many more, Robert Key knows what it is like to be controlled through the payroll vote, but defends it vigorously. 'The best thing for any government is for 100 per cent of all MPs to be on the payroll or party hacks. Whipping is extremely important not just because it ensures a government majority but also because it conditions people to believe that they will only be rewarded for good behaviour. On balance whipping is a good thing. Without it you could not maintain a party majority. There are two circumstances when you are allowed to defy a Three-Line Whip: when you have a strong constituency interest, like fishing rights, and matters of deep conscience.'

'But would it not be better to have voting without pressure?' I asked.

'You can't have pressure-free voting. There are huge interests and secret voting would not help. You have to live with yourself and your conscience – for example over capital punishment. Constituency pressures can be real but are often used as an excuse. Then there are pressures from the party. You can't be an expert on every issue. Then there are pressure groups which are blossoming at the moment and I think are very bad for democracy. Small single-issue groups. There is a huge career structure for people in pressure groups. I see it all the time. Directors move around from one cause to another as hired advocates. It is very expensive – even answering all the mail – and these people are unelected and unaccountable yet raising vast sums from people. Then there is church lobbying and religious bigotry – when you are told you are the devil incarnate.'[166]

While there will always be campaigning on issues for as long as there is free speech in a democratic state, it is also clear that the public pays great respect to MPs who listen and are prepared to break party rules for the sake of what they believe is right.

As a prominent dissident, Teresa Gorman has received many letters from people who say they admire 'principles, integrity, and courage'.[167] Many of them have told her: 'We've never voted Tory in our lives but we admire what you're doing,' or 'You've got guts.' Then they have often followed that with a paragraph of utter contempt for the Cabinet. And then some have said, 'If you were Prime Minister, we would vote for you.'

I asked whether that was because of her anti-EC stance.

'Personally I think it's an anti-sleaze reaction. People hear nothing good about their politicians so it is not surprising that they hold us in contempt. Then suddenly a group of us stood up for our beliefs. The response was phenomenal.'

In an earlier interview an anonymous MP described a system run by Whips which seemed to rely on a comprehensive index of 'sleazy' rumours about rebel MPs, but he said that he had no direct evidence of a 'black book', apart from gossip in Westminster.

Then in May 1995 a former Tory Whip spoke candidly to a television crew about a secret dossier. He described how MPs would come to the Whips for advice when in trouble over allegations, whether financial or sexual, even involving 'sex with boys'. The Whips were usually protective and would do what they could to help. However, the details would be recorded. If there was trouble with that MP's loyalty some time later, he or she would be approached and threatened with exposure.

A former Whip confessed that a wide range of 'scandalous' stories were collected, many of which were pure gossip, for the express purpose of blackmail. 'When you were trying to persuade a Member that he should vote the way he didn't want to vote, it was possible to suggest that perhaps it would not be in his interests if people knew something about him.'[168]

The researchers then went to see Lord Whitelaw, who also confirmed the existence of a list of scandalous rumours in his day. The gossip was collected, analysed for damage potential, and stored for possible future use, regardless of whether it had any basis whatsoever in fact. 'I mean, the Dirt Book was just a little book, in which you had to write down varying things that you knew or heard about people.'[169] Another Whip said: 'We knew everything about everybody.'[170]

I myself asked Lord Whitelaw about the whipping process. Lord Weatherill seemed to have been painting rather a rosy picture of whipping as it was some years ago. I described what Lord Weatherill had said about standards of integrity then, and how the Whips recognised their duty in opposition to let people vote for measures which would clearly benefit the country, even if the party was officially opposed.

Lord Whitelaw said: 'I don't even know exactly how it works now. There is still no way you can force people. You've got to try and work with them.'[171]

I also asked the then Chairman of the Conservative Party, Jeremy Hanley, about whipping and whether a secret dossier existed. 'I've never heard of this gentleman [the Whip], I must admit. I've read the article.'

I challenged him about the experience of people I had met who were savagely whipped over Maastricht.

'Is this by one party only? You're not giving the impression, are you, that only one party does this?'

I explained that I was under no illusions about the Labour Party, but I had come to talk to him about his own people.

'I know not of this book,' he replied. 'This is absolutely true.' Jeremy Hanley continued: 'I've never been a Whip.

I've never been subjected to the pressure of Whips. I have never been threatened by a Whip in this way. I do know that there were certain people who went into print in newspapers saying they were apparently threatened.'

'But now a former Whip is saying. . . .'

'Who I've never heard of – so it must be an awfully long time ago. I've been in the House of Commons now for twelve to thirteen years. I wouldn't in any way want to denigrate him or to say that what he is saying is untrue. All I'm saying is that what he is talking about, his experience, is many years ago.'

'But isn't it just possible that he is the only one who can speak, because the others are still in government or are MPs?'

Jeremy Hanley thundered back: 'I can tell you absolutely from my own experience and from my own knowledge, I don't know anybody that has been threatened in that way, although if I were a Whip and I desperately wanted to get a government's programme through, it might be my task for me to persuade people to do so. And what they use as powers of persuasion might be many and varied. I have never experienced it myself, although I have voted against the government on a Three-Line Whip. I have even Telled [counted the votes] in the Chamber against the government on a Three-Line Whip. Two Whips came up to me and they shouted and screamed at me before and after the event, but they never threatened me.'

However, he said he did recall a Minister threatening him that he would never get on in government. 'And if you're not man enough to stand up for your convictions when you are voting against the government for which you were elected then you are not serving your constituency.' Jeremy Hanley blamed the press for creating an image of politics that was 'fantasy' according to his own experience.[172]

Jeremy Hanley clearly had no knowledge whatsoever of a

secret dossier and its existence is unproved. In this regard it is interesting to note that shortly before this book went to press a Commons researcher told me that his MP had been talking to a Conservative MP and happened to mention that another Conservative MP had been behaving in a thoroughly dishonest and disreputable manner regarding parliamentary expenses. The very next day the colleague bounded up to thank him profusely. 'I told the Whips Office straightaway,' she said, beaming. Her purpose was not to ensure justice but to increase the Whips' power.

I asked Lord Ennals, as a senior Labour Peer with years of Commons experience, what his perspective was on whipping. He felt that one answer was to have greater honesty by candidates before election. 'When I was elected it was on certain policies, a manifesto. There was a certain certainty about what positions we were going to take. It was also understood there were certain subjects which were a matter of conscience: hanging, age of consent. I agree there will be changes and so too there ought to be changes but they voted for a particular set of policies . . .

'The public is entitled, if I have voted differently from what I said I would do, to an explanation. If the government decides to impose a Whip on something not in their manifesto, then they owe an explanation to the country. If there are differences in your own point of view, then you should say so in your own personal manifesto. The national structures should have waivers written, where MPs will not be voting with the government. You do have to have discipline so that the government is able to do what it said it would do.'[173]

So, heavy-handed whipping is a way of life at Westminster and destroys integrity because its sole aim is to bully people to vote against the things they believe in. On the other hand very few MPs are able to imagine how any government could survive without any kind of discipline at all. While there is clearly a need for communication of policy and for order in any party, what we have seen is disturbing evidence of abuse.

We will return to whipping in the final chapter, together with a vision for a very different kind of democracy, but we now need to look at another area which weakens men and women of integrity: ministerial office, collective responsibility and Cabinet secrecy.

8

Secrets of Ministers and Civil Servants

'The Secretary of State was obsessed with secrecy. In a dictatorship I would have been bumped off – I knew too much.' Former Minister, 1995

'Many Ministers only have a clear conscience because they have a poor memory.' Anonymous MP

'By the way, you ought to know that my public pronouncements bear no relation to my private views.' Sir John Foster, former MP, casual comment after TV interview

'If I had to say which was telling the truth about society, a speech by a Minister of Housing, or the buildings put up in his time, I should believe the buildings.' Kenneth Clarke, Minister

A government Minister told me, 'Corruption is not the problem, it's incompetence,' but what is the evidence for that? The truth is that there is plenty of evidence of both, but both are well protected by secrecy so the truth is always hard to establish.

For obvious reasons secrecy is likely to invite abuse when it covers the actions of a large number of people with great collective power. Yet in Britain the Official Secrets Act means that it is almost impossible for an ordinary citizen to get hold of basic information, and even harder if you are a member of the press. I have many examples from my own experience where I know exactly which official has a particular piece of information, but I cannot get hold of it.

An example for me as a doctor has been the figures showing numbers of adverse reactions to measles vaccination – important in giving accurate health advice. I knew whom to ask and had spoken to the person on the phone. However, I found that the only way to get this information was by asking an MP to file a Written Question to the Minister of Health. The disadvantage of this method is that it is slow (a response can be expected in a week or two), and often gives only the exact barest minimum needed to answer the precise question. There is no prospect of discussion and no way to be certain from whose desk the answer has been prepared, unless as I had done, some preliminary work has been carried out. The Press Offices are staffed by people who know little more than the content of recent press releases by Ministers. Such secrecy is oppressive, threatens democracy and is condescending.

One expression of official secrecy is 'collective Cabinet responsibility' which means simply that Cabinet members are sworn to absolute secrecy and loyalty to the agreed 'party line' from the moment they are appointed. This makes sound sense from a management point of view but can be fraught with ethical difficulties. It means that the only way you can expose something you believe to be wrong is by resigning, which may well remove any real influence you have in doing anything about it. So you either remain and continue the deception or cast yourself out into the political wilderness. There is hardly a middle way without being forced to resign.

I went to see a former Minister for whom I had great respect. He talked very freely about what life was really like in government and then dropped a bombshell concerning a major scandal he had discovered relatively recently. It has never been exposed although several other Ministers and senior civil servants know about it, including the Secretary of State and the Permanent Secretary (the most senior civil servant in the Department).

Even now that he is out of office, he is worried about the repercussions to himself and his family should the documents he has deposited in a bank vault ever see the light of day, which at the moment is unlikely to happen until after his death. He was not involved in the scandal directly but realises he could now be open to criticism for not resigning the moment he found out and exposing the situation from the back benches.

He told me under the strictest promise of complete anonymity: 'As a member of the government I came to the point of seriously considering resigning because I realised that I was being lied to and so was everyone else on major issues of national importance – a whole series of issues. Civil servants knew it too and were prepared to go along with it. Other Ministers were aware as well and we discussed it together but we all decided to keep quiet.'

'When did the alarm bells begin to ring?' I asked.

'I was always wary when I found a tricky issue buried deep in a mountain of several hundred letters waiting for signature.' He was working steadily through the pile on his desk at the Department when his suspicions were aroused over trends in answers about a particular subject.

'The standard paragraphs finally got to me. I summoned the civil servants responsible to explain this policy – the Grade Threes (intermediate level) or indeed Fives – and gradually my hair started to curl. Many of them are incompetent. That is the problem with the British civil service. On technical issues the people doing the work are the Grade Sevens, but they are rarely allowed into the presence of a Minister so as not to show up the Grade Fives and Grade Threes. Grade Threes appear with a brief they have read only half an hour before.

'I just felt in my bones that what I was being asked to sign up to was morally wrong. And then I realised it was also unsustainable, but it was still being sustained after very many years, and everybody knew it.'

'And these answers that were going out were untrue?' I asked.

'No. They weren't lies. They were just not the truth. They could have been and should have being saying almost the opposite.' (Laughter.)

'So they were a long way from the truth?'

'No, no. They weren't lies but they were not the truth. Not the whole truth. And this was the dilemma. One gradually realised one was living in a very shadowy world. But the implications of allowing a change in policy would have been dramatic.'

'So what did you do?'

'I sought to change a number of policies.'

He told me of his conversations with other Ministers after which it became clear that they too were aware of the problem but did not want to do anything about it. The Secretary of State was unmovable.

'What scale of shaking of government do you think there might have been if it had been exposed?'

'I don't think it would have resulted in ministerial resignation – after all, the Permanent Secretary was supporting the state of affairs. I just think there would have been a major row in Parliament. One of the problems was that the opposition was so pathetically weak that they would have been too stupid to have done anything about it. And that has been a problem in recent years.'

'How many Secretaries of State have been involved in this?'

'I have no idea. Many – but they may not have all known. And this is another worry. Because civil servants outlive politicians, they are the guardians of continuity of policies and they are the guardians of the secrets. And their game is to let the politicians know as little as necessary.' He described how papers of a previous administration are locked away as soon as there is a change of government so that Ministers have to start again with a blank piece of paper in any investigation of their own. 'The most powerful meeting of the week is arguably not the Cabinet, but the meeting of the Permanent Secretaries with the Cabinet Secretary on Wednesday mornings. This is the establishment. They are the guardians of the traditions of the civil service.'

'So how did you decide whether to stay or to expose the situation and resign?'

'I knew I should stay in, but it was rationalising it that was difficult. I knew there must be a lot of other Ministers in a similar situation to me over a range of issues, who were finding the going quite tough. But I felt that if I left, it really would be a rat leaving the ship – not that the ship was sinking which sometimes surprised me. It really did get to my conscience though. It is quite wrong to suppose that politicians don't have consciences. They do.'

'So have you ever talked to anyone about it?'

'To be perfectly honest I have never burdened my wife with political issues – we've got better things to talk about. But I was clearly very worried. I was not behaving normally and she realised something was seriously wrong. And so I told her what had been going on. I said I really thought the time had come to depart, but her reaction was very swift:

"Don't be so daft," she said. "If people like you go, it is only going to get much worse." And so I stayed.'

'But it sounds as though it was a real dilemma.'

'Yes, but I didn't have any hesitation in carrying on after I had thought it through – and shared it. Of course the difficulty is that it is very difficult to share these sorts of things with anyone.'

'It must be a very lonely place.'

'Except, you see, you put these things to the back of your mind because you are so ridiculously busy as a Minister. There are always a thousand other things waiting to be done. However it did shake my faith in all sorts of people and institutions.' He told me of a number of situations both inside and outside politics which have combined to make him far more cynical about trusting other people today. He also felt strongly that his experience was important for people to understand.

'So who else have you told about these events you describe apart from your wife?'

'I told no one else although I kept an account of significant events as they happened which is now in a safe place – but what do I do with it? Burn it? I can't show it to anyone. I always believed that history was bunk and now I knew it was true. The most important facts were never recorded anywhere. Even minutes of Cabinet meetings record neither who said what nor what was said. They record the wishes of Number 10. It was a standing joke to see how the Cabinet Office had concocted the minutes of the last meeting.'

'What would have happened if you had "gone public"?'

He replied that although no crime had been committed under British law, 'the consequences of telling the truth after all these years would have been profound. Citizens might expect millions of pounds in compensation, and successive governments and parties would have had to admit they had been wrong for years. It was not a cover up because it was never uncovered in the first place. It was always secret. The problem was compounded by the fact that the Secretary of State was obsessed with secrecy. He trusted no one – neither fellow Ministers nor civil servants.'

The former Minister described to me how the standard response on many issues was, 'Why do they need to know?' or, 'We'll just keep that to ourselves.' The Secretary of State was powerful and intimidating, and knew he had the means to utterly destroy the career of any junior Minister who crossed him. The effect on the former Minister was profound and disturbing: 'He sapped all my confidence as a politician. After six months I wanted to go.' He described to me how other Ministers had also suffered at various times.

He felt he was being gradually squeezed out of office, got rid of as a dangerous man. 'I was a delver. Some people just take things as they are, they accept uncritically what they are told, but I tend to ask questions. I would ask for a set of background papers behind a decision or a policy, and if I felt I still wasn't being told the whole story, I would ask for more papers, delving down layer after layer to get at the truth. In a dictatorship I would have been bumped off – I knew too much. Instead I was sacked – suddenly.'

I asked him if he was tempted to seek redress. 'If you could, would you like to see the Secretary of State named over what has happened, particularly in view of other reservations you have about his general conduct in a number of different situations?'

'No. I am not a vindictive person at all. I have no desire to expose him. I don't want him identified. I hope it won't come to that.'

Since then he has tried to get on with normal life, but the memory of what is in the vault continues to occupy his thoughts.

'Every ministerial and political career ends in tears. After being sacked, what was my reaction? To get on with life, represent my constituency and involve myself in special interests. Ironically, after I left, ___ nearly stumbled on the truth and the Department is now shit-scared and reviewing its position. In general civil servants outlive Ministers and they like nothing better than a quick turnover, and in this case there was a high degree of civil servant continuity through a number of changes at the top. I can't understand why the Permanent Secretary didn't say anything.'

He then described the freedom he felt on leaving government, and how it was only then that the issues became clearer. 'It is an extraordinary sensation leaving office because the burdens of state really do fall from your shoulders. One becomes objective in one's judgements again to a very large extent. The Whips really hold no fear over you because they don't any longer control your destiny, whereas they did before you got into office. You become more dangerous to the Whips and one of the problems of the Conservative government is that there are so many ex-Ministers on the back benches. It means that your politics become far more clearly orientated towards your own beliefs and the needs of your own constituents, in a very healthy way.'

Perhaps the former Minister was wise to keep quiet, having not immediately resigned on discovering the scandal. David Amess has strong views as a back-bencher on what a Minister should do in such circumstances, which I suspect are typical of many other MPs, and nothing compared to the severity of the opinions of the nation as a whole. 'I think if you are a Minister and you are unhappy with a policy, or you think you've uncovered something that is either dubious or criminal, then you should make a statement in the House of Commons. If they say, "Look, you're going to be chucked out if you open your mouth about that," then you must state your case in Parliament.'

However, he agreed that it could be very difficult when in the situation to know what to do. 'Everyone must make his own judgement. I do not believe in resigning lightly. I much prefer to fight from within and it's up to each individual how much they can tolerate. It is a dilemma but if you feel passionately that you have uncovered something you believe is disgraceful and cannot persuade anyone to listen to you, then I support that person in resigning and then making it known publicly.'[174]

Another (nameless) Tory MP added that he thought there were now so many leaks that a serious cover up would be impossible to maintain for long. 'I've noticed increasingly that it's pretty impossible for the government to get away with anything really. You've got letters being leaked, minutes being leaked – it's just hopeless.' However, this MP had never been a Minister: as we have seen, the truth can be hidden successfully for years, if revelation would be embarrassing to many of the individuals who know the information.

A second former Cabinet Minister told me that he too had a deeply troubled conscience. This time the issue was over arms sales, weapons which had been used against the country's own people, a situation not covered by any of the recent inquiries. After some discussion on a broad range of topics, with the tape still running we moved to some of the dilemmas Ministers faced.

Without more than a second or two of hesitation he began to unload his heavy burden. His confession is reproduced here unedited as he originally intended it to appear in his lifetime. He knew he was a sick man and that his time was short and that he was faced with a great personal dilemma. I sought to let him tell the story at his own pace and in his own words. He knew the story had to be told, and he wanted it to be told, but agonised over how and when the country, place and time should be revealed. He was comforted at the thought that the truth might one day be made known, together with other broader matters, in the context of a book which addressed some of the common dilemmas of ministerial life.

'I now know that an answer that I gave as a junior Foreign Office Minister about the supplying of arms to X which were subsequently used in Y was an incorrect answer. And I know that the answer that I gave then has been repeated time and time again by subsequent Ministers years ago (albeit in good faith).

'If I really decided to go to town on this and explore it, and I am under pressure, bearing in mind what my knowledge now is, what my views now are on the question of arms to X. I know that what I said then was not only incorrect but very damaging. And so I have been pressed to write to Douglas Hurd [then Foreign Secretary] to [warn him not to use] the words which I used x years ago because (as he obviously does not realise) they weren't true then, as I have now established, and they are not true now. I haven't done this. I'm considering it. I'm afraid I'm just taking my time over this. There must be others [in the same situation]. From the moment I accepted [the Written Answer] I held responsibility for it.'

He agreed that similar incorrect answers could have been given out by him in good faith a hundred times a year, more than half of which he might never have known anything about. He agreed that Ministers could sometimes be in danger of building in their answers a fantasy land created by their civil servants.

'... which is the great advantage of having political advisers. They ought to be checking to be making sure that advice given to Ministers is actually correct. I had a political adviser who was a party man, a very smart fellow. He was a ****. He was paid to be a **** . . . to ask, "Are you sure what you are being given to say is true because I happen to think that it isn't. Have you thought of the consequences. Because if it isn't true, what you're saying will give it credence, and will give rise to the sort of situation I've just described to you."

'These people thought that I gave them an assurance that I would write to Douglas Hurd and ask him to stop using my words [that he has been repeating in good faith]. Well, I didn't say anything like that. Well, they're now getting very angry with me, because . . . but I said I didn't say that. I said I would consider all this and I am considering.'

I asked him if he was under pressure that they would go to the press. Had they threatened him in any way?

'There is an element of risk [that they will go to the press]. They haven't said that or I would be more worried than I am. But I am worried to do the right thing. As you have pointed out this is a very serious, very serious problem. If foreign policy is going to be made by statements made x ago, by civil servants . . . how would you ever find out who they were? Civil servants could become so frightened of saying anything that you would create frightened civil servants going around cowering because they were frightened that what they were saying . . . they would be more inclined to say nothing. It would get even more boring. You would get answers that weren't answers. It's bad enough as it is. It would get even worse.'

This then was the interview as it might have appeared, but for one important fact: shortly after our interview, just over sixteen weeks later, I received the sad news that Lord Ennals had died. I therefore, in accordance with his wishes, have felt able to tell more of the story for the sake of a terrorised people in a far-off place that few have heard of, a people who have been savagely oppressed by an appalling regime using British arms, a people who much occupied Lord Ennal's thoughts in his last days. The place is East Timor, the aggressor is Indonesia, and the arming of this regime by Britain continues to this day.

I have known David Ennals for many years, long before

my own work in the AIDS field which he warmly supported as a Peer. He is well regarded for his involvement in health issues, and his pioneering work with the charity MIND, but he had many other interests, particularly in foreign policy. He was a veteran of the Normandy landings – he arrived on French soil before the main assault, and was badly wounded by a sniper shortly afterwards. As a result he had a lifelong interest in the armed forces.

From 1966 to 1967, he was Labour's Parliamentary Under-Secretary of State for the Army, and Minister of State for the Foreign and Commonwealth Office from 1974 to 1976. I remember him staying in our home in Washington DC in 1975, when my father was part of the British Embassy there. It was around this time that the troubles started with Indonesia.

So what was it that caused the former Minister to be so deeply troubled in conscience when I saw him? What was it that he had become aware of? After our interview he had promised to 'look up the details' if I wanted, and we had agreed to meet again, but that was not to be. As a doctor I had been in no doubt as to his frailty as I sat there listening to him, and as we got up to say goodbye I realised it was very likely that I would never see him again.

As I returned home I decided not to rush back for a second interview, because I felt that he had already taken a large step in saying what he did, and I did not want him to feel that he was under pressure to give more details then than he wanted. He knew that if he were to die, he had already told me more than enough to make sure the plight of the East Timorese would be acknowledged.

However, after he died I began to trawl back over years of parliamentary business, reading and re-reading every Parliamentary Written Answer he gave throughout 1974 to 1976 relating to Indonesia or Timor. I have also examined similar answers from Ministers in the 1980s and 1990s. There is no trace of a written answer given by him that appears obviously wrong unless, as with other situations we have seen, the problem was just that the answer was appallingly incomplete. But if so, what was missing? What fact was omitted? What were those immensely damaging words that were first used innocently by David Ennals and then repeated innocently over the years, and were still used in good faith by Douglas Hurd in 1995?

The first two answers recorded are unpromising:

22 May 1974: On relations with Indonesia:
'It is the policy . . . to strengthen relations with Indonesia . . .'

The background is important. On 30 September 1965, General Suharto overthrew the democratically elected government and then over the next few months put to death many hundreds of thousands of his political opponents, communists in Java and Bali.

1 November 1974: How many warships will be sold to Indonesia? 'Negotiations are still in train [for four corvettes] . . . it is the intention . . . to let this order go ahead.'

However, there were already growing concerns about the continued oppressive nature of the regime. On the same day David Ennals was asked to ban further goodwill visits by the British Navy until the fate of 70,000 political prisoners had been determined. He refused for reasons he did not state. Civil war then broke out in neighbouring Timor, which was still a Portuguese colony, but moving towards independence. In 1975 the British government was well aware that tensions were growing with Indonesia and some say that there was advanced warning that Indonesia was poised to invade, a process which began that autumn.

On 22 December 1975, the Security Council of the United Nations passed a unanimous resolution condemning Indonesia's aggression. Just a month later David Ennals said relations with Indonesia were 'satisfactory', but there was a storm ahead. There were reports that two British members of a film crew had been executed by an Indonesian firing squad after being arrested by them in East Timor where they were reporting on the conflict. David Ennals said he had seen contradicting accounts and could not verify what had happened.

5 April 1976: On the future of East Timor:
'Our prime concern, of which the Indonesian government are fully aware, is that the people of East Timor should be able to decide their own future.'

This is hardly controversial.

On 17 July 1976, the country was formally annexed by Indonesia, and Portugal promptly recognised the action. Some 200,000 people, or a third of the population, were massacred. To this day the oppression of the East Timorese continues. Farmers have been moved to areas where soil erosion has been so great that they have starved, teenage girls have been rounded up and sterilised against their will, and there have been many summary executions.

I am unable to find any Written Answer that explains David Ennal's personal concerns about arms. However I have detected one common element, which could possibly have had immense military significance starting in 1975 and continuing twenty years later: sales of Hawk aircraft to Indonesia. Hawk aircraft were top of the range state of the art. The Labour government set up the first of many rolling contracts which are still running, to supply these lethal fighting machines 'for training purposes'. This means that they were supplied without range-finding and weapon-release systems but were otherwise identical in every way. However it is not difficult to convert such an aircraft back to an offensive role, even if the weaponry and aiming devices are a little crude.

But what was the purpose of trainer aircraft? Was it just, as the Indonesian airforce persuaded Ministers over twenty years, merely to train pilots? Why should so many trainer aircraft have been needed?

British export policy covering defence sales to Indonesia is quite clear. Take for example Alan Clark's replies on 16 January 1992:

'As regards defence sales [to Indonesia], all applications to export military equipment are carefully scrutinised on a case by case basis. We do not allow the export of arms and equipment likely to be used for repressive purposes against civilians. In the case of Indonesia, this covers the possible repression of the population of East Timor.'

When asked to detail licences approved for export of arms to Indonesia since 1979 (under the Conservatives), he gave the standard reply: 'It is not our normal practice to disclose details of United Kingdom defence sales to particular countries . . . All discussions between my Department and United Kingdom defence suppliers are conducted on a confidential basis.' This has been a consistent position of all recent governments. Lack of detail is the accepted rule.

On 25 June 1991, Alan Clark was asked about yet more sales to Indonesia of Hawk aircraft, this time an upgraded version. He replied: 'It is not our practice to comment on defence exports to specific countries.' On the same day, the Prime Minister was asked if he had raised the plight of East Timor with Indonesia's Minister for Research at their meeting. He replied that he had not.

On 2 March 1992 Peter Lilley gave a Written Answer in

Parliament that no information was available on the proportion of UK annual exports to Indonesia each year from 1975 that were arms deals requiring export licences. Again these replies are standard practice.

Shortly before I saw Lord Ennals, the following question and statement was made in the Commons. I have no doubt that it was this matter that so troubled him.

22 November 1994:
Mr Mullin (Labour):
'It is common knowledge that a huge arms deal is being negotiated with Indonesia . . . one of the most odious tyrannies in the world . . . it came to power on the back of a bloodbath that has been matched only by Pol Pot in Asia in recent years. Has not much of the hardware that we previously sold to Indonesia been used for internal repression and will not some of the hardware that we are about to sell also be used for internal repression?'

Mr Freeman (Conservative Minister) made it clear that the government had received firm assurances from the Indonesian government that the aircraft would not be used against civilians, and that the government had received no evidence that such an assurance had been broken.

Mr Mullin continued:

'Since the illegal occupation of East Timor, more than 200,000 East Timorese people have been killed by Indonesian forces. Further information has now been published by the Timorese people showing that Hawk aircraft are used to bomb them and their positions. Is that not evidence enough to stop any further arms sales to an appalling regime which has perpetrated such a bloodbath against the Timorese people?'

Of course, anecdotal accounts by one side or another in armed conflicts can be very unreliable, as experience in Bosnia has shown, and are no substitute for 'hard' intelligence, which, as Mr Freeman's statement indicated, was lacking. Nevertheless, such anecdotal reports coming direct to Lord Ennals may have troubled him greatly.

A week after this exchange came further questions about the proposed sale of Scorpion light tanks to Indonesia.[175] There were unconfirmed rumours that Indonesia had signed or was about to sign a $2 billion arms deal with Britain.[176]

We can therefore begin to understand why Lord Ennals was so appalled. It is more than likely that he became aware that these aircraft were easily converted into an offensive role and were being used as such. The East Timorese may have been supplying both him and Christopher Mullin with eye-witness accounts of Hawk attacks.

The Scott Inquiry into arms-for-Iraq (see next chapter) discovered that Conservative Ministers were themselves aware by the late 1980s that supplying Hawk trainer aircraft to an aggressor nation was providing them with 'defensive capability', but that is not the same as saying such aircraft are likely to be used in this way or that they have been. An important distinction.

Iraq wanted to buy Hawk aircraft or manufacture them under licence. As Prime Minister, Margaret Thatcher received a briefing in July 1989 warning her that 'we could not guarantee that it would not be used at some point for internal repression or even for chemical warfare attacks'. Another briefing paper said: 'Although Hawk is designed as a trainer aircraft, it has defensive capability.'[177]

On his first day as Foreign Secretary (19 June 1989), John Major also received a memo about Hawk for Iraq. He argued at the time that Hawk should not be sold to them: 'It was a big order. It was technically worth a great deal of money . . . but although *technically* Hawk itself *could* be used for peaceful purposes, Hawk amended could have been used for more war-like purposes' (my italics).[178]

Therefore by July 1989, at least, one Conservative Minister and the Prime Minister herself knew that the same Hawk trainer aircraft supplied to other countries such as Indonesia could just as easily have been the primary motivation behind purchase of these aircraft.

The question is, why did they continue to sell Hawk aircraft to Indonesia? The reason for continued sales is presumably that Ministers felt, on balance, that the risks of the aircraft being misused were very small and worth taking to win a major order and help keep our arms industry alive. This is consistent with Alan Clark's reply on 16 January 1992: 'We do not allow export of arms and equipment likely to be used for repressive purposes against civilians.'

While the above may be considered speculation, there is no other military deal which has linked Indonesia with Britain over nearly twenty years, where there has been so much controversy over arms being misused for internal repression. It weighed heavily on Lord Ennals and it is possible that the implied or perceived threat of exposure by a group representing the East Timorese people, may have hastened his death. He felt a great empathy for that part of the world, even adopting a child from Vietnam who tragically died in early adult life.

We may never know the full truth, but Lord Ennals' own account is a vivid illustration of the pressures of office, and of how signing just one piece of paper 'in innocence' can set in train a long trail of events affecting thousands of other people. I am sure that similar stories can be found every year in every Department.

One of the key issues is 'collective responsibility'. We all stand or fall together. We all own every decision and defend every decision.

Cabinet member Peter Lilley told me: 'Collective responsibility is primarily about confidentiality – keeping the nation's secrets. Normally the issues classed as issues of morality and conscience are free votes. Two questions: [first] can you go along with collective responsibility? Every detail I may not have done quite like that, nevertheless in principle I support it or [secondly] do you think it's wrong in principle? In which case you can always leave. But what wouldn't in my mind be honourable would be to go along with something in public and then leak in private.'[179]

Another Minister told me: 'You've got to have a clear personal line beyond which you cannot go. Without it, matters of conscience get pushed to one side. There must be room for private disagreement and if necessary for public resignation.'

Lord Weatherill says it is vital that Cabinet discussions are not reported to others, but decisions should not be concealed once made. 'While policy is being formulated you can't have public debate. The one crime, please let me underline this with all the force at my command, there is only one absolute crime and that is to lie to the House. If you get found out doing that, you have absolutely had it.'

But what exactly is the definition of a lie? Lord Weatherill admits that in many cases civil servants may feel it is more important to protect the Department and their Ministers than to serve the public. 'I don't mind a partial answer [in Parliament]. Very frequently you can't give a full answer. That is not a deliberate lie. I don't think there are deliberate lies. If the public gains that impression then it's all up. . . .'

But surely that *is* the impression the public has today. That is the problem.

Lord Weatherill is disturbed by this. 'I would be passionately against dishonesty in answers. It's a crime to mislead the House. I believe in honour. But I've never been in a Department so I don't know. You will have to consult others about this.'[180]

So I did. On another occasion I went to Number 10 Downing Street. I explained that former Ministers had already told me that they had sometimes faced dilemmas of conscience, about whether to keep something secret and deceive people or whether to 'come clean'. What was the official policy on lying? Were there any circumstances when telling a complete falsehood was acceptable?

I was informed by someone close to the Prime Minister that as far as the government was concerned, there were two circumstances where it was both necessary and morally right to lie to the public and to Parliament. One example was to quell market speculation about an imminent change in interest rates. Another was over issues relating to national security.

National security can however become a convenient blind behind which to hide a great number of embarrassments. And it is rather unfortunate that the only way to steady the markets is to tell them the exact opposite of what you have decided, because next time they will believe even less. It does the image of politicians no good at all.

Surely it would be better to have an agreed understanding in Parliament, the media, the public and the markets that 'no comment' is always the standard response on market-sensitive matters, and that this is a completely neutral statement rather than a sign of an imminent change. At present 'no comment' is seen as a warning, while denials are met with deep cynicism.

On 31 October 1995 new details were given to Ministers of public interest 'escape clauses' under which they could continue to withhold information. In new additions to 'Questions of Procedure for Ministers' it was made clear that defence, security, international relations, information about internal discussions (eg Cabinet meetings), communication with the Royal Household, Budget advice, prejudicial information about legal proceedings and assessments of recommendations for Honours, would all be used in future as defences against openness.[181]

These criteria clearly cover a vast amount of government activity. One thing is abundantly clear therefore: partial answers and suppression of the truth will continue to be a way of life in government. Few would argue for total openness. The issue is over abuse of power to strangle the release of information which might be embarrassing or damaging to those who have that power.

Returning to the issue of secrecy and collective responsibility, Alistair Burt, then Under Secretary for Social Security, believes you can have perfect integrity as a Minister without agreeing with everything that happens.

'I do not believe that government would be possible if everyone had to agree with every decision and no one was prepared to take hard decisions. If you are not prepared to make hard decisions, then you have no business to be in government. But there will be points beyond which you cannot go. If you have no stopping points whatsoever, then I think you are thoroughly dangerous and with any luck you will never be elected to a position of any seriousness.'

I asked him what his advice would be to someone who inherited a terrible decision.

'If you find yourself landed with decisions that other people took then your responsibility is clear. If the government has a line, then defend it publicly. But you should be moving heaven and earth to say to colleagues, "This ain't going to work. I don't know what so and so was thinking of, but I'm not content to leave this be." You may then find after you go through a re-evaluation process that there's no escape route; that really every other option is worse than the one you've got. But if you are concerned about a policy, you should follow this process. You may find there's a chance of a change.'

But what about the possibility of being fed wrong information by civil servants and then having to take the blame?

'Although your information comes largely from the civil service you have to use your own political antennae, your own advisers. And if you are serious that you are being given a "bum steer" and you can prove it, then your officials are in serious trouble. If work is badly done then somebody is moved. We are all aware of civil servants who have been moved because they are not up to the job.'

However, Alistair Burt says that in his own experience 'we all make mistakes' which need to be faced up to honestly and admitted to. He gave as an example his own involvement in the notorious Child Support Agency (CSA), set up to extract payments from absent fathers, which largely went to offset the costs of benefits for single-parent mothers.

'Ministers had not been warned in the period 1991 to 1992 [when I took over] that the administration of the CSA was not robust enough to withstand a certain amount of pressure. If they had I would not have been able to go before the [Select] Committee and say, "Look, we genuinely didn't know. We believed we had set it up right." '[182]

However, the whole system is very intolerant of mistakes, and this intolerance is seen every day in aggressive debates as well as in the media. The result of this intolerance is not that fewer mistakes are made, but just that most of them remain well hidden. This is the case even when the mistake is one that is not human error or incompetence so much as a poor decision based on inadequate information, or short-comings due to lack of resources.

Honesty, humility and openness about poor decisions would make a refreshing change from half-truths, arrogance and guardedness. Such a culture would require consensus among all parties but would lead to greater respect, because it would be based on integrity.

The alternative is yet more absurd theatricals every time something goes wrong in a Department – for example, calls for a Minister to resign because a prisoner escapes. This is hypocrisy at its worst since opposition leaders know full well that they will face similar embarrassing moments when in power, not least because the entire civil service and public bodies will continue with existing staff under a new government.

Anyway, what is truth and what is a right decision? These things are often so subjective. A former Minister told me: 'Truth is a matter of judgement in so many issues. If people resigned every time a truth was discovered, there would be no Ministers left. I have been quite shocked by senior civil servants who have made serious errors. One Permanent Secretary said he spent the whole time making excuses for Ministers. I thought that was a bit rich! I thought I spent all *my* time making excuses for civil servants.

'Every now and then a civil servant martyr emerges who blows the whistle on a Minister – but the other nine out of ten will always be prepared to give the wrong advice to a Minister and when the Minister changes, rapid shuffles add to civil servant power.'

As a Secretary of State, Peter Lilley is upset at accusations of government dishonesty, which he feels are wrongly founded: 'I think there's a presumption that British standards in public life are low and getting worse. I don't agree with either assumption. I think standards are very high. Of the opposition generally I have found them to be of great integrity. They don't tell lies. They may say things I don't agree with or things I know to be wrong. They don't deliberately set out to tell a lie and I rather suspect that they would say the same about me and most of my colleagues.

'The process at Westminster is designed to make it very difficult for you to get away with telling lies. If you say something, your words will be reported the next day in *Hansard*. You will be torn apart if they are untrue. There is much more rigorous quality control than many people say. The reason the public out there think we're lying all the time, is that we often are seen to promise a better world, and they themselves hope we will be able to fulfil things governments can't achieve.'[183]

Another MP with ministerial experience told me: 'I think I can say that I have never been party to anything I would regard as unethical. Things may have been suggested but actually they've not been pursued.'

I asked Lord Whitelaw whether he had ever been in the situation described above of feeling he had to endorse decisions or situations which he knew were unethical.

He said: 'You have to take the rough with the smooth. You can make changes. You can admit it. Of course these are the things that happen and you just have to go along with them and try to work out the best way forward.'

But had there been any great dilemmas of conscience?

'No. Great anguish as to wisdom of what I was going to do, yes.'

'Not anguish about the wisdom or otherwise of what someone else had done?'

'Well, if they did it or had done it, you just had to get on with it in the best way you could.'

'But isn't it hard?'

'I suppose it is but I never found it really quite like that. Some things happen that you don't like – you either have to resign or go on with them.'

'What about when it's not a question of policy but a question of ethics?'

'I don't think it is. Most of the things that I've dealt with have been things of policy not of ethics. There *are* some great issues. But if you've been in government and changed your job from one job to another you probably know about them anyway.'

Sir George Young was fortunate to find that he was not a Minister when faced with his greatest dilemmas, which were over the Poll Tax. 'Happily I was not in government. It wasn't just wrong politically. It was morally wrong – moving taxation away from the better off towards the worst off. I felt very unhappy. I voted against the party, defied how many Whips, I don't know. If it had happened when I was in government I don't know what I would have done.'[184]

I asked him about partially truthful parliamentary written answers.

'Answering a parliamentary question in a misleading way, there's a code, rules and you try to stick to it. And civil servants are the ones who will warn you if what is proposed is likely to be misleading to Parliament. Misleading Parliament is actually quite serious. If you do mislead Parliament it is a resignation matter. At the end of the day all a politician has got is his integrity. And if that goes, that is your goodwill, that is all you have. The extent to which you get anywhere in Parliament, in government, is because of your "reputation".'

I asked at what point a Minister needed to resign.

'If he hasn't got the confidence of the party.'

Another Minister agreed: 'If you've got the Party with you [you can survive]. The Whips are the arbiters of that. If the message comes back that the Party in the House is behind you on this one, then even if the media are against you, the Labour Party is against you and to some extent the country is against you, you're probably OK. If you've got the Party in the House with you then you've probably got a big chunk of the public with you.

'At the end of the day [the Whips] will let the Prime Minister know if a member of the government no longer commands the support of MPs in the House. And that is the black spot, and then you've probably had it.'

A secret civil service

While secrecy by Ministers is one thing, secrecy by civil servants is another. My father was a civil servant for years. My family has been steeped in the tradition of political neutrality. To this day I have no idea which way my father has voted in any election. In the same way, there are very few people indeed who know which way I have voted over the last twenty years. For him, the idea of allowing strong political views to affect civil service conduct would be totally wrong.

However, such civil service neutrality can only work if there is agreement that advice to Ministers remains confidential. Otherwise it could be hard to work with an incoming administration after a change of government. So then, the argument for secrecy in the case of civil servants is that it prevents their politicisation, although it also helps protect Ministers from sabotage by selective leaks.

Teresa Gorman thinks that the civil service is far too powerful: people with jobs which will outlive perhaps a dozen Ministers and several governments. 'This country,' she says, 'is run very largely by civil servants, not hereditary or elected members nor appointees. As a Minister you are very dependent on their advice, because if you make a mistake your career can be over in a very short time. Unless you have very strong views, their ideas will prevail. Every civil servant has a drawer full of them.

'They can fill your every waking and sleeping hour, so inevitably you will sign some papers without knowing what is in them. Sitting there until the small hours with several red boxes and piles of documents. A system that requires an individual to work from six in the morning until midnight as a Minister and then expects him to take home two boxes containing many hundreds of letters is absurd. The vested interests in the system will remain long after you have gone and can finish you off.'[185]

One feature of the last seventy years has been the dramatic growth in the number of civil servants and in the scope of government responsibilities. In 1913 a mere 12.1 per cent of the gross domestic product was spent by government Departments, but by the 1987–8 financial year the total budget had already exceeded 40 per cent. This expansion of government power is one reason why pressures on Ministers have grown to the point where proper supervision and control of their Departments has become almost impossible.

While civil servants are supposed to be kept out of the limelight, providing confidential advice to Ministers who then take responsibility for decisions, sometimes these boundaries have been confusing. Some civil servants have been asked to play a very public and political role, which has worried not only civil service unions, but also senior politicians. Lord Weatherill explained his concerns over a recent controversy in Australia. 'I can't understand it. Sir Robert Armstrong sent to represent the government on a highly controversial matter in order to explain a ministerial decision in Australia. I can't believe it. It is a question of personal integrity and personal honour. If you put yourself up for public office, then the public has an absolute right to expect very high standards.' Lord Weatherill's worry was that civil servants were increasingly being asked to defend policies for which they had no executive responsibility.

A former British Ambassador with many years' experience in the Foreign Office told me that on the whole he thought he had never been placed in a position he could not accept ethically. 'If I had, I would have told them where to go. The ultimate threat is to go straight to the press.'[186]

However, another senior civil servant agreed that integrity was often hard to maintain. Civil servants were often in a real dilemma: do they bury their consciences and just go through the motions of churning out papers providing a hundred arguments in favour of things they believe are morally wrong, or do they risk declaring their own positions in private discussions and arguing the case? 'Ministers are supposed to ask officials to prepare a case, information on which a decision can be made. But all too often they ask for arguments to back up a decision which has already been taken.'[187]

I remember a very curious episode, many years ago, when I was being advised on how to draft the most effective lobbying letters for MPs to send to a Minister about an issue which concerned me. The most remarkable thing was that this unpaid help was coming not from an MP, nor a lobbying consultant, nor from a political activist, but from the very same civil servants who would later be drafting the replies to these MPs for Ministers to sign.

Thus the whole exercise changed gradually from a simple campaign to something of a civil service game, beginning and ending in a junior official's office, and designed to impress upon the Minister that a particular change in policy was needed. The process gave the civil service some extra ammunition with which to load their arguments.

Ken Livingstone says: 'You expect civil servants to conspire against you . . . in that case you replace them. You sack them.'

I asked whether it was possible after winning an election to see the papers of the previous administration, for reasons of continuity and audit, to help prevent corruption.

'You don't see previous decisions. You have no access to any previous administration. You have to appoint a barrister which is what I did at the Greater London Council. My own view is that if there is any evidence of corruption then it should immediately be exposed.'[188]

Lord Ennals pointed out, from his own experience in a Labour Cabinet and subsequently, that sometimes the decision to answer in a certain way comes from a Minister, not a civil servant, but then all are compromised. 'Sometimes a Minister has required of civil servants that they give an answer which is basically not true.'[189]

A conspiracy between Ministers and civil servants

Edwina Currie has particular concerns about how Ministers and civil servants may operate together to protect departmental interests or the interests of those they represent.

'One of the key things about government is to protect people from threat. Health Service regulations are all part of that. If a government knows of a threat to health and safety and is involved in a denial, then there is tension.'

Her own experience was as a junior Minister in the Department of Health where she was provoked into action over the growing numbers of people made ill every month by salmonella food poisoning related to poultry and eggs.

'My concern was that the government knew of 500 confirmed cases a week of people sick enough to need samples taken. Most were of the new strain, the main cause of the increase. Rapid spread, virulent, people hospitalised for weeks, one death on average every week. I was particularly upset about a nine-year-old boy who died in September 1988. The problem was how to handle the situation. The first step was to warn the public, and also to encourage people to take care over the preparation of food.

'Sir Donald Acheson, the government's Chief Medical Officer at the time, issued five different warnings about under-cooked or raw eggs from summer 1988. The Health

Authorities issued three public warnings. One Health Authority stopped using eggs altogether – I felt that was excessive.'

Her greatest worry was that there would be a long hot summer in 1989 with rapidly spreading infection, leading to a major epidemic. She was asked by the media if there was a problem and she said, 'Yes.' She was asked the way to tackle it: 'Handle with care,' she replied. 'But the following week 6 million families stopped buying eggs.'

Edwina Currie's one-liners have often caught the public eye. Everyone remembers the campaign comment on the risk of HIV on holiday: 'Take the wife.' She described how events spiralled to the point where she was forced out of her job. 'My personal sense of alarm was reserved for the Ministry of Agriculture, Fisheries and Food (MAFF). My officials and MAFF officials were in frequent contact. MAFF officials denied the problem existed at all.'

I asked Edwina Currie about government ethics generally. She feels the system works erratically and very largely depends on ethical views of Ministers and civil servants and a view of what damage is done by a particular course of action, in comparison with another.

'You only have to look at how different countries have handled the issue of liability over HIV-contaminated blood and blood products [causing AIDS]. In medical terms the information was available around the world simultaneously. We took the view that we must not use such blood. If anything went wrong we [Ministers] would get blamed. [But] when it came to salmonella I felt we were compensating the wrong people – compensating farmers instead of sick people. Farmers should have sued MAFF for failing to do its duty, failing to test contaminated animal feed. MAFF officials were not doing their job properly. BSE has also been handled by the same officials.

'In order to reduce the cost of animal husbandry, experiments had been going on for some time over diverse animal feeds and cheaper forms of protein. For years it was known that there were risks in feeding animal protein to herbivores – and infected animal products to herbivores even more so – for example the ground up remains of sheep [with scrapie, fed] to cattle which probably caused BSE. The last thing you should do is feed animals with products from the same species. Yet, ground up dead chickens with salmonella were fed to chickens – which probably accelerated spread. When I asked awkward questions I wondered why the MAFF was being so defensive.

'Their defensiveness seemed [in part] connected with the way the bugs had entered the system. There was inadequate mass testing of animal feedstuffs, commercially produced. It should have been apparent that such feedstuffs were a biological disaster waiting to happen.'

So what happens when two Ministries are in conflict? Presumably someone has to resign – in this case it would either have been Edwina Currie or her opposite number Richard Ryder (later to become Chief Whip).

'There is a long standing tradition that Ministers defend Ministries. You are a bit stuck when the Ministry is indefensible. You can't go against your civil servants. If you are part of a team and there is a weak link in the team, then everyone is compromised. If the situation has been there a long time it can take a major upheaval to change it.'

Edwina Currie fears that history may now be repeating itself over BSE, which has already done enormous damage to the industry – pointing out that even as long ago as in the Gulf War, British beef sent to the troops in Saudi Arabia was banned because of the disease. 'When people say they are resigning on principle it is sometimes only a part of the story. It is six years since I left government. I declined to rejoin it. You can come to your own conclusions.'[190]

A Minister's role is changing rapidly. Although government spending is still huge, power over decision making is being progressively lost to Brussels. As EC control increases, more and more decisions depend on European policy, while as we have seen, quangos have grown and so has the role of civil servants. This feeling of powerlessness has led to a different attitude when things go wrong. In the past a Minister would have taken responsibility and resigned. Now the reaction often is 'Why should I resign? I'm not responsible.'

So Ministers and civil servants alike can face enormous moral dilemmas where the answers are very unclear. It is possible to become a government Minister with great hopes of being able to maintain the highest standards of integrity, but sometimes it can be difficult to do so without resigning.

From the day they are appointed, Ministers can become locked into the history and culture of the Department they are supposed to be leading. The volume of routine work generated by civil servants, together with Cabinet meetings, Parliament, European delegations, constituency matters, party campaigning and media interviews, all combine to erode time and energy for proper scrutiny. The pressure of having to maintain a Cabinet line in every media interview can be hard for a free thinker with strong views.

However, if there is one area more than any other which has consistently raised most difficult questions of secrecy and integrity it must be arms deals in a world complicated by embargoes, ethics and clashes of opinion on both. This is the subject of the next chapter.

9

Trade Scandals and Arms Deals

'We have reached the stage where every man and woman in this House is an object of suspicion.' Sir Edward Heath (1916–)

'An MP is someone who stands for what he believes others will fall for.' Anon MP

'The greater the power, the more dangerous the abuse.' Edmund Burke (1729–1797)

In November 1992 a High Court Judge became increasingly concerned about a case he was trying at the Old Bailey. Every day he was being presented with more evidence against three men from a company called Matrix Churchill who had been charged with selling arms-related equipment to Iraq, in breach of strict government controls.

However the public perception was that the government was taking elaborate steps to withhold a large number of important documents vital to the defence of the three. The Scott Report found this impression was unfair. Ministers had signed special secrecy certificates in good faith, seeking public immunity from legal proceedings, although the final decision about release remained with the Judge.

In the Matrix Churchill case the men faced almost certain prison sentences, but if the documents proved them innocent, the public scandal would rock the government to its very foundations. The men claimed that they were trading with secret government backing, in co-operation with military intelligence. There was a risk of a serious miscarriage of justice.

Eventually the Judge became convinced that these men were correct in what they were saying. The prosecution case collapsed. However it would be several years before the whole truth was exposed by the Scott Inquiry, not just about Matrix Churchill, but about failures and misjudgements at many levels of government as well as within the civil service. By the time the report was published, many of the key players had moved on from government to other things. There were no resignations and very few apologies of any kind.

In order to understand what happened, we need first to look at the events leading up to the prosecution. Most of the many recent scandals involving massive overseas contracts have been to do with arms or oil or both. It is disturbing that one of our biggest exports is the killing industry: weapons designed to slaughter humans, maim, injure, destroy. It is even more disturbing that the buyers are often non-democratic states with a terrible track record of human rights abuse.

The root of the problem is imperialism: the dying British tradition of being a great military power able to span the globe. The reality is that our own arms purchases are now far too small to keep British manufacturers in business. Defence budgets of some £23 billion continue to fall, with a 22 per cent cut in the strength of the armed forces by the mid-1990s.[191]

The sensible thing perhaps would be to buy arms from the US, and encourage these enterprises to diversify into non-military production. Instead government-owned arms producers like British Aerospace have been privatised (BAe sale raised £390 million) and we see Prime Ministers promoting British arms exports at every opportunity. The reason is that arms sales are one of the largest contributors to our balance of payments.

British Aerospace is just one of many arms producers, and is Britain's third largest manufacturer with a turnover of £10.5 billion a year. It is also one of the three largest arms manufacturers in the world, and in 1992 exported three-quarters of its military production. For example in 1992 a £5 billion order was made by Saudi Arabia for forty-eight Tornado bombers.[192]

The argument goes that other countries are going to get lethal weaponry or other military equipment from somewhere so they might as well buy it from us. This is the reason for the Iraqi arms scandal. There was a formal ban on Saddam Hussein buying British arms but since other nations were willing to sell to him, and as the potential orders were so huge, Ministers took a relaxed view of discrete exports of items that were not strictly lethal weapons.

In fact there would later be great debate about how 'arms' were defined; for example, radar and radio communications equipment, or night vision equipment or components of weapon systems, or complicated machine tool equipment capable of being used to make arms locally.

The security forces realised that Saddam Hussein's 'shopping list' would make interesting reading. What was he short of? How many missiles did he really have? So the three men from Matrix Churchill were recruited. Not only were they told that they could break the embargo, but they were also assured that they would be doing the country a huge service, by relaying back priceless military intelligence.

But then the trouble started. Customs and Excise were unaware of who these men were and were also unaware of the encouragement they had been given. They uncovered the secret trade and arrested the businessmen. A huge outcry followed the collapse of the trial but who was to blame? There were rumours that the trail led right into the very heart of the government.

Lord Justice Scott's inquiry began in 1992. It took more than two-and-a-half years to unravel the complicated maze of half-truths and deceptions by members of the government and civil servants alike. He was quickly buried under an avalanche of paper: 200,000 pages of documents and submissions from 278 witnesses, of which 81 were invited to attend a hearing. This was not a criminal investigation, nor a civil suit, but a public inquiry, and it cost almost £2 million.[193]

The issues were so complicated that Sir Richard realised that if he allowed lawyers to cross-examine every witness in an adversarial process, the inquiry would slide into oblivion with countless detailed diversions, and might have taken until well beyond the millennium.

So instead, each witness was interviewed in an inquiry, the aim of which was to establish the facts. Each was allowed a legal adviser present, and legal assistance was given to people so they could comment on drafts. People were also allowed if they wished to make an application to cross-examine any witness who had made damaging statements about them. However no one took up the offer.

Sir Richard Scott has been much maligned by senior Conservative politicians. In particular he has been accused repeatedly of unfairness to witnesses, who it is said were unable to defend themselves properly against statements made by others.

My own view is that Scott took every possible effort to be fair to all, within the constraints of a three- to four-year time-scale for the whole process. A full legal process would not have been in the public interest – we would have had to wait until beyond 2000 for a verdict on events which took place in the late 1980s.

Scott's method was to study documents in great depth, and then question witnesses where he needed clarification. In many cases people were surprised that he appeared to have a firm view on what had happened before he had spoken to those involved. The reason is that he felt that the written records often spoke for themselves. Indeed, they were perhaps a more reliable and complete source than the memories of witnesses for events many years ago.

Christopher Muttukumaru assisted Lord Justice Scott throughout the Inquiry. He wrote afterwards in the Report of the difficulties they had faced. 'How were we to break into Whitehall's magic circle? How could public concerns about what was alleged to be a covert government policy to relax defence sales policy best be allayed? How could the Inquiry meet the concerns of those who alleged that, having brought prosecutions, the Crown had sought to prevent disclosure of material that would assist the accused men to establish their proper defence? It was plain that we had to go back to basics.

'There is a paper-trail in Whitehall whenever important decisions are taken, whether at ministerial level or official level. The Inquiry began a paperchase to reveal decisions that were taken and the basis for them. The papers came in boxes, in triple-sealed envelopes and even in sacks marked "HM Diplomatic Service". And once the paper mountain had built up (some 200,000 pages of documents) there began the process of sifting and analysing the material. The trail led us to a labyrinthine complex of committees and sub-committees . . .

'The Inquiry had an unrivalled insight into the whole picture. This kind of insight was not even available to the participants in the drama themselves, who would only have been aware of part of the picture. The documents often contained very good evidence of the facts.'

A complete set of the transcripts of oral evidence alone fills a shelf some six to eight feet long. However it is fascinating to read, whether the questioning of Lady Thatcher, John Major, William Waldegrave or other well-known politicians. Senior civil servants also found themselves being taken through memos and letters they had written, line by line, by detailed and probing but courteous interrogation.

The first confidential draft of the Scott Report was so damning of a number of Ministers and civil servants that publication was delayed for several months to allow their own legal advisers to argue the case for changes. Prestigious legal firms were employed at public expense to defend the Ministers and civil servants, and there were a number of key changes in legal representation at the last minute, which caused yet more delays as new legal teams caught up with events.

The legal bill for representation had already reached £568,000 by June 1995.[194] The trouble is that with every month of delay the public memory faded and the chances increased that there would be no justice. Month after month of a tedious inquiry inevitably led to boredom and confusion about the real issues and the public lost interest.

The normal punishments in these sorts of cases are Ministers being forced to resign from office and humiliation in the House of Commons. But if Ministers have already moved on, and perhaps are no longer even MPs, then such sanctions become meaningless. There are rarely sanctions against civil servants. Until the Scott Inquiry, their work was so well sheltered by official secrecy that it was almost always impossible to tell which named official had been responsible for advice or action taken.

Tory back-bencher David Amess said before the Scott

Report was published that 'no one in my constituency could give a jot about it – what this chap Scott has found, however many millions of pounds it has cost to take evidence. It's a waste of time.'[195]

However, despite many delaying tactics, the contents of the Report began to leak out from several sources, causing great outrage from those criticised who felt that they had not been able to defend themselves properly.

One reason the process took so long was that the Inquiry uncovered no fewer than twelve similar cases to Matrix Churchill where prosecutions were brought or considered.[196] Here is a summary of the main ones.

SUMMARY OF MAIN CASES

Matrix Churchill[197]

In 1991 Paul Henderson and two other directors were charged with sending equipment to Iraq, knowing that it was almost certain to be used to make shells and missiles. The £54 million turnover company was Iraqi controlled[198] and employed 700 people but went into receivership when the three directors were charged. They said that the trade was approved and they were working with British intelligence. Before the trial at the Old Bailey in 1992, Public Interest Immunity Certificates (PIICs) were signed in good faith by Michael Heseltine, Malcolm Rifkind, Tristan Garel-Jones and Kenneth Clarke.[199]

On 4 and 5 November 1992, Alan Clark, former Defence Minister, was cross-examined. He admitted in court that they had been 'economic with the actualité' and the trial collapsed. He later described the whole prosecution as 'dotty'. He said that he had made no secret of his view that Britain should sell as much conventional military equipment to Iraq as possible, and that the implementation of the guidelines had indeed been subtly changed.[200]

Ordtec[201]

In 1992 Paul Grecian, Bryan Mason and Stuart Blackledge were convicted at Reading Crown Court for sending artillery fuses to Iraq via Jordan. They received suspended prison sentences while Colin Phillips, from the trucking firm EC Transport, was also fined. They pleaded guilty. Public Interest Immunity Certificates were signed in good faith by Kenneth Baker and Peter Lilley.

Paul Grecian had also been supplying intelligence data to the British.

Euromac[202]

In June 1994 Ali Daghir and Jeanine Speckham had their convictions dismissed by Lord Taylor, after they had been found guilty for exporting electrical capacitors said to have been suitable for 'nuclear triggers'. Lord Taylor said that the original Judge had misdirected the jury.

Sterling[203]

In 1985 Reginauld Dunk and Alexander Schlesinger were fined for trying to smuggle 200 Sterling machine guns into Iraq via Jordan. Staff at the British Embassies in Jordan and Iraq went back on their assurances that they would speak up if there was trouble, so the men were left without any defence. However, the Scott Inquiry found clear evidence that embassy staff had been told to keep quiet by Foreign Office officials assisted by Customs and Excise.

BSA[204]

In November 1991, Keith Bailey was charged at the Old Bailey with supplying shell-making equipment to Iraq in 1988–89. However just three days after the collapse of the Matrix Churchill case all charges were withdrawn.

There were further delays in final publication after the sensational eleventh hour 'discovery' of vitally important documents held by the Ministry of Defence Police. They related to the arms company BMARC. Those involved in running the Inquiry were furious at what seemed to be another attempt to delay things. One Minister commented: 'You can hardly blame Whitehall for fighting back and trying to throw a spanner in the works.'[205] There was some antagonism between Scott and senior civil servants. The Permanent Secretaries were said to be horrified at the way relatively junior civil servants had been dragged into the public arena, breaching all previous codes of anonymity, and risking a politicisation of the service.

During the delays there was a hostile campaign by a number of political figures against the Inquiry, pointing out what they saw as fundamental weaknesses in the approach Scott had taken. They said repeatedly that an adversarial approach would have been fairer. As the publication date drew nearer, the negative comments grew louder and more strident. Lord Nolan's Inquiry into standards in public life had suffered a similar fate.

The government strategy seemed to be: if criticised heavily, set up a formal inquiry and build up great public confidence in the process; then string out the inquiry itself and delay publication of the report for as long as possible and at the last minute launch a hard-hitting attack on every aspect of the inquiry; if all else fails, then be ready to move those about to be criticised out of office as fast and unobtrusively as possible.

The final Report was published in early 1996. The main text ran to no fewer than 1,800 pages with an extra 450 pages of appendices, 2,250 pages in total. A bargain perhaps at just £45 a copy for members of the public, but who was going to bother to read such a massive thesis? Most who actually did so were surprised to find no executive summary at the beginning and it was extremely hard to try and work out what Sir Richard Scott's conclusions were.

Although summary paragraphs were scattered throughout the text, they were often expressed in confusing or contradictory language. Indeed the language of the Report as a whole is densely written, with tortuous sentences and clumsy phrasing. Many verdicts on the actions of individuals are interwoven with the main narrative, and are expressed in convoluted terms.

Because there had been so many leaks of the early drafts over the previous eight months, and because there was such a breakdown of trust between leading members of the main parties, the government decided not to let opposition MPs see a single word of the Report until minutes before an official statement was made to the House of Commons, indicating the government response to the Report.

There was a concession. After a huge row, the government agreed that designated members of the opposition could see it earlier in the day, so long as the person was guarded in a room with no telephone or fax and no visitors whatsoever. In the event, only one opposition member was willing to accept such strict conditions.

In stark contrast, senior members of the government received their own copies a week before, giving them urgently needed time to digest the Report thoroughly, reflect on the large number of criticisms, and prepare an aggressive damage-limitation exercise.

I was in Parliament on the day the Report was published. I watched John Major sweep smiling into Westminster precincts in a packed black limousine at high speed from 10 Downing Street. I felt the tension among MPs and Peers of all parties as they gathered in the corridors. I saw and heard their anger as they were each handed their own copies of the green-covered six-volume Report, large enough and heavy enough for two briefcases. I watched them as they marched into the Debating Chambers carrying the reports stacked high in both hands. There was a palpable feeling of disgust. The whole performance seemed to indicate only one thing: that the government had been scared stiff at the damage Sir Richard Scott's words could do.

I listened to the official statement as it was given to packed Upper and Lower Chambers simultaneously. And then I watched a feeble opposition response. Television networks that night carried a full-bloodied Conservative attack, dismissing Sir Richard Scott's greatest criticisms out of hand, but there was very little opposition comment of substance.

Having read 1,500 pages of the Report, my own view is that the government summary that day was shockingly poor and dangerously misleading, and to my mind bore little relation to the actual contents as a whole. Media reporting was also very confusing, then and in the days following. It was a prime example of the parliamentary adversarial system at its very worst. Both the main parties quoted selected passages out of context and the balance of the Report was almost entirely lost as a result.

So what did Sir Richard Scott actually say, and what were his conclusions? What was his verdict after such a colossal review of the way government had worked?

The Scott Report

The Report is very disturbing reading. The difficulty is doing justice to it all in a book of this length. Sir Richard Scott not only summarises the evidence and his verdicts, but also contains pages of original documents, letters, memos and other records. It is a very important historical record of how government works. Rather than form a bland digest of the entire Report, I have reproduced sample extracts to give some flavour of what it is like to sit down and read it. The paragraph lettering is exactly as it appears in the Report, and each extract is in Report order. The facts speak for themselves.

In September 1980, Iraqi forces invaded Iran and so a war began which continued until August 1988. There were massive casualties, Iraq used chemical weapons, and Iran armed children as infantry soldiers. When the war started, Britain took a position of strict neutrality in the absence of any United Nations embargo on defence sales.

From 1980 to 1984 the government in Britain found itself watching as large arms contracts were fulfilled for Iran, under agreements dating from the time of the Shah of Iran, before the Iranian Revolution in 1979. When the Islamic Republic came into being that year there were still seventy-nine contracts outstanding.

A big question in the early 1980s was whether to allow these contracts to proceed. Then there was the crisis over American hostages in Iran, and over four British hostages, as well as tense relations between neighbouring countries such as Saudi Arabia and other Gulf States. All this made the trading climate perilous and controversial, although exports of all goods to Iran still totalled £700 million a year in 1984.

In contrast the traditional arms purchases by Iraq were from the Soviet Union and other Eastern bloc countries. When war broke out Iraq became a huge potential market; it seemed less likely that sales to Iraq of military technology would land up in the Soviet Union and sales were encouraged by the British government.

(D1.10) As early as 1981 a Cabinet Committee agreed that although lethal arms and ammunition would not be sold to either side, 'every opportunity should be taken to exploit Iraq's potentialities as a promising market for the sale of defence equipment; and to this end "lethal items" should be interpreted in the narrowest sense and the obligations of neutrality as flexibly as possible'. Scott adds: 'It is a question whether this attitude to defence sales in Iraq was consistent with the public stance of impartiality and even-handedness.' So even in 1981 we see the beginning of a gap between actuality and public statements on this matter.

In 1984 the so-called Howe Guidelines were introduced, covering arms sales to Iran and Iraq, introduced when the two were still at war. How the Guidelines were interpreted, particularly after the war ended in August 1988, is the heart of the whole affair. But how do you define what arms are anyway? Sir Richard Scott gave his own description as follows.

(D1.1) 'The word "arms", in a military context means weapons. The "arms trade" is, strictly, a trade in weapons . . . But the ability to conduct war . . . requires a wide variety of equipment and facilities which are not "arms" in the strictest sense . . . tank transporters, mine detection and mine clearing apparatus, computers to guide missiles . . .'

He pointed out that 'defence' usually has a wider meaning than 'arms' and 'defence-related' is the widest of all, applying also to 'dual-use' items where there could be a function for civilian purposes. These are subtle but vitally important differences which led to the huge rows and allegations of deception.

(D1.11) Lord Howe explained to the Inquiry: 'It was very important that we should not be perceived in Iraq or Iran or elsewhere in the world as having departed, consciously or inadvertently, from a position of neutrality, impartiality and even-handedness. Any such perception would have been extremely damaging to foreign relations with a number of countries.'

(D1.27) Scott is critical of the way questions of Ministers by MPs on arms exports were met with a standard blocking reply: 'It has been the practice of successive governments not to make public details of export licence applications.' He said of such a typical reply given in 1984: 'Failure to supply, in broad terms at least . . . information, cannot be justified.' However, such answers were certainly in keeping with previous practice over the years.

There was a major disagreement between Scott and Ministers over whether a subsequent relaxation of the application of the Guidelines in favour of Iraq, and a tightening against Iran, was a policy change. Scott is clear: by any common sense view of government, there was a change in what was allowed for exports and what was forbidden as a result of decisions taken, decisions which were not made clear to the public.

Indeed, a decision had been made to keep the Howe Guidelines as far from the public eye as possible in the first place. In the event they were only announced in October 1985, having been agreed in 1984.

A new argument began to emerge: while nothing should be done to prolong the war, perhaps there was nothing wrong in evening up the two sides, so if one was short – say – of small boats, then export permission might be given to redress the situation. Again these sorts of discussions were not made public.

(D3.19) In 1988 a draft paper was submitted to Lord Howe outlining various changes, which he was reluctant to put forward, because of the publicity it could have attracted, according to Scott.

'Lord Howe's objection to the draft paper (1988) and the recommendations for a more relaxed application of the Guidelines was not taken on substantive grounds. Lord Howe's objection was presentational. He did not want it to "become known" that the line on arms sales to Iraq had been relaxed . . . His objection that "it would look very cynical if, so soon after expressing outrage over the Iraqi treatment of the Kurds, we were to adopt a more flexible approach on arms sales", was no more than an objection to the new approach becoming known. He was prepared for the new approach to be adopted but not for it to become known . . . Lord Howe's mistrust of the public and unwillingness to run the risk that public debate might embarrass government policy was consistent with his evidence . . . that there was "nothing necessarily open to criticism in incompatibility between policy and presentation of policy".'

(D3.34) When it came to Matrix Churchill and machine tool exports, a briefing for Lord Trefgarne in December 1988 said, 'Intelligence sources indicated that the lathes were to be used for making shells and missiles.' We will follow this strand of Scott's Inquiry later.

(D3.42) A letter from William Waldegrave's office to Alan Clark's office on 7 February 1989 said: 'Mr Waldegrave is content for us to implement a more liberal policy on defence sales, without any public announcement on the subject.'

(D3.47) However, William Waldegrave said that he would not have expressed it quite that way, and referred to a 'fine modulation' of an existing policy. Yet Scott argues: 'Contemporary documents make it impossible in my opinion to quarrel with the expression "a more liberal policy" as being a fair and accurate description . . . Mr Waldegrave did not find the phrase jarring at the time. He did not do so for the simple reason that the words, "a more liberal policy", describe in ordinary and common sense language the reality of what he and his colleagues were discussing.'

(D3.115) A Ministry of Defence Minute dated 18 November 1992 recorded: 'They agreed to change the Guidelines to take account of the ceasefire [between Iraq and Iran]; and at the same time that their application would be relaxed. They also made a conscious decision (set out most clearly in a letter from Mr Waldegrave) not to make any announcement. Their reasoning seems to have been that any announcement, however carefully drafted, would upset somebody. Arguably this was not misleading Parliament, but it may be represented as culpably failing to inform Parliament of a significant change to the Guidelines of October 1985.'

(D3.123) Scott describes Waldegrave's viewpoint as 'one that does not seem to correspond with reality'. He goes on, 'To describe this revised formulation as no more than an interpretation of the old is, in my opinion . . . so plainly inapposite as to be incapable of being sustained by serious argument.'

(D3.124) However, before one becomes too critical of Mr Waldegrave, Scott adds: 'I accept that Mr Waldegrave and other adherents of the "interpretation" thesis did not . . . have any duplicitous intention.' Nevertheless, 'the description of that decision as being merely a flexible interpretation, or flexible implementation, of the Guidelines is bound to be misleading to anyone who does not know the substance of the decision'.

(D4.3–7) Then there was the question of answers given to MPs which were 'untrue'. From May to July 1989, William Waldegrave signed twenty-six letters containing the words: 'British arms supplies to both Iran and Iraq continue to be governed by the strict application of guidelines which prevent the supply of lethal equipment or equipment which would significantly enhance the capability of either side to resume hostilities.' Also, 'The Government have not changed their policy on defence sales to Iraq or Iran.'

Scott condemns these letters as 'not accurate'. He explains: 'The inaccuracy should have been noted by Mr Waldegrave, who had been one of the midwives at the birth of this new formulation . . . The statement, "the Government have not changed their policy on defence sales to Iraq or Iran" was untrue . . . Mr Waldegrave knew, first hand, the facts that, in my opinion, rendered the "no change" policy untrue.'

However, once again, in case you feel too critical of Mr Waldegrave, Scott adds: 'In his evidence to the enquiry, he strenuously and consistently asserted his belief, in the face of a volume, to my mind, of overwhelming evidence to the contrary, that policy on defence sales to Iraq had, indeed, remained unchanged. I did not receive the impression of insincerity on his part.'

(D4.15) '[Mrs Thatcher] had received and read the MOD paper dated 20 July 1989 on the Hawk project in which references were made to the "more flexible interpretation of the guidelines for Iraq [but not Iran]" and so can be said to have been placed on notice that a more liberal approach to defence sales to Iraq was being adopted than had previously been the case. But the paper had been concentrating on Hawk [aircraft] and I do not think Mrs Thatcher can be blamed if, when signing the letter of 21 August 1989, she did not recall the implications of the references to the Guidelines.'

(D4.16) 'Mr Major said: "I think the government's approach was impartial . . ." However on 25 July 1989 he received his first brief as Foreign Secretary . . .: "Since the ceasefire in August 1988, the Guidelines have been applied with greater flexibility for Iraq [but since last February with much greater rigidity for Iran . . .] our public presentation of our policy on arms supplies to both countries has, however, stayed broadly the same. . . ." This briefing did, as it seems to me, put John Major on notice that Iraq was receiving more favourable treatment than Iran so far as export licensing was concerned, a state of affairs that, in my opinion, calls into question a continuing stance of impartiality. . . . In any event, the briefing was directed to the Hawk project, and as with Mrs Thatcher, I do not find it very surprising that Mr Major did not avert to all the implications of the briefing on other issues. I do not doubt Mr Major's evidence that he signed the letters believing the statements they contained to be accurate, but I do not accept that they were in fact accurate.'

(D4.22–23) William Waldegrave wrote to MPs saying: 'It is untrue to suggest that Britain is selling arms to Iraq,' and again 'Britain is not selling arms to Iraq,' and again, 'Britain does not sell arms to Iraq.' Scott points out that these are technically correct if you consider only lethal weapons, but not if you include general military equipment. However, other letters signed by him said the following or similar: 'We do not supply arms to Iraq; strict guidelines were introduced in 1985 to prevent the export of military equipment to Iraq and Iran while the Gulf conflict was taking place.'

Scott says: 'The suggestion is, to my mind, clearly conveyed in the three letters in question that no military equipment had been sold by Britain to Iraq during the Gulf conflict and that none was being currently sold. . . . The assertion . . . could not truthfully have been made. . . . Officials . . . should have noticed the inaccuracy. I think it in the highest degree likely that Mr Waldegrave did not notice. . . . But I think he ought to have noticed, particularly as many of the members of the public whose letters he was dealing with were not confining their complaints to the sale of lethal weapons.'

Others also signed misleading or inaccurate letters but Scott concluded that many of them were unaware of the changes that had been made to exports allowed.

(D4.42) Scott goes on: 'The answers to parliamentary questions in both Houses of Parliament, failed to inform Parliament of the current state of government policy on non-lethal arms sales to Iraq. This failure was deliberate and was an inevitable result of the agreement between three junior Ministers that no publicity would be given to the decision to adopt a more liberal, or relaxed policy, or interpretation of the Guidelines . . . Having heard various explanations as to why it was necessary or desirable to withhold knowledge from Parliament and the public of the true nature of the government's approach to the licensing of non-lethal defence sales to Iran and Iraq respectively, I have come to the conclusion that the overriding and determinative reason was a fear of strong public opposition to the loosening of the restrictions on the supply of defence equipment to Iraq, and a consequential fear that the pressure of the opposition might be detrimental to British trading interests.'

(D4.58) Scott was damning of the whole system of statements which only disclosed part of the picture, whatever the subject might be. 'The withholding of information by an accountable Minister should never be based on reasons of convenience or for the avoidance of political embarrassment and should always require strong and special justification.'

(D4.61) The trouble is that in an adversarial political system, the asking of questions and the giving of answers becomes a political game. Sir Michael Quinlan told the Scott enquiry that it was seen as a competitive activity between the opposition whose function is to give the government a 'hard time' and to 'seek to extract information which they can use to portray the government in a bad light'. Therefore, 'the reactive purpose of the government is to avoid having a hard time. . . . The game has been played in essentially the current way by every government and opposition in living memory. And though the participants may sometimes be blameworthy, the fact that the competition works to the detriment of balanced public understanding rests less with individuals than with the dynamics . . . of the Westminster system itself.'

(D4.62–63) However, Scott rejects the notion of a game utterly. 'Government statements made in 1989 and 1990 about policy on defence exports to Iraq consistently failed, in my opinion, to comply with the standard set by . . . 'Questions of Procedure for Ministers' and, more importantly, failed to discharge the obligations imposed by the constitutional principle of ministerial accountability.'

The same disturbing patterns of behaviour are found when looking at Hawk aircraft sales, lathe sales and a host of other related issues. On almost every page of the lengthy Scott Report there are indications of multi-layered confusion, lack of openness and sometimes of error, at every level of government operation examined. Let us look for example at the proposed sale of Hawk aircraft to Iraq, and other matters.

(D6.27) '. . . in the letters to which I have referred of the government's decision on Hawk to the Guidelines is a very good example of the FCO's preference for the presentationally convenient, as opposed to the factually accurate.'

(D6.98) 'This was the second FCO submission to Ministers which contained important inaccuracies.'

(D6.102) 'The content of the submission to the Minister was not, I conclude, a subject to which he gave any close attention. This inattention was consistent with his general approach to line management.'

(D6.103) '. . . failed to put before the Minister a balanced recommendation . . . The Minister was ill-served on this occasion.'

(D6.120) 'Mr Waldegrave, in my opinion, should have been told about it.'

(D6.133) More seriously for the Matrix Churchill case, the DTI took the view that they had never been informed of the intended use of the machine tools to make military goods. This was based on a 'misleading' summary of an intelligence report, which had contained ample evidence of probable military use.

(D6.135) 'The submission [to the Secretary of State of DTI] was . . . highly unsatisfactory.'

(D6.182) 'It is an unfortunate fact that the . . . report did not come to the attention of. . . .'

Scott concludes that there was an ongoing conflict between the DTI, keen to preserve a Midlands-based machine tool industry, and the Foreign Office, concerned with political and presentational consequences of sales to Iraq. Between them was the Ministry of Defence whose recommendations about individual orders often swayed the approval process. The culture within the Ministry of Defence changed when Alan Clark was a Minister, as we will see, and became more relaxed about arms exports to Iraq in particular.

(D8.9) When it came to export licences for machine tool manufacturers Scott said: 'In a number of cases it was known to the would-be exporters that the intended use of the machines was the production of armaments or munitions. In these cases the imprecise statements in the application forms constituted a deliberate concealment of the known intended use. This deceptive practice was attributable in part to the belief by manufacturers that they had been encouraged by Mr Alan Clark, in his remarks to them . . . to stress, when applying for licences, the potential civil purposes to which the machine tools could be put. The deceptive practice was attributable also to a belief by the manufacturers that the government was aware that the likely use of the machines would be munitions production and was complaisant about that possibility.'

(D8.11) Scott describes 'Nelsonian use of a blind eye' in the light of the 'cumulative volume of intelligence'.

(D8.16) 'The failure of the government to be forthcoming in its public statements about its export policy to Iraq precluded public debate on this important issue. . . . Parliament and the public were designedly led to believe that a stricter policy . . . was being applied than was in fact the case.'

Then there was the case of the Iraqi supergun: Project Babylon was an almost unbelievable project, the aim of which was to build a vast high-velocity gas-driven gun capable of launching massive artillery shells into the upper atmosphere.

The first (smaller version) would have a range of 600 miles. The original design was by Dr Bull of the Space Research Corporation who was mysteriously shot dead on 16 March 1990. Ten tapering sections of the giant barrel were made in

Britain. One of the clues to the real purpose of these immense tubes was the extremely tight tolerances used in making the bores, and the unusual finishing of the internal metal surface, using techniques associated with artillery production.

The question is when the government knew about it, was enough action taken, and was Parliament properly informed? In the event the tubes were seized just before they left the country, but do the facts fit with what Ministers told Parliament? Scott devotes a great number of pages to answering these questions.

(F4.26–27) On 18 April 1990, Nicholas Ridley made a statement to the House of Commons describing the seizure of eight large tubes at Teeside, as they were about to be shipped to Iraq. He said: 'Until a few days ago my Department had no knowledge that the goods were designed to form part of a gun. If my Department had known, then it would of course have advised that licences were necessary, and they would not have been granted.'

(F4.28) Scott says: 'First the statement that the government had "recently" become aware of the Iraqi project to develop a long-range gun was a far more elastic use of the word "recently" than was warranted by the facts. The project had been known to the intelligence services since at least September 1989. Moreover, information about the project had been disseminated to government Departments [in] intelligence reports on 30 November and 5 December 1989.'

(F4.29) 'Mr Clark accepted in evidence . . . that the use of the word "recently" was an "exaggeration".'

(F4.40) 'The text is consistent with an attempt to avoid criticism of the government for not acting sooner than it did.'

However Scott was unable to discover all those responsible for drafting the statement, particularly who added the word 'recently'. This sort of problem was common.

Often a Parliamentary Written Answer would have been drafted and redrafted by many different people, sometimes including legal advisers. Any one of them might change a word or a phrase. A common source of error was when one person made a very minor change, subtly altering the meaning in a way which was very important, although the significance was not realised at the time by the person concerned. Each subsequent alteration was not always vetted again by all those who had previously approved the wording.

(F4.80) So how did the supergun parts come so close to slipping through the net in spite of intelligence reports? Scott concludes: 'There were omissions. There were failures. . . . Muddle undoubtedly had a part to play. But it went even further than muddle.' Proper records were not kept of various briefings and there was poor communication. '. . . There is clear evidence that, some time before October 1989, government officials had had clear information which raised the suspicion that Walter Somers' tubes were probably intended for use as artillery gun-barrels. . . . The evidence indicates suspicion that an Iraqi long-range artillery weapon with unusual features was in contemplation. Parliament should have been told this.'

Nevertheless, what actually happened was that Ministers were not properly informed and statements were not made.

Then there is the vexed issue of the Public Interest Immunity Certificates signed by various Ministers. Were they trying to prevent the truth about the Matrix Churchill case from coming out in court?

(G10.11) Scott says: 'A Minister ought not to sign a Certificate unless satisfied that the production of the documents or the giving of the information in question would cause significant damage to the public interest.'

(G10.15) But there were other ways in which the Matrix Churchill defendants could have had difficulty with their defence. For example, documents could be moved from one Department to another in an attempt to hide them from the public gaze. Andrew Leithead of the Treasurer Solicitor's Department wrote on 22 August 1991: 'It is likely to be easier to prevent the disclosure of these documents if they are in the hands of the DTI . . . who could resist a witness summons on "Cheltenham Justices" grounds as well as public interest immunity [than] it would be if the documents are in the hands of Customs and Excise as prosecutors who have to obey the Attorney General's guidelines.' He explained that the view was that the documents referred to were in any case irrelevant to the defence case.

(G10.19) Scott asked Andrew Leithead: 'Was it not in fact the aim here that you and Mr Hosker were trying to achieve, to make it harder for the defendants to obtain the documents?'
    'Yes.'
    'Even though the position was that the prosecution had the documents?'
    'Yes.'
    'Yet there is a duty under the Attorney General's guidelines to give copies of prosecution documents, unused, to the defendants, apart from the exceptions in PII?'
    'Yes.'
    'This was a way not to be bound by that duty?'

'Yes. . . ' He added: 'It was thought to be the right way of dealing with it at the time.'

(G10.21) However, Andrew Leithead later sought to alter his oral evidence in a written submission. Scott remarked: 'He should, he now says, have answered "No" instead of "Yes" to the relevant questions cited in paragraph G10.19 above . . . [He] has also in his written comments said that certain passages of his letters are incorrect.' Mr Leithead wrote later: 'I regret that I wrote in such incorrect terms. . . . With hindsight and the experience of the years that are now passed, I can clearly see that these paragraphs are wrong.'

(G13.32) On one of the PII certificates signed by Tristan Garel-Jones were the words 'unquantifiable damage' that could be caused if certain documents were released. Scott was very concerned about the misleading impression given by this phrase.

'In his evidence to the Inquiry, Mr Garel-Jones explained . . . "unquantifiable damage" . . . as covering both "unquantifiably large" and "unquantifiably small".' He said: 'It could be a mixture of both. I mean there could be some information where the damage would be unquantifiably large and may be leading to someone's death, and another instance where the damage could be unquantifiably small.'

'Minuscule in other words?' asked Scott.

'Yes, and there could be a mixture of both in the same document.'

'The judge would read that, do you think, as covering both?'

'I think he certainly would. I think judges are well practised in knowing when words can be interpreted in two different ways, I would guess . . .'

As a judge himself, Scott disagreed. 'I suggest the suggestion that the references would be understood to cover damage that was "unquantifiably small" as risible.'

(G13.33) Scott quotes from a letter between government officials about Michael Heseltine, President of the Board of Trade. Unlike some other Ministers, he had 'needed a great deal of persuasion to sign the certificate. At first he refused to sign *any* certificate. He seemed to think it would be unjust to the defendants. It was of course pointed out to him that [the judge] would decide whether or not the claim would be upheld. But Michael Heseltine was only finally persuaded after he received a stiff letter from the Attorney General saying that it was his duty to sign.'

(G13.46) In comparison, Malcolm Rifkind acted exactly as advised and signed a certificate, saying to Scott afterwards: 'I understood the rules to be quite straightforward and to be very, very longstanding, that if a Minister was satisfied that certain papers came within the category of "advice to Ministers", or ministerial documents or departmental papers, or intelligence papers then he was obliged to sign the certificate to that effect.'

(G13.54–57) Michael Heseltine said to Scott: '. . . when I first read the submission . . . I said "Up with this I will not put . . ."' I was being asked to sign a document which would deny these documents to the proper trial . . . I did not know the details of the defence case; but I could not believe that this was not relevant to it.'

(G13.76) Sir Nicholas Lyell, the Attorney General, gave firm advice to Ministers on signing the certificates. Scott remarks: 'He did not read any of the documents that it was supposed

[Mr Heseltine's] certificate should protect. Indeed, at the time he gave oral evidence to the Inquiry, 24 and 25 March 1994, he had still not read any of the documents.' Instead, he relied on the briefing of another colleague that 'there was nothing in the documents that in any way called into question the fairness of the prosecution'.

(G13.84) Michael Heseltine was asked to sign a supplementary certificate. He complained that he was about to leave the country and had been unable to consult with other Ministers. 'I realise the pressure,' he wrote at the time, 'but it is quite intolerable to present me with these issues when I have no time to explore them more fully.' In the event, none of Michael Heseltine's concerns was adequately communicated to the judge.

(G13.123–125) Scott writes: 'Major responsibility for the inadequacy of the instructions to Mr Moses (QC) must, in my opinion, be borne by the Attorney General. . . . I accept the genuineness of his belief that he was personally, as opposed to constitutionally, blameless. . . . But I do not accept that he was not personally at fault. The issues that had been raised by Mr Heseltine's stand on the PII certificate did not fall into the category of mundane, run of the mill issues that could properly be left to be dealt with by officials in the Treasury Solicitor's Department without the Attorney General's supervision. . . . These are difficult questions. The answers are not obvious . . . I would not have expected Mr Heseltine, a non-lawyer, to have articulated them. But I would have expected the Attorney General to have done so. . . . There was, in my opinion, an absence of personal involvement by the Attorney General that Mr Heseltine's stance . . . had made necessary.'

(G17.29) The Matrix Churchill trial collapsed after Alan Clark gave damning evidence, not of Matrix Churchill involvement, but of government behaviour and attitude. Scott reviews what Alan Clark said under cross-examination in court: 'You knew the Iraqis would not be using the current orders [for machine tools] for general engineering purposes but would be using them to make munitions?'

'The current orders, yes,' replied Mr Clark.

'If you had said of course the Iraqis will be using the current order for general engineering purposes that could not be the case to your knowledge?'

'I do not see that the fact that they are using them, were using them, for munitions, excludes them using them for general engineering purposes more than the other way round.'

'But here the writer of this minute [ie the DTI note of the 20 January 1988 meeting] is attributing to you the statement the Iraqis will be using the current order for general engineering purposes, which cannot be correct to your knowledge.'

'Well, it's our old friend being economical, isn't it?'

'With the truth?'

'With the actualité. There was nothing misleading or dishonest to make a formal or introductory comment that the Iraqis would be using the current orders for general engineering purposes. All I didn't say was "and for making munitions", if I thought that they were going to say that . . .'

'You knew that the machine tools would be put to, were currently being put to, a munitions use and that the follow-on orders so long as the war lasted were likely to be put to a munitions use?'

'Could be put, yes.'

'. . . You invited the companies to agree a specification, ie get something in writing, the customer to highlight the peaceful use to which the machine tools would be put, even though to your knowledge it was at least so long as the war lasted, very unlikely they would be put to a peaceful use?

'Yes I would agree with that.'

Later the exchanges continued as follows.

'You didn't want to let anyone know that at this stage these munitions and their follow up orders were going to munitions factories to make munitions?'

'No.'

'And the emphasis on peaceful purposes and general engineering and so on would help keep the matter confidential?'

'I do not think it was principally a matter for public awareness. I think it was probably a matter for Whitehall cosmetics.'

'A matter for Whitehall cosmetics to keep the records ambiguous?'

'Yes, yes.'

Later again they continued:

'So the signal you are sending to these people is: "I am a minister (sic), I will help you get through these orders and the follow ups through the rather loose guidelines and the rather Byzantine ways of Whitehall. Help me by keeping your mouth firmly shut about military use"?'

'I think that is too imaginative an interpretation. I think it was more at arm's length than that.'

'But in any event it was how they would help, by not, as it were, making Whitehall cosmetics run, rather by keeping quiet; stating nothing military?'

'They got it by implication?'

'Yes, by implication is different. By implication they got it.'

(G18.1–12) Scott concludes that the Matrix Churchill trial was 'a trial that ought never to have been brought'. He lists a considerable number of criticisms and weaknesses of several Departments. However he does not conclude that there was a conspiracy to allow innocent men to be sent to gaol, despite widespread speculation and accusation in the media and by opposition MPs.

(G18.54) Scott also expressed concerns about the blanket way in which PII certificates were used. He attacks the idea that Public Interest Immunity should always be invoked even when a Minister believes there are overwhelming reasons why documents should be disclosed in the public interest, particularly as in this case, to ensure fair justice. He points out that there is little precedent for the use of such certificates in criminal cases.

(G18.104) 'Class claims were made which were not, in my opinion, warranted by authority, and which ought to have had no place in a criminal trial.'

The overwhelming impression gained by studying the oral evidence, and the Report itself, is that Ministers often have only a partial understanding of what their own Departments are up to, that Ministries are bad at talking to each other, and that individual civil servants also tend to have only a partial picture. It is also very clear that much time and effort are given to how a course of action will be presented publicly: will it be explained at all, or in part, or dressed up as something slightly different?

Ministers are given complex briefings, but so many of them, on so many different issues, that they are unlikely to read them all word for word, and even less likely to recall all of them in any detail some months later without help.

It is clear that the risks of being a Minister are huge. You are vulnerable to criticism all the time, signing letter after letter prepared by others. A key issue is responsibility. How can a Minister possibly hope to keep a grip on a Department when almost every person in it is a civil servant who may have his or her own agenda and failings? The volume of work is far too large to allow proper scrutiny. The issues are too complex. The system is too powerful.

A major error can be made in seconds; in the signing of a single letter, sitting there among hundreds of others. How can a Minister be held fully responsible for an inaccuracy if the letter has been drafted by three or four civil service 'experts' and is referring to a highly specialist area? It is particularly difficult where Ministers are shunted around from one Department to another after only short periods in post. Ministerial turnover is dreaded by many civil servants because it takes so long for a new person to 'come up to speed' regarding – say – every aspect of the health service. However, turnover also means less oversight, less leadership, and greater control by departmental officials.

But if Ministers in today's complex system of government cannot reasonably be held responsible for all the decisions they take and for the accuracy of statements they make, then who can be? Are we moving to a form of government which is wholly unaccountable, or are we going to have to move to a situation where senior officials advising Ministers are also held publicly responsible?

If I ever found myself running a Department, and had the power to do so, the first thing I would do is hire several of the highest calibre executives I could find, paid to help oversee policy development, check advice, probe, ask questions, and generally make sure that every statement made and every letter signed is a true and fair reflection of the facts. In turn they would be expected to be publicly accountable for their own errors. This means that they have to accept responsibility for advice given.

In my view, politicisation of the civil service is inevitable and necessary, although it will continue to be fiercely resisted. But as we have seen, the current system is no longer working and is unsuitable for twenty-first-century government. It encourages 'buck-passing', yet the buck all too often lands up in the murky anonymous world of 'official advice'.

But anonymity will never be the same after the Scott Inquiry. A civil servant from now on will always know at the back of his or her mind that a private and confidential note written today may become part of a very public inquiry tomorrow, and all those whose names are on that note could well be called as witnesses for detailed interrogation. The days of impartial and secret advice are over.

Of course, Scott also identified a number of other situations where Ministers were far from ignorant, only too well informed of what was going on, and where a deliberate decision was made to mislead the public with partially truthful statements.

Despite all the criticisms in the Scott Report, not one person resigned, nor was there any apology for the way in which the public was misled. On the contrary, speeches were made which vigorously defended the government's position, making it abundantly clear that Ministers felt that they had the absolute moral right to disagree with Scott, and to reject as many of his conclusions as they liked.

But if that was the case, what was the point of getting him to do three years' work in the first place? A very expensive exercise for nothing. If the Cabinet were going to make their own verdict binding as regards future action, then they should have announced their own final decisions years before. Of course, the reason they did not dare to do so was that there would have been public outrage. There was an urgent need to reassure people that there was not going to be a cover up.

In that regard it was unfortunate that the government gave itself such a long time to study the report, and allowed so little access to anyone else. It made its position far worse in the eyes of the public. It would have been far better to have allowed both government and opposition leaders equal access for a far shorter time before official publication, even if opposition members had to submit to some sort of controls to prevent leakage.

My own view is that the criticisms levelled by Scott against William Waldegrave and against the Attorney General, Sir Nicholas Lyell, are so serious that they should have resigned on the day the Report was published. I believe that Scott's conclusion that the Attorney General was at fault made his position untenable.

Mr Waldegrave may not have had any 'duplicitous intention', but his descriptions of the interpretation of guidelines were 'bound to be misleading to anyone who does not know the substance of the decision'. To me, this indicates a lack of understanding of the public perception that ill becomes a government Minister.

Alan Clark should also have resigned (if still in government) for being economic with the actuality. However, he was no longer even an MP when the Report came out. Others were also criticised, but in less serious ways.

Without doubt, Sir Richard Scott did a great service to the nation. He took to pieces the whole business of government, exposed its shabbiest features to public gaze, and also revealed some of its greatest strengths. He raised many questions, and challenged the prevailing culture of arrogance and half-truths.

The lesson is that the British public *do* want to know in some detail what government is up to, especially over areas affecting the public conscience such as arms sales to dictatorships. The nation's elected representatives ask thousands of written questions every year, and deserve accurate, clear and informative replies. However, it is also true that long inquiries and weighty reports can create confusion and boredom.

Unless there is a rapid move towards far greater openness, there will be irresistible moral arguments for legal measures such as Freedom of Information legislation. I do not believe that the British people will tolerate the politics of deception much longer. Politicians in power who fear a Freedom of Information Act had better start communicating more fully.

In exchange, opposition MPs need to treat information with greater maturity, rather than using every snippet as out-of-context ammunition to score cheap points, when they know full well that the real issues are complex and the choices are rather limited for whoever is in government. That is the reality.

10

The Changing Culture

'No one pretends that democracy is perfect or all-wise. Indeed
it has been said that democracy is the worst form of
government except all those other forms that have been tried
from time to time.' Winston Churchill (1874–1965)

'Now they are avid for office or they've failed. They're much,
much more ambitious – increasingly so and I find it almost
nauseating.' Lord Weatherill (1920–)

'Freedom of the press in Britain is freedom to print such of the
proprietor's prejudices as the advertisers don't object to.'
Hannen Swaffer (1879–1962)

'Thou god of our idolatry, the press . . .
Thou fountain, at which we drink the good and wise;
Thou ever-bubbling spring of endless lies.' William Cowper
(1731–1800)

It is clear from all we have seen in previous chapters that
there has been a fundamental change in parliamentary life.
Attitudes have altered while standards have fallen. Before we
look at proposals for reform, we need to probe further into

the way in which the culture of both Westminster and the media has shifted.

The old 'Club' culture may still be a dominating influence on the lives of new MPs entering the House but that influence is no longer what it was. To some extent the reshaping of expectations and practices in Westminster is a reflection of changes in the nation as a whole.

One of the first changes that struck me on talking to many older politicians has been the acceleration of the pace of life. Forty years ago, MPs spent far more time hanging around the precincts of Westminster. Few had secretaries or offices, and people like Lord Healey recall that they did most of their correspondence by hand on their laps. Now each MP receives so much mail that more than one secretary may be needed to deal with it all.

Lord Whitelaw says, 'I became a Member of Parliament in 1955. The difference now from then is quite simple: it was a much more friendly place. You got to know people. I don't think the people in the House of Commons today do know each other. They don't see each other.

'When I was Chief Whip in '64, I used to go along to the smoking room every single evening at six o'clock, if I could possibly make the time, and from six to seven-thirty I sat and talked to members. And at half-past seven I had a table of my own and I used to ask three people to come to dinner with me.

'Now nobody goes in any of these places. It's because everyone sits in their offices. It's very odd. They spend all their time in their hutches, with all the equipment they have now. It's a much less friendly place at every level. In the earliest days after the war the two parties had a coalition and the senior members of the parties knew each other very well indeed. Parliament was a place where people used to talk, people used to argue and you got to know generally what people were thinking. It was a community.'

Older 'Club' members passed on the great traditions and ways of doing things. The unwritten 'gentleman's code' lived on, reinforced through informal conversations.

Now, Lord Whitelaw feels, 'They are completely hooked into their own thoughts and their own ideas and they don't really listen. That is a really major change in the whole way that Parliament works.' In contrast, the House of Lords was a far more friendly place, maintaining the old patterns of life, welcoming new faces with hospitality and courtesy.[206]

The second change has been the advent of the career politician who drifts perhaps from school or university to a research job in Westminster, and never leaves. Lord Weatherill says that this is a serious weakness and many MPs are motivated by ambition, rather than by a desire to serve their country. Politics should be a calling, not a career.

'What has happened in recent years is increasingly a tendency to become professionals and there's hardly anyone there who's actually done a job outside. I'm not a politician. I describe myself as a businessman in politics. I didn't even get here until I was forty-three. I'm a tailor by trade. But what has Mr Portillo actually done? It's not his fault, he's young.

'We're trying to redress this. In the Industry and Parliamentary Trust of which I am Chairman, we have today twenty Chief Executives or former Chairmen of companies, between fifty and sixty who have indicated to us that they would like to enter Parliament, who would do so as a service and not for the money, for the Conservative Party and for the Labour Party, and the Liberal Democrats, but we can't get them past the selection committees. The members ask, "What canvassing have you done? How many doors have you knocked on?" Today [the younger generation] are avid for office or they've failed. The whole culture has changed.

They're much, much more ambitious – increasingly so and I find it almost nauseating.'[207]

There is less class division than there was. Lord Healey remarks that he can hardly tell these days who is Labour and who is Conservative by the way they dress or how they talk, whereas it was very obvious when he was first an MP. Despite the mixing of backgrounds across the parties, and the fading of class distinctions, MPs are often far more polarised and dogmatic than they were, and more prone to point-scoring for the sake of it.

The Second World War had a great impact on the generation that entered Parliament in the 1950s, and it affected the way they saw politics. 'Those who were in the services, who were interested in politics, were determined to create a better world,' Lord Healey explained. 'We had all learned from experience that we depended on one another, that we sink or swim together, and also the better off people had a great natural sympathy for the worse off. Idealism or a sense of purpose was a prime motivation for the wartime generation to go into politics and a lot of them made big financial sacrifices.' He recalls that just after the war he earned less than his wife did as a teacher, and teachers were poorly paid.[208]

There was general agreement after the war that a social revolution was needed, with such measures as the introduction of the National Health Service, and the nationalisation of such industries as coal, gas and electricity. Consensus ruled Parliament and there was a consistency of policy regardless of who was in government.

Sir Edward Heath sees a greater intolerance of other views today: 'Looking back we were a very tolerant party. In fact, both parties were tolerant. Sometimes this is missing today. Let us not try to hide this fact. It is true very often in the House of Commons.'[209]

Another shift has been created by the growth of parliamentary lobbying through the 1980s, which many politicians see as a dominant and distressing feature of parliamentary life today, although still affecting mainly the Conservative Party. Many practices which have been widely accepted recently, would have been regarded as unthinkable just twenty years ago.

The functioning of Parliament has also been profoundly affected by the relatively large size of government majorities over the last few years, apart from the 1992 election. Landslide victories can create arrogance and complacency, while tiny majorities tend to keep governments far more sensitised to public concerns.

It can be unhealthy for the same party to remain in power too long. A government can become blind to its own defects, believing itself 'immortal'. A government can also run out of quality people with losses after every Cabinet reshuffle, so that the team becomes more lightweight. The power of patronage is wielded by one party, so that many power structures such as quangos become unbalanced. A government continuously in power also has no time or space to think, or to develop fresh vision. It is possible that there would have been less of a credibility crisis over lack of integrity in Westminster if different parties had been alternating in government over the last sixteen years.

There is another factor which has had a huge effect on Parliament and that is the introduction of television, which only began in November 1989. The suggestion had first been made thirty years earlier. 'It's killed debate,' said one Peer. Many MPs are greatly influenced by the possibility of getting a twenty-second 'sound-bite' on to the airwaves. There are two different images imprinted on the public mind as a result of television. The first is a Chamber that looks empty despite the fact that a Minister is giving what is supposed to be an important speech. The second is a Chamber during Question Time that is crowded, noisy and full of rude interruptions. Neither of these images is positive.

However, Lord Weatherill is relaxed about accusations of disorder. 'Behaviour is infinitely, infinitely better than it has ever been. Read the history books. Take Disraeli's maiden speech when he was shouted down. It would be unthinkable today. He made the famous comment, "The time will come when you will hear me," but they wouldn't hear him. On another occasion, in 1883, the *Hansard* editor gave up and wrote across four pages in Victorian scrawl, "The house proceeded in indescribable disorder!"

'During the course of this indescribable disorder, Speaker Brand just had time to lean forward and whisper to his learned clerk: "What do I do next?" The clerk just had time to give him some very wise advice. "Sir," he said, "I should be very cautious." '[210]

Disorder can detract from debate. Tony Blair feels that Prime Minister's Question Time is an occasion where the House of Commons needs reform.

'The atmosphere is so charged in there. I am physically more nervous before that than anything else I do. Harold Wilson used to be physically sick beforehand. It's partly because you have one minute to put across a point and that place is like Romans and the gladiators and the lion. You hesitate for a moment and you die in there. It's a real pantomime in many ways.'[211]

How new MPs find their feet

If the culture is changing, and new rules are being proposed, then it is even more important that new MPs have a proper induction. How else will they discover how they are supposed to behave? Simon Hughes is an interesting character:

widely respected, minority party front bench, younger generation, fresh and radical in thinking, yet not a Liberal Democrat Party hack by any means. I asked him what kind of training or induction there was for new MPs.

'In short, none. None at all,' he replied. 'There is never a proper induction programme. All that happens – and it happened to me, I suppose in 1983 – is that for a day the Chief Whip at the time takes you to the most important places of all; you are shown your pigeon hole; you are rehearsed for taking your seat; you are given a little bit of information about a couple of things.'

'What about a copy of Erskine May's book of procedures?'

'No,' he replied. 'Nothing really. I don't think I was given a single piece of paper. The fees office now sends new MPs an envelope in which they say, "This is the position regarding your salary and your pension rights and the office costs allowance." There wasn't even a compulsory meeting with them.'

'What about information on declaring Members' Interests?'

'No. Nothing at all. I wasn't even given a book saying "Rules for new boys and girls." '

'Or procedures about addressing other Members of the House?'

'No. You were told to go in and sit and watch like good apprentices, like a pupil barrister who has no rules either. You just followed someone around and picked it up by watching. So you went into the House and watched what other people did. I took my seat on 1 March and made my maiden speech on 21 March and by then I was meant to have worked out what to do.

'It is an extraordinary place, and even today it may be better but I am still very conscious of the fact that it is more a matter of chance and luck and hazard as to how much support a new MP gets. It may depend on whether they have friends already in the House. It is very much a case of, "Come in and see how it goes – we've all learnt it that way." There is no training.'

I asked him what he thought about Lord Whitelaw's comment that MPs now live in their 'rabbit hutches' and hardly know each other.

'Certainly it has changed a lot. I think that there is increased pressure to be constituency MPs. Coming from your constituency, living in your constituency, doing your surgeries. MPs prefer that as well in a way because in a constituency you are an MP, whereas in Westminster you are just one of 651 MPs who may get a chance to say something or may not. And so apart from big "set piece" occasions you can probably be perceived as doing more out there on the ground. The media are more demanding so the number of requests for radio and TV is growing all the time.'

A number of those I have talked to describe a Debating Chamber that is in serious decline, emptied by the growth of Select Committees and other office work, the lack of competent speakers, and general apathy. Many MPs certainly have very poor communication skills and are boring to listen to. Set piece debates, with powerful charismatic speakers, used to be an exhilarating and entertaining experience, but the Commons is bereft of many such characters today.

There are few people who can draw a crowd when their name comes up on the screens around Westminster. Some MPs already watch debates from their offices so there is less need to go rushing back to hear a debate. In fact there is little point in being there unless an MP wishes to contribute, or a vote is called. Hughes again: 'People don't have a worldview in the same way as they used to. The Whips are much more tough on people so the chance to develop your own thinking, free thinking ideas, seems to me to be limited. Nowadays the assumption is that when you come here, you come to do a full-time job. Increasing numbers of people don't find it appealing and some of the great public figures of our day wouldn't consider it financially remunerative, or wouldn't consider that the balance of work, the grind of constituency work as against shaping the policies of the nation is something that inspires them. So people of vision and insight, worldview or national perspectives probably say "I would be better being the editor of the *Economist*, or being the director general of the CBI," and therefore we don't attract the same range of people as we probably once did.'[212]

I asked one MP what words of wisdom she would give to someone interested in going into politics. She thought for a moment and smiled: 'Don't bother,' she exclaimed. 'If you want to join one of the best clubs in the world, as they say, which is what a lot of the chaps want to do, then come, but don't think you're going to change anything.'

Low morale, poor self-image and a critical public are all symptoms of the general malaise, yet some manage to remain reasonably cheerful. Lord Weatherill does not think there is much wrong with the Commons, looking back on his time there. 'Parliament has been brought into disrepute and we must deal with public perception of these matters, [but] I'm passionately against rules. I think we should operate by self-discipline, and that MPs should always conduct themselves as Honourable Members.'[213] He has seen many so-called reforms and says that each was meant to solve a problem but created another.

David Alton strongly disagrees with the supposed merits of self-regulation, based on his experience as part of the Privileges Committee: 'Parliament is incapable of self-regulation. It's obvious from the way that the Privileges Committee has operated over the last year that although many of its members are highly conscientious and estimable individuals, Parliament itself cannot satisfactorily deal with excesses which are committed by other parliamentarians. The watchdog is too closely identified with the process. It would be far better if there was an independent Standing Committee. Impartial people, perhaps a couple of High Court Judges. Ultimately we would still sit in our own court in judgement on our own colleagues, but I don't think the investigative process should be conducted inside the House.'[214]

We have seen that there have been dramatic cultural changes within Westminster, but what about the world outside? As far as many parliamentarians are concerned there is one factor above all which has more than anything created the crisis of confidence within Westminster today, and that is a change in the culture of the media.

It is true that without a free press, most of what you have read would have remained secret for a generation. However, we have also seen many cases recently where the press have invaded privacy and libelled people who have sometimes been powerless to defend their reputations. The media may well be operating in a more hostile way towards politicians than thirty years ago, but is that such a bad thing?

The media war with Westminster

Sir George Young is a mildly spoken Minister compared to many others, yet even he says that what the media are doing now is 'evil'. 'A lot of Ministers and MPs have seen what a media witch hunt can do to a colleague. There are no saints in politics; there are no saints anywhere. And everybody makes mistakes, small ones and big ones. And when you see an error of judgement or a relatively small mistake magnified, distorted and a witch hunt to find out what other mistakes may have been made a long time ago, you can see it destroy a chap. I think that's evil.

'There are all too many examples of colleagues who have been hounded out of government, many of whom were very good Ministers. I think it's what the media have done to the wives and the family rather than what they have done to the individual. Quite often the wife and the family are totally innocent bystanders who loyally stand by the chap. I think that does put good people off politics. I believe in the freedom of the press but they have a responsibility.'[215]

Another Minister pointed out that the result of media aggression is that 'politicians will simply play safe, they will simply parrot the line to take, clam up, because the game is "spot the gaff"; and instead of people honestly answering a question as to what their view is, they have to remember what so and so said yesterday about this. As a result politicians are becoming more defensive, less honest. They tend to shelter behind what the line is. In the long term that is bad for democracy.'

Lord Whitelaw also slams the press. 'I think the press have stirred things up far too much . . . after all, Parliament and party political leaders are just the same as other people. I don't think it is that much worse. I think it is worse because the press are hunting after people. I think probably there were many very big figures in the twenties who were up to all sorts of activities. Nobody knew. None of us are absolutely sure figures and therefore I dislike the hunting of politicians, particularly the sex hunting, which I think is very unattractive.'

Lord Whitelaw is depressed that issues are often overshadowed by personality conflict, and rarely reported. 'Every day The Times, The Guardian, the Mail, always had a column on what was happening in Parliament. Today you won't find a word on anything that happened in Parliament. Only if there is a row. The press are now determined to hunt things out. All their people aren't writing about issues, they are writing about people.'

However, he is against controls. 'I have never been in favour of forcing things on the press. I think the press have gone wrong. I think they have wrong values and I think they are going to have to find their own values back again. I don't think it is for Parliament to force them into it. I thought one of the worst hunts was David Mellor. It was a monstrous thing. I mean, he was very silly. He went far too far but I do think in spite of that he really was victimised. I think the press hounded him to an extreme.'[216]

There is no doubt that media now set the agenda. News of dogs biting children led to the Dangerous Dogs Act; the Hungerford massacre led to the Firearms Amendment legislation, and the Dunblane school massacre led to further calls for firearms controls; salmonella in eggs led to the Food Safety Act; live animal transport to new EC regulations and Greenpeace campaigns led to reversing a government backed decision to dump an old oil rig at sea. However, those in the media would say that they are simply a mouthpiece for the views of the nation.

One MP complained that when it comes to leaders in the nation, even those with integrity are vilified. 'The private lives of everybody are torn to pieces, however exemplary they may be. They will find an angle on it which they can turn into three pages of copy which of course they hope will sell more copies. It's a scandalous state. On the bright side they do scrutinise, they do scan the small print, so there is an enormous public debate on the issues in the media as well as the House.'

Peter Lilley believes that the 'hysteria' will probably subside. He too is very cautious about new controls. 'The chances are that they won't work because it would be seen that politicians were trying to protect themselves from the press. Protecting ordinary people from the press would be fine [but] the first journalist that falls foul of a Privacy Law, because he exposes some infidelities [of an MP] and pleads national interest, will become a hero, go to gaol for a little while, and the law will be changed again.'[217]

However David Amess sees the current situation as 'crazy', intolerable and one that must be regulated. 'And now the media say "Who shall we bring down next?" They say "Boo!" and we jump. It's crazy . . . They're destroying politicians. They're destroying the monarchy, they're destroying the church, they're destroying the judiciary. They will eventually destroy themselves. I would legislate, because all this code of practice is a cop out. I'm not a lawyer but I think it is wrong to print in newspapers allegations which are not substantiated by an action through the courts. Most Members of Parliament do not have money to fight one of these actions.'[218]

Robert Key is also 'appalled' by low journalistic standards. 'Many journalists are quite happy to lie and are regularly peddling lies in what they write – and there is no redress.'[219]

Some Conservatives are convinced that there is a Labour-inspired plot behind the anti-sleaze crusade. Jeremy Hanley told me, 'This campaign that Labour is playing on so-called sleaze is all part of a destabilising campaign which they have learned from the Democrats in America. They have studied dirty tricks in America. They have studied very hard indeed.' As an example, he cited a broadcast by the Labour Party (May 1995) where the Prime Minister was called a liar no fewer than fifteen times. 'The attacks on individuals are all part of American political theory.'[220]

Unfortunately it is far too easy to dismiss media pressure

as part of a vindictive campaign. We have already seen that the public are utterly fed up with the sleazy reputation of politicians in general and want higher standards. The reality is that both press and politicians are populist driven: they have to respond to the mood of the nation or perish. The difference is that the media do seem far more in touch with public opinion on these matters than those at Westminster.

Harry Greenway is another of the growing number who have felt the pain of false allegations in the press. 'It is extremely important for the press to be obliged to stick to established facts, to be prepared to defend what they say under law and to face really severe penalties if convicted of half-truth, malevolence, unfairness and so on. An apology in the paper one inch by ten inches long is not enough. Newspapers can pressurise the authorities into bringing actions which are baseless or for which they have the flimsiest of evidence – in spite of established rules of at least 50 per cent chance of a successful prosecution.

'I believe these rules can go right out of the window as hysteria builds up against an individual. There is then a "no win" situation: if the "revelations" are ignored, then Ministers are accused of taking no action. If the case goes ahead but is lost, or dismissed for lack of evidence, there is a suspicion of cover up, so a situation can be reached where the only way the public will be satisfied following trial by media, is with a successful prosecution.'

In Harry Greenway's case, allegations were made which led to a court case that hung over him for three-and-a-half years, during which he had to fight an election. The case was eventually dismissed. 'All charges were withdrawn and I was awarded expedited costs by a distinguished High Court judge. The law could be tightened up. The media should only be able to print if a criminal charge is made – not the gossip before. It is better surely to bend over backwards in fairness. It isn't for the press to be judge and jury in these matters. We would then be more in line with the Continent.'[221]

Jeremy Hanley described the very personal nature of press attacks. 'I have got a thicker skin [now] than I ever thought I possessed. The insults completely wash over me now. Last September [1994] I think actually I was very deeply affected by the press. For instance my son, because he was my son, was dragged through the *News of the World*, and as a result lost his job. Then I certainly did feel the press were getting at me. But I don't react now. [However] my wife does find it difficult to pick up newspapers now.' Jeremy Hanley is convinced that Labour will find the media hunting about in their own private lives when they are in government.

In the meantime he feels that the aggression of the press is putting people off entering public life. 'You ought to see what has happened to our candidates list. There was a time when being a Member of Parliament was actually respected. We used to have more than a hundred people willing to stand for Parliament, [for a by-election]. Now we're lucky if we have twenty and the quality [is less]. There are fewer with experience, willing to lend that experience to the nation. It's a tremendous cost.'[222]

Tony Blair also feels this acutely. Asked if his wife Cherie was pleased that he had become Leader of the Labour Party, he said, 'She was torn. She felt pleased because she thought it was the right thing. But you wouldn't be human if you didn't fear what it would do to your family. It's the thing that worries me more than anything else.'[223]

There are several ethical issues which the media face other than merely reporting accurately and fairly, or confining inquiries to legitimate means. One such issue is the Lobby system. This is a code of practice which allows someone like the Prime Minister to be as rude or indiscreet as he or she likes to a bunch of journalists, with the absolute guarantee that the remarks will be reported anonymously.

For example when you read that 'a source close to the Prime Minister' has said something insulting about another politician, the truth may be that the interview was with the Prime Minister himself. It could be argued therefore that by definition the Lobby encourages lack of integrity at best and deception at worst. It allows people to speak opposites out of both sides of their mouths at the same time; to be loyal and damning with flattery and flannel.

Media 'interests'

Another ethical issue is whether or not journalists should have to declare their own interests in some way, or be governed by a code of conduct which forbids accepting favours that may influence what they write. These questions were highlighted following revelations about press hospitality from Mohammed Al-Fayed. The Al-Fayed family gave elaborate and generous hospitality to many journalists during the 1985 battle for the takeover of the House of Fraser. One reason was to convince the British press that they were a long established family of established and respectable wealth.[224]

The former deputy editor of the *Sunday Times*, Ivan Fallon, who strongly supported the Al-Fayed bid and wrote a book about it, freely admitted that he had stayed twice at the Paris Ritz free of charge, although he denied that it had compromised his journalism. He said he went strictly for work and did not stay at weekends.[225]

Brian Vine of the *Mail on Sunday* also admitted that he had spent a night in the £6,000 Windsor suite at the Paris Ritz and wrote about it for the travel page. 'I did not expect to receive a bill for reviewing a hotel suite.'[226]

Jeremy Warner, later business editor of *The Independent* said he had been sent a 'card' but had not used it.[227]

We also need to look at the issue of so-called 'justifiable subterfuge'. Was it right for *The Guardian* to send a forged fax on House of Commons letterhead to try to establish the truth about a hotel bill relating to a stay at the Paris Ritz by Jonathan Aitken? A majority of 275 MPs voted in favour of referring the editor to the Commons Privileges Committee. Edwina Currie remarked: 'Scrutiny by the press is one thing but subterfuge is another, and that's the issue at the heart of *The Guardian*'s bad behaviour.'[228] Similarly, should the *Sunday Times* have been disciplined in some way for entrapping MPs with cash offers for questions?

Peter Bottomley urged caution: 'Criticise them, get involved in arguments by all means, but don't try to use the Committee of Privileges for trying to control what journalists do in their legitimate role of acting as vacuum cleaners, picking up all the dirt, sifting it out and making mistakes and often getting it right in what they decide to put out to the public.'[229]

He told me recently of the appalling way in which he had been libelled in the late 1980s over malicious allegations entirely without foundation, and of other libel and harassment. Despite these things he is not bitter, and believes things may change as the public begins to react against it all.

Despite the technological revolution in publishing, over the last fifteen years there has been a significant decline in the circulation of many newspapers generally, and the tabloids have suffered along with the rest. The so-called 'circulation wars' have heightened the media frenzy over 'scandals' as well as narrowing profit margins.

If you are libelled you can take court action – in theory. In practice, it is very expensive because you have to pay heavy costs as you go, and legal aid is not available, however poor you are. Even if you had a guarantee of winning damages and costs (and it is never certain), you could run out of money very quickly before getting anywhere near a court hearing. Thus libel actions are really only for the rich; the rest are in most cases unable to defend their reputations.

But even if the legal costs are no problem, many would argue that you are very unlikely to clear your own name even if you win. There are many reasons for this. First, far less media coverage is given to successful court actions than to the original allegations. An example of this was the libel action against the *Independent on Sunday* won by Said Mohammed Ayas, after settling out of court. The action was summarised in fourteen lines hidden at the end of a larger article about Jonathan Aitken on the bottom of page two.[230]

The only way to get more coverage is to refuse to settle out of court and go for a bloody public battle. This can be very unpleasant and time-consuming. Every possible excuse will be given for the libel, which may well include restating the original allegations and a host of other negative comments. What is more, every word said in court can be freely reported under British law without the risk of another libel action.

The aim of the press defendants will be to throw so much mud in the air that the jury will lose patience and decide the story was justified. What started out as a single article on the inside pages could become a front page in many national papers, every day for two weeks. A libel read by fewer than a million people and readily forgotten, may now become a major concern in the minds of 10 million. These are the reasons why most people who are libelled take no action. Too many people have left court having lost their actions and their wealth as well as their reputations, despite the fact that they may well have had a genuine case of grievance.

Simon Jenkins wrote in *The Times*: 'If you are innocent, never sue. If all the hobgoblins of Fleet Street chase you down the road to hell, never sue. If they libel you, defame you, pester your children, call your wife a whore, never sue. If they goad you beyond the bounds of decency and tolerance, still do not sue. If learned friends assure you of unlimited riches, do not sue. If bewigged judges swear they can imbue your name with the sweetest odours of the Orient, do not sue. Never sue for money, fame, status, reputation. Just never sue.

'But if you are brazen and a gambler sue. Sue the newspapers to the skies. You will almost certainly win. You may not clear your name, that is asking too much, but the odds are that you will make a lot of money. Remember that in law a newspaper is guilty unless it can prove itself innocent . . . I know of almost no big defamation case during my professional career in which that court yielded anything like a just verdict . . . Indeed so terrified are most parties of the waywardness of libel law that they settle out of court on terms that are usually a travesty of truth.'[231]

It could be said that Simon Jenkins, as a veteran of the press, is hardly likely to write comment pieces encouraging the libelled to take newspapers to court, but his points are well made.

The Conservative Party has shown itself extremely wary about new press controls. The government hoped that self-regulation by the Press Complaints Commission would be seen to work. Its Chairman, Lord Wakeham, also warned against further regulation, while the then Conservative Party Chairman, Jeremy Hanley, declared that 'no government can win' on legislation against the press. Who wanted such a massive issue to flare up in a pre-election year?

The White Paper was expected to recommend new measures to protect individuals from damaging comments, new measures against bugging and telephoto lenses for 'spying on people and a civil remedy for invasion of privacy'. One official was quoted as saying: 'The work has all been done.

Major knocked it back and didn't want to risk taking on the press.' Legislation against 'kiss and tell' or entrapment was ruled out because it would wipe out 'many books which are on the bookshelves and in public libraries'.[232]

Chris Moncreiff, Lobby Correspondent of the Press Association told the Nolan Inquiry: 'In recent years the Press, including television, has become far more aggressive in its approach to MPs, to seek out what they consider wrong-doing. Indeed in some cases as we know, the Press has resorted to acting as an agent provocateur, perhaps even as an imposter to find out what they consider to be the truth. They say that the end justifies the means. It is something that thirty years ago would never have happened – a move by a newspaper or any part of the media to try to entrap an MP into doing something which he should not do.'[233]

There is another side to the arguments over libel and privacy. While libel laws are there to protect people from unjustified character assassination, there is no doubt that they restrict public access to the truth. Many may say that is a small price to pay for protecting civil liberties, but it can be disturbing if it means the corrupt or incompetent are unfettered by criticism.

Writing in *The Independent* recently on the publication of a 'revealing' biography of Mark Thatcher, Peter Koenig wrote: 'Something happens. A large number of people know it happened. But no one can say it has happened, explore how it happened and what it means and stay on the right side of Britain's libel laws. So the pursuit of telling what happens deteriorates into a game that preoccupies politicians and reporters but bores the public. Years later, when it no longer makes a difference, the facts dribble out, by which time they serve as little more than cheap entertainment, and in so doing, confirm the public's deep seated cynicism about politics and the media.'[234]

As I have discovered myself, in practice libel lawyers are extremely nervous about any comments which may be considered in any way harmful to the reputation of wealthy and powerful people, and book publishers are even more so.

Newspapers tend to be seen as here today and thrown away tomorrow, so those who are upset by an article may decide to let matters rest. However, books hang around on bookshelves for a decade or more. Newspapers make an instant return on a sensational story with added circulation, whereas a book publisher could be faced with a court injunction before a single copy has been sold. The result is that newspapers publish material you will never find in books.

While there have been many media abuses of press freedom, there have been many excellent examples where revelations have been a service to the nation. The question remains as to whether the end always justifies the means, especially when it comes to invasion of privacy.

There is evidence that journalists have sometimes had more power than even the police in pursuing an investigation, yet they are far less accountable. An example is over entrapment, where police evidence obtained would never be heard by a jury, but the same method can be used by a journalist and information broadcast to the nation, even though it may destroy an individual's reputation.

I have studied carefully the Press Complaints Commission Code of Conduct. This was drawn up as a last ditch attempt to head off strict media regulations by trying for one last time to show that self-regulation can work. It followed the Committeee on Privacy and Related Matters chaired by David Calcutt QC, and the abolition of the Press Council.

It is full of reassuring phrases but they may be worse than useless in practice for a very important reason. Here are a few of them: intrusions and inquiries into an individual's private life are not generally acceptable; journalists should not obtain or publish material obtained by using clandestine listening devices or by intercepting private telephone conversations; journalists should not generally obtain or seek to obtain information or pictures through misrepresentation or subterfuge; documents or photographs should be removed only with the express consent of the owner; journalists should neither obtain nor seek to obtain information or pictures through intimidation or harassment.

However, every single one of these noble principles is all but destroyed by an exception clause allowing all the above to be forgotten if it is deemed to be 'in the public interest'. So if the public interest needs to be satisfied, then a journalist, or anyone else connected with the media, can go ahead to bug people's bedrooms, their cars or their offices, burgle their homes and places of work, steal or copy papers, letters, photographs and computers; they can intimidate people and harass them, deceive and bully, with full immunity from censure.

The central and urgent question therefore is defining where the public interest lies. But this too is defined in the Code of Conduct. 'Detecting or exposing crime or a serious misdemeanour', or 'protecting public safety' seem clear enough, but there is a third category which is vague and is a passport for media intrusiveness. The third definition of the 'public interest' is 'preventing the public from being misled by some statement or action of an individual or organisation'.

This final category could be interpreted very widely – and has been in the past. Presumably it could be used to justify bugging an entire government Cabinet's homes and offices if it were suspected that some Ministers were not always saying in public exactly the same as they were saying in private on any matter of 'public interest'.

Listening devices are cheap and widely available from shops in the centre of London. For a few hundred pounds you can acquire a highly miniaturised bugging system or a phone tap. It has never been so easy to probe into people's personal lives, and there has never been so much money available to snap up stories of 'scandal'. There is thus a lucrative market for any private investigator who wants to make a living out of invading the privacy of those in public life. If he or she is caught with nothing to show for the effort, then they will be 'on their own' without a friend in the world, but if they find something out, the press will beat a path to their door.

The current Code of Practice would seem to permit breaking into the homes of many of the people mentioned in this book, and stealing diaries, notebooks, telephone books, financial records and personal correspondence. But where does it stop? Presumably prominent back-benchers are fair game too, and those who run quangos – and so the list goes on.

If we define the 'public interest' as what interests the public, whatever sells newspapers will be a good guide. But what if the public interest is instead equated with the national interest? Harry Greenway suggested recently that the definition of the public interest should be the public good, but that leads us to a very different place.[235]

If it were shown that the country is in danger of being starved of quality leadership because many potential MPs are not prepared to see their spouses, their children or themselves aggressively pursued by the press, then we might conclude that the current hounding of those in public life is very much against the national interest and should cease.

Both France and Germany are around a hundred years ahead of us on these matters. While we argue over press controls, we forget that France has had a legal right of reply since 1881. If a newspaper writes something about you, even by implication, and you object, you can ask for a correction or insist that your own views are published. Replies of up to 200 words must be printed uncut, unless the words are libellous or likely to incite racial hatred. In Germany a similar right of reply has existed since 1874. Both countries have healthy democracies and few would be able to argue convincingly that the public interest has been greatly harmed in any way.

Newspaper editors may point to the many other restrictions on journalists: the Official Secrets Act, the Draconian 'D notice' banning unauthorised disclosure on receipt of official information, stricter libel laws than elsewhere, the Criminal Rehabilitation of Offenders Act of 1974, and Contempt of Court to name but a few. Nevertheless, it is hard to argue for external regulation of the conduct of MPs without some similar measures for the media as well.

As we have seen, many politicians I have spoken to despair of ever taming the media, particularly now that ownership is dominated by a few very powerful players. For them the answer lies in pressure from the public, from advertisers and from proprietors. Public reaction can have a sobering effect, as the *Sun* newspaper found after an offensive article attacking Liverpool supporters after the tragic Hillsborough disaster in Sheffield, at their match against Nottingham Forest.

The Press Council 'condemned' the article which appeared on 19 April 1989, just four days after the deaths, and up to 300,000 people in or near Liverpool refused to buy the paper. For a time it was hard even to buy a copy as many newsagents refused to order it. I have talked to people in Liverpool recently who tell me the paper has still not been forgiven fully.

In conclusion, then, we have seen that the culture of both Westminster and the media has changed, and that there are arguments for changes in the way both operate. We now need to look at measures that can be taken in the light of the many concerns raised by this book.

11

Rebuilding the House

'Politics are too serious a matter to be left to the politicians.'
Charles de Gaulle (1890–1970)

'We cannot legislate for integrity.' Betty Boothroyd, Speaker of
the House of Commons, 1995

'I am fed up with being called a sleazebag.' Anon MP

'It is the necessary nature of a political party in this country to
avoid as long as it can be avoided the consideration of any
question that involves a great change.' Anthony Trollope
(1815–1882)

'Where there is no vision the people perish.' Proverbs 29:18

Problems are easier to identify than solutions, but the more
serious a problem becomes, the more urgent is the search for
a way forward.

In May 1995, Lord Nolan's Committee published its first
report on standards in public life, with a wide range of
recommendations, including a ban on payments for lobbying
and new controls on quango appointments. It followed several

239

months of written submissions, as well as oral evidence before a large committee in a televised public hearing at Westminster Central Hall. Lord Nolan is a quiet, reserved and shy man who was deferential and kind to witnesses, to the point where some who watched him in action began to worry that the Inquiry would have no 'teeth'. However, others on the Committee were less accommodating, and early leaks left no doubt that the final report would be quite radical and incisive.

Despite first indications from the Prime Minister that the report would be fully implemented, it met vigorous opposition from MPs, led by Sir Edward Heath and others who were in no mood to make major changes. Lord Nolan watched expressionless from the Gallery while section after section of his carefully reasoned proposals for major change were shredded and lampooned.

For example, many MPs were bitterly opposed to any notion of some kind of independent body to rule on any aspect of parliamentary ethics. They insisted that self-regulation continued at all costs. They also attacked any suggestions that selling their services in well-established commercial arrangements was in any way unethical. The report was referred to a House of Commons Committee, which began a long watering down process, before a full debate in Parliament. The Committee rapidly split along party lines, as did the House of Commons.

However, as has been said, you cannot legislate for honour or integrity. Codes of practice or votes to ban certain behaviours may be useful in defining what is acceptable, but they have limited value. They may help resolve the war between press and politicians, by laying down clearly where the wandering line now lies between right and wrong in public life. Nevertheless, guidelines will be ignored if people think that they can get away with it, unless there is a deeper transformation of attitudes and culture.

It is hard to see how anything other than radical measures will restore public confidence. Only utter fools would dare ignore the devastating vote of no confidence in politicians revealed by opinion polls. People still believe passionately in democracy, but not as they currently experience it, while some politicians continue to live as though the media have made up the survey results. Others take the position that politicians have always been unpopular and it hardly matters. Indeed, the future of democracy at Westminster could be threatened by failure to take action.

I am convinced that nothing less than a radical overhaul of the parliamentary system will work, and that the process may take several Parliaments, perhaps even a generation. The need is urgent and the pressures for change continue with every fresh allegation. I am convinced therefore that a political revolution of sorts is inevitable, while the timing and process may be uncertain. Such a process may require a new political movement which transcends party divides in a quest for common values.

It could be argued that the revolution has already begun. Parliamentary history was made in a watershed vote on 6 November 1995 when 587 MPs voted to ban all commercial lobbying arrangements and related consultancies, with only two MPs voting against.

This was a decisive change, a body blow to accepted culture and a sure sign that Westminster had been rattled to its very foundations. The vote was followed minutes later by another, forcing MPs to disclose details of how much they earn from outside interests. This was carried by 322 to 271 votes, a firm majority, despite disastrous last minute waverings by John Major who said he was against that particular measure. The result was therefore embarrassing to him and the whole Conservative Party, despite being technically a free vote. He was portrayed in the press as opposing anti-sleaze reforms, comments which were both unfair and unfortunate.

The significance of these votes can hardly be over-emphasised, and lies in the fact that such results would have been totally unexpected just twelve months previously. All the rancour and discord, which had been aimed at the Nolan proposals when unveiled just a few weeks previously, had suddenly melted away. Many MPs no doubt had consulted with their constituency colleagues, to be told in no uncertain terms to 'clear up the stinking stables of Parliament or lose our support'. One MP summed up the feelings of many when he said: 'I am fed up with being called a sleazebag.'

But have one in three Conservative MPs been truly con-verted in their hearts, or only in their heads as a means of sur-vival? It is hard to believe that all those with parliamentary consultancies have radically changed their worldview in such a short time. That is perhaps one reason why John Major was caught out. The Whips warned him just days before that Conservative MPs would not support earnings disclosure, but opposition collapsed at the last minute.

The votes were dramatic and historic, but mere votes may not be enough to change the habits of a lifetime. One MP immediately declared that he might refuse to abide by the new rules, which had no basis in law. Another made it clear that he was not too worried about new measures when it came to accepting cash for arranging a meeting with a Minister. In the future it will simply be a question of MPs making sure they are not caught, with little grounds for excuse if they are. In any set of regulations there are loop-holes, and in the complex world of Westminster there are many ways to disguise activity.

I am convinced that substantial change at Westminster will require more than a vote or two. It will take a new generation of dynamic visionary leaders. The trouble is that many outstanding men and women of integrity are dismayed at what they see as wide-scale political corruption and moral decay in Westminster, and are not yet prepared to sacrifice their lives and the future of their families for it.

As I have talked with many MPs and Peers I have been struck by their sense of paralysis: the notion that nothing can change. The traditionalists are a powerful group and may be in the majority: they worship the glorious past with a selective memory for all that was good; they live for the old atmosphere; the fading memory of grand speeches; the power of Churchill and Gladstone. For them, the buildings, the archaic method of working and the elaborate procedures are all part of the magic and the mystery; they almost worship the semi-sacred cathedral of power.

They are a self-selecting group of Westminster enthusiasts, which is why they are there. On the whole they are a disappointing lot, with notable exceptions, lacking weight and calibre. As we have seen, the place is also seductive and intoxicating through the atmosphere of privilege, pressure of patronage, and through persuasion to conform by established members. Radicals can quickly lose their cutting edge.

However, while bored back-benchers sleep through irrelevant debates and while Ministers hurry from the Chamber on urgent business, a second political revolution is already in progress. Step by step the traditional power of Westminster is being transferred to a European Parliament and Regional Assemblies could be a reality within five to ten years.

The crisis over BSE in beef and the subsequent ban on British beef in the EC was a further example of loss of power from Westminster to the European Parliament. This relentless process is threatened by nationalism and tribalism within nations – although sub-national groups also find the EC rather attractive because it gives them a hope of direct representation in the future if a country disintegrates.

There are a few anarchists in Parliament who would happily sweep much of the system away, who despise any tradition based on a wealthy élite, and who see Westminster traditions as a means of perpetuating the worst kinds of patronage and discrimination. Yet they are widely regarded as eccentric, misguided, and disloyal members of the 'Club'. The danger is that 'Club' members are losing touch with reality; the world has moved on and left their culture behind.

My purpose now is to draw together various options which could be taken to help place Westminster on a healthy foundation for the next century, assuming of course that by then European Parliament has still left something for Westminster to do. Some of these will find wider public support, while others are more controversial. Most of them may find a hostile reception from politicians, but as a whole they could form the basis of a renewed democratic process. Some, as we have seen, are already becoming a reality.

Lord Nolan's Committee has suggested seven principles of public life which should govern every word, action and decision of those at Westminster, whether MPs or Peers. These principles express values which are important, which one might wish could be taken for granted, but which need to be spelled out in the light of the current crisis. They are the bedrock on which a healthy society is based. The wording from the Nolan Report is reproduced here in full in bold, with extensions of each, and one addition.[236] Many of these basic principles are expanded later in more detailed proposals. They should apply where appropriate to Peers as well as MPs.

Eight principles of public life

1. Selflessness

Holders of public office should take decisions solely in terms of the public interest. They should not do so in

**order to gain financial or other material benefits for
themselves, their families or their friends** nor to gain
advantage for their party. Public office should be seen as a
high calling to serve the nation as a whole. Elected representatives should always bear in mind their duty to take into
account the views of the whole electorate, not just those who
voted for them.

2. Integrity

**Holders of public office should not place themselves
under any financial or other obligation to outside individuals or organisations that might influence them in the
performance of their official duties** or might give the
impression of influencing them or of placing them under an
obligation. Neither Members of Parliament nor Peers
should work for lobbying companies, nor accept consultancies or any other remunerated roles which relate to their
parliamentary function. This wholesale prostitution of the
parliamentary process should cease. They should however be
free to pursue unrelated interests outside the House (see
below).

Candidates for election have a responsibility to inform
their electorate what policies they will support or not support
if elected, particularly where their views may not coincide
with their party manifesto.

Regarding Whips and whipping, it is unethical for holders
of public office to attempt to pervert the democratic process
by placing undue pressure on others to support measures
which they believe are wrong and have said before election
that they will not support.

It should be accepted that in a healthy democracy, debate
should influence the views of those in public office.
Therefore admitting an altered perspective may be a sign of
integrity rather than of weakness. The alternative is a

Parliament of unreasonable people who believe that every opinion they have is so correct that it will never change. Care should be taken to represent differing policies and views of others fairly and accurately.

3. Objectivity

In carrying out public business, including making public appointments, awarding contracts, or recommending individuals for rewards or benefits, holders of public office should make choices on merit, after a proper process of independent consultation not influenced by political affiliation, race, colour, creed or any other factor such as Freemasonry which might undermine public confidence. The power of patronage must not be abused.

Therefore all quango appointments should be advertised widely and subject to independent review. Publicly funded contracts should be awarded on an open basis. Civil service jobs and remuneration should be independent of any political pressures. 'Party political' honours should be greatly reduced so that the majority of politicians are nominated by an all-party group, for consideration alongside others who have provided outstanding service to the nation.

Membership of any political party, involvement in political activities and membership of the Freemasons or any other 'secret society' should be declared by candidates for public appointments. One might argue that candidates for Parliament should also declare links with secret societies.

4. Accountability

Holders of public office are accountable for their decisions and actions to the public and must submit themselves to whatever scrutiny is appropriate to their office, remembering at all times that they are public employees whose sole task is to serve the public. They should not be accountable merely to each other. Therefore, particularly where there are public concerns, external audit should replace self-regulation, and independent inquiry should replace internal investigations. The new Parliamentary Commissioner for Standards may well be able to fill some of these roles.

5. *Openness*

Holders of public office should be as open as possible about all the decisions and actions they take. They should give reasons for their decisions and restrict information only when the wider public interest clearly demands. Secrecy is so embedded in public life that this is unlikely to work without a Freedom of Information Act.

6. *Honesty*

Holders of public office have a duty to declare any private interests relating to their public duties and to take steps to resolve any conflicts arising, in a way that protects the public interest and maintains confidence in public office.

Peers as well as MPs should be required to register all interests from which remuneration or other benefit is gained directly or indirectly. The approximate value of the interest should be recorded in several categories – say £5,000 bands – as well as the approximate time commitment. A proposal for declaration of earnings related to a parliamentary role has already been implemented.

(It has been said that this will 'obliterate the professional classes' from Parliament, so that the only people who remain are millionaires using Westminster as a club and those who have never earned a living outside politics. This is clearly nonsense. Many company directors have salaries that are published, so why not MPs?)

Roles or responsibilities which are unremunerated but which are likely to create a sense of obligation should also be declared, as well as possible future interests where relevant. Parliamentarians should take all possible steps to ensure that their duties are not likely to be seen to confer undue material advantages to relatives or spouses, for example through commercial arrangements. The utmost care should be taken that all statements made are accurate and not misleading about personal matters, and contain enough information to quell speculation and rumour, with due regard for privacy.

7. Civility

The seventh principle is civility (not on Lord Nolan's list). **Holders of public office should make every effort to care for the reputations of others as they would like to be cared for themselves.** They should endeavour to seek common ground for the good of the nation, so that policies may be built on consensus rather than confrontation. They should take care to avoid insulting or derogatory language about people, and should avoid abusing parliamentary privilege to say things that would normally be libellous, except in very exceptional circumstances of overwhelming national interest.

8. Leadership

Holders of public office should promote and support these principles by leadership and example and should ensure that at all times in public or in private that they do not act in such a way that might risk bringing public office into disrepute. At present the House of Commons is ruled by partiocracy. The party is everything. However, the duty of each MP should be to uphold the honour of the House and to serve the nation. These should be a higher calling than party loyalty.

Disciplinary Committee

Standards need to be maintained by a Disciplinary Committee which is independent of Whips and party executives, and which commands public confidence, as a reference point for advice and action on ethical issues. Members (whether politicians or others) could be proposed and elected on a free vote in the House of Commons. In the current climate, confidence is unlikely to be restored by continued self-regulation, through the Privileges Committee for example. However a return to self-regulation may be possible once public confidence in Parliament as a whole has been rebuilt.

The Disciplinary Committee should include outsiders, perhaps in the majority, as well as MPs, and be chaired by a judge, while remaining a manageable size to enable rapid decision-making. The new eleven-strong Select Committee on Standards and Privileges is too large. Previous investigations by similar committees have taken too long and have split down party lines.

Many politicians have protested at the suggestion that anyone other than MPs can sit in judgement on MPs, and the same with Peers, because by constitution Parliament is the highest court of all. While that is true, Parliament has the power to choose to delegate whatever powers it likes – and has already done to a European court over many issues. In any case, there is always a built-in safeguard because delegated powers can always be withdrawn if seriously abused.

On balance, so long as the interval between accusation and verdict is short, it is probably better to have private hearings with full publication of oral and written evidence when the verdict is announced. The alternative is a full-scale public hearing which may not be helpful for many minor cases. If an MP is found guilty of misconduct by the Disciplinary Committee, then a range of options can be recommended by it for Parliament to act upon, of which one is an amnesty or pardon.

1. Amnesty and pardon

It is clear that there has been genuine confusion over a number of 'grey' areas relating to lobbying in particular, and also the declaring of interests. The public may be served best by defining a range of minor breaches of behaviour committed before a certain date, for which an amnesty could be granted. This will allow MPs, who still fear that various minor undeclared interests will be discovered, to bring them all out into the open, in order to set the record straight. A pardon could also be considered for various offences in exceptional circumstances for compassionate reasons.

2. Fines

A second response could be a fine. However, the last time an MP was fined by Parliament was in 1666.[237] Fines could be a very useful sanction. In 1967 the Committee on Parliamentary Privileges recommended that legislation be passed to give the Commons statutory powers to levy fines. This call was repeated in 1977 by the same committee but nothing has happened.[238]

My view is that such a step is long overdue and should be introduced at the earliest possible moment. A fining system would allow disciplinary action which falls short of other more drastic steps, and would enable the public to feel that justice is being done, particularly since many of the 'crimes' seem to have a root in financial greed.

3. Ministerial suspension or resignation

The Committee should have the freedom to recommend that a Minister resigns or is immediately suspended from office pending an inquiry in the case of more serious allegations under investigation. It is unwise and perhaps an unfair burden to leave such matters entirely to the discretion of a Prime Minister. In all these measures the aim is to restore the highest public confidence. In law there are some problems over a Minister handing over the Crown's mandate for his or her Department while still technically in office but 'suspended'. However, this is allowed for in the case of serious incapacity through illness, and a similar allowance needs to be recognised here.

4. Suspension or expulsion of an MP

There have been many examples in the past where MPs have been thrown out of the Debating Chamber and barred from the precincts of Westminster. In practice, the greater punishment is loss of face with other members of the Club, and media ridicule. However, longer-term suspension deprives electors of effective representation, and the means to do anything about it. One alternative for serious offences could be expulsion, which forces a by-election, so that the MP's own constituents can give their own verdict. It has happened in the past that such a disgraced MP has been immediately re-elected (Bradlaugh in 1882) and returned to take his seat.[239]

In the past, Members of Parliament have been expelled for being in 'open rebellion'; having been guilty of forgery; of perjury; of frauds and breaches of trust; conspiracy to defraud; corruption in the administration of justice, or in public offices, or in the execution of their duties as Members of the House; of conduct unbecoming the character of an officer and a gentleman; and of contempts, libels and other offences against the House itself. MPs have also been expelled for fleeing from justice, regardless of whether they have been convicted.[240]

5. Imprisonment for most serious offences

Although the Lords have always retained the right to send people to prison, whoever they may be, the right of the House of Commons to do the same for its own Members has fallen into disuse. In 1967, it was recognised that even if a prison sentence were to be imposed, it could probably not be extended beyond the end of that parliamentary session – which might vary from a few weeks to a few days. This power could be redefined and exercised, within that limited time constraint, for without a fuller range of the normal powers open to the judiciary, the only way to ensure proper punishments will be by trial in a conventional court, and this may not always be necessary or appropriate. An example of where imprisonment might be appropriate would be in the case of accepting a large bribe.

Some attention will also need to be given to a similar system of sanctions for Peers who transgress.

Proper remuneration and contracts for MPs

Then there is the question of remuneration for MPs, possible restrictions on outside earnings and proper auditing of expenses.

1. Increased pay for MPs (above June 1996 levels)

Bearing in mind job insecurity, almost complete disruption of normal family life, the difficulty many back-benchers find in returning to other employment, and the urgent need to recruit men and women of calibre who have a track record of success, MPs have not been adequately paid, until the historic July 1996 26 per cent increase, which many may agree pushed the argument the other way in favour of a pay cut.

Some people argue vigorously that the salary for MPs was already higher than the national average, and that it is vital that such important public service is carried out by people who are prepared to make a financial sacrifice. However such increases become more reasonable in return for some kind of trade-off for a ban on consultancies and paid lobbying, and for pro-rata salary reductions for time spent on other employment (see below).

On balance I am convinced that substantial pay increases were necessary to encourage the most outstanding leaders of the nation to enter political life. It was a curious situation indeed when a Parliamentary Commissioner was recruited in November 1995 on a salary of £72,000 a year for four days a week, to supervise such things as the Register of Members' Interests, for MPs paid less than half that figure.

However, a condition of higher pay should have been some kind of scaled reductions, taking outside earnings into account. So how could this work in practice?

2. Increments for age and experience

It is absurd to have a new flat rate for MPs which takes no account of age or experience, particularly now at the high level of £43,000 a year. It would have been far better to have had a basic 'package', perhaps at June 1996 levels, for new Members, which increased with every year at Westminster, up to a maximum 'seniority rating'. Allowances for backbenchers would remain unchanged.

I hesitate to mention exact figures because to do so may invite controversy, distracting from the proposals as a whole. However, it is necessary to do so in order to illustrate how pay scales might work, and to show that the overall 'salary' bill should not have been much larger when deductions were allowed for. What changes the most is the distribution of income between MPs.

Let us take for example a yearly increment for experience of £1,000 increasing to a maximum of £20,000 for someone with more than twenty years in the House. There could also be an extra adjustment for age which allowed a new entrant – say in his or her late fifties – to have more income than a new thirty-five-year-old, bearing in mind how useful 'life experience' is to the House.

Let us suppose that a starting salary of around £35,000 is increased for MPs over the age of thirty-five, by £2,000 per five years of extra age. The maximum could be set at a certain level – say £55,000 for any MP, however old or experienced. This is better than a flat rate of £43,000.

Ministers on appointment could gain an increase on top of whatever their MP's pay would normally be. The amounts could vary from £15,000 for a junior Minister, to £40,000 for a Prime Minister. The new increase to more than £140,000 is probably too high. Ministers leaving office should have a full year before the ministerial allowance ceases, to compensate for strict controls on what jobs they may accept in the two years afterwards, unless they have been forced by the Disciplinary Committee to resign.

Examples of incremental scales:

1. 35-year-old – newly elected	£35,000
2. 55-year-old – newly elected	£43,000
3. 48-year-old – elected at 40	£45,000
4. 68-year-old – elected at 38	£55,000

5. 60-year-old Minister – elected at 45   £80,000

6. 55-year-old Prime Minister – elected at 40   £92,000

These new figures above assume continuous service in Parliament. If the total increments gave an average of £10,000 extra per MP per year, then that figure multiplied by 651 gives a total of £6.5 million, less savings on outside interest deductions which could come to £5.9 million (see below), giving a net cost increase of only £0.6 million or 2.7 per cent on top of the pre-July 1996 total bill of around £22 million instead of 27 per cent approved by Parliament, or £6 million addition. These figures do not include national insurance, or pension contributions or increases for Ministers.

3. Formal conditions of service

There is no written contract at present between an MP and the State, and therefore no terms and conditions of service. The reason is that an MP is elected by constituents to represent their interests, and that has been the description of the entire working relationship. In practice the MP's role has been defined by precedent, as described in Erskine May's authoritative but complex guide to parliamentary practice.[241]

There should be a formal statement of terms and conditions of service which every MP has to sign before receiving any remuneration. Electors can send whomsoever they like to Parliament, but if money is going to change hands, then it should be on a properly determined and legally binding basis. Such terms and conditions should state the expectations for attendance, general behaviour, ethical code, outside interests and other matters including management of staff.

Disciplinary procedures should be explained and agreed to as a part of the signed contract. For instance the contract could state that the MP agrees to accept the recommendation

of the Disciplinary Committee as immediately binding.
Failure to do so would lead to freezing all remuneration payments.

4. Ban on paid lobbying and parliamentary consultancies

Outside interests are important to keep Westminster healthy.
It is essential that we do not encourage a Westminster ghetto
– with its own culture, mannerisms, sense of humour, language and attitudes – out of touch and out of control. It is
vitally important that longer-standing Members continue to
have experience of the 'real world'. This is less so for those
who have just entered the House after a full non-political
career, yet essential for MPs who have had no experience
other than working in local or national politics. Nevertheless,
outside interests do need regulating.

It is quite acceptable for MPs to continue part-time interests outside the House, but not if they gain financially from
employment as a direct result of being in Parliament, as is
currently the case with 30 per cent of MPs.[242] However, there
is nothing to stop them offering their time to whomever they
like, as an unpaid public service, nor to stop companies
employing former MPs as advisors.

5. Deduction of income for time on other jobs

Even if MPs earn from unrelated fields – say as a part-time
doctor or dentist – the time spent on these activities should
be declared. It is relevant to their electors because it affects
their availability. In the light of the recent huge increases in
remuneration, it seems very reasonable that a proportion of
their state income should be deducted, if the person is regularly unavailable for parliamentary business due to outside
commitments.

Thus, taking the examples above, an experienced MP
working an average of two days a week as a solicitor, with

twenty-five years in the House, would receive £30,000 instead of £50,000. This is fairer on MPs and fairer on the tax-payer. Electors should also be told in campaign literature how many hours a week each candidate proposes to spend on parliamentary or constituency business. Relevant outside interests should be declared in debate, and when asking written questions, as well as listed appropriately and promptly.

Assuming an average MP has a day a week of work outside the House, and the new salary structure above, then around £9,000 would be saved per MP each year or £5.9 million. This would offset some of the cost of allowances forage and experience.

6. Restrictions on ex-ministerial appointments

There should be an agreement that Ministers do not take up jobs for up to a two-year period in which they or their employers might benefit substantially from their recent time in government. (Lord Nolan has suggested this should only apply to Cabinet members, but this is illogical. The restriction applies already to senior civil servants and should apply to junior Ministers too.) An independent vetting committee should decide when this ruling should apply. The minimum time from ministerial office to appointment in any case should be three months.

7. Standard terms and conditions for staff

There should also be standard scales of pay for MPs' staff so that their rights are protected and so that it is easier to ensure where allowances are spent. Such staff should be on a proper Westminster payroll and enjoy similar pension rights and other benefits to those of the civil service. The value of the allowances for staff should not be increased above the level of inflation.

Reform of party funding

No reforms will be complete without addressing party funding. As we have seen, the current system of fund-raising invites accusations of corruption because sources are often not revealed, and where they are made public, it is possible that undue influence is being exercised. There is also a danger that if campaign expenditure helps win elections, and if a 'party of the rich' tends to have a greater budget than a 'party of the poor', then wealth will buy votes, power and a Prime Minister.

1. Partial state funding and spending limits

A first step would be to limit national election spending. Constituency expenditure is already fixed – at £3,370 per candidate, not including candidate expenses. A further step would be to provide a state contribution towards new national limits, perhaps half, which could be topped up by voluntary donations. The level of support could be calculated by the share of the votes at the last one or two elections. Local costs would continue to be raised locally.

Another option would be to match voluntary contributions pound for pound with state funds up to the permitted total. The budget should be set quite low. One of the reasons that such a vast amount is spent on political advertising is in order to outdo the influence of the other parties. The only ones who gain are advertising agencies and sellers of space.

In a media-dominated age there is already huge coverage of the issues at election time. A better use of resources would be to use state funds to print summaries of each manifesto and send them to every household with candidate details, all on the same document, and let people decide for themselves, rather than batter the public with emotive one-line slogans on hoardings. The candidate details should indicate the issues on the party manifesto which the prospective MP will not be supporting if elected.

2. Stricter controls on donors

Then there is the controversy over the secret source of many donations. While personal donors have a right to privacy, the public also has a right to be certain that an entire party is not being hijacked by the generosity of a few large donors, or even by a foreign government. Therefore it seems reasonable to suggest that all donations above a certain size should be publicly declared – say over £50,000 – and that the maximum donation allowed from any source should be £1 million annually. There should also be a complete ban on political funding from organisations abroad, or from individuals, unless they are entitled to vote in a British election. It is true, however, that this would be increasingly hard to police in our global village with so many transnational money flows.

The costs of state funding would be around £10 million every five years divided across the parties roughly in proportion to the share of the national vote at the last election. That sum works out at less than 4 pence per person per year – hardly a massive strain on the national purse.

Reforms of the House of Commons

1. Reform of whipping

We have seen how the abuse of whipping has been another factor bringing Parliament into disrepute. We saw in an earlier chapter that the only purpose of whipping, apart from telling MPs which way the party leadership intends to vote, is to bully MPs into voting for things they do not believe in and which they think are wrong or against the interests of their constituents or of the nation. The process of whipping needs some reform but this is unlikely without reform of patronage, which is linked with it.

In an ideal world each debate would be won or lost on the merits of its arguments, and a good speech would be expected to alter MPs' voting. At present, debates are won or lost on the party majority, and sometimes when majorities are small, on the basis of loyalty through whipping. It is almost unknown, therefore, for a vote to be swayed by debating, and so it could be argued that the proper function of the Chamber has been largely lost. Many speeches are made for little purpose other than to impress party hacks, for the television lens, or for local supporters back home.

There should be a complete and immediate ban on so-called 'death bed' votes as described in Chapter 7. Proxy voting should be allowed by the Speaker on medical grounds, allowing seriously ill or dying MPs the dignity of remaining in hospital or at home with proper care without the stress of being blamed for a major defeat in a decisive vote.

2. 'Integrity voting'

There is a radical alternative which I have called 'integrity voting', where all sides agree that their Members will be informed of a party line but that on most debates there will be a free vote. MPs will be allowed to decide each motion on the basis of the arguments. No longer will we have the absurd situation of a Bill being passed because those who hated it in the majority party voted for it, while a smaller number of those who agreed with it in the opposition voted against it.

'Integrity voting' means that candidate selection is far more important, and constituency parties would need to take greater care in finding out a whole range of opinions before agreeing to adopt a person. As I have said above, election details should indicate the main points where a candidate is expected to differ from a party line if elected. This will deal decisively with the great argument for whipping, which is that pressure is needed to make MPs vote for the policies on which they were elected.

However, many votes are taken on matters not directly referred to in a manifesto, or on issues which have emerged since the manifesto was written, or in circumstances which have changed, so there must always be room for some flexibility. It can also be argued that few voters have seen, let alone read, a manifesto from any party and can hardly expect their MPs to be held to all the small print. The complete Conservative manifesto for the 1992 election takes some reading: it is around a third of the length of this book.

3. Government by consensus rather than decree

Many MPs say that government like this would be impossible. It would certainly be harder work. The result would be less legislation, but more co-operation and more communication. Perhaps better legislation would be the result, with the support of the majority of all parties. The Poll Tax would have been thrown out at the first hurdle. Strong measures would be those known to command support of the majority of all parties.

'Integrity voting' would lead therefore to government by consensus rather than by decree, and there is a great deal of hidden consensus at the moment. That is why so many are finding it harder than ever to tell the difference between the policies of the major parties on many issues. Why should this be such an embarrassment to party leaders? Surely it gives us some hope for the future, for more consistent government and more considered opposition.

'Integrity voting' would encourage MPs from different parties to see each other as potential allies on a number of issues instead of adversaries on almost everything. It would encourage proper debate where speeches are made in the expectation of winning or losing votes. It would command public approval.

Opponents may argue that such a suggestion is 'hopelessly naive' and could never happen. However they have no better suggestion than continuing to whip MPs into voting for what they may believe strongly is wrong for the country. There has to be a better way.

'Integrity voting' also takes into account that in a constituency of 60,000 voters, only 25,000 may actually have voted for the successful candidate or for that party. Yet all 60,000 people are totally dependent on that MP for representation. If an MP takes his role seriously, then the first obligation will be to his or her total electorate, and that will probably mean supporting policies 'of the centre' rather than the extremes of left or right. After all, those are probably what the electors would vote for if they had been given a proper choice, other than a two-party system with 'first past the post'.

The number of MPs on the 'payroll' with no voting freedom should also be reduced. The strict payroll vote should include only those in paid positions – ie Ministers, not Parliamentary Private Secretaries.

4. National referenda on constitutional issues

One way to avoid aggressive whipping battles would be to carry out a national referendum more often than in the past, to settle an issue of national importance. For example, over further integration with Europe, or the formation of national assemblies in Scotland, Wales and England. This would also prevent elections being hijacked by single issues. Such national votes are expensive however, and not to be undertaken lightly. Perhaps in the future cable technology may allow simultaneous low-cost electronic voting by people at home on a massive scale.

5. Discipline in debate

There is widespread unhappiness not only with whipping, but also with the way business generally is conducted in the House of Commons, ranging from objections to 'animal noises' and 'yah-boo' politics, to gratuitous insults, blocking devices used to thwart the wishes of the majority of MPs, or lack of discipline over the use of debating time so that some debates go on into the night. The overall impression is not good.

One may argue that attempting to tackle such issues in the context of sleaze or integrity is taking things too far. However, the way Parliament works does convey an important message to the nation about values in democracy, together with how MPs are seen to behave and the way they organise their business. Unless the pattern of life changes, those who find it unattractive, distasteful and demeaning will continue to boycott the place. Yet those are the very people the country needs to restore integrity to public life.

6. Reform of Prime Minister's Question Time

An example of this is Prime Minister's Question Time on Tuesdays and Thursdays, which is undoubtedly a major tourist attraction judging by the people in queues, but serves little useful purpose. The Prime Minister is fired a range of questions with no notice and is forced to waste considerable time each week rehearsing bland answers across a vast field of interest.

Of necessity the result is superficial point-scoring which makes good theatre but is bad for democracy. A primary aim in Question Time is to trip up the Prime Minister with some slip of the tongue or half-guarded comment. This is the politics of the classroom or playground rather than the vital business of the nation.

Parliament and the country would be far better served by a more structured time when particular questions are put down in advance, after which related points can be taken from the floor. The time for this could be extended from fifteen minutes to half an hour. Question Time could then become a show-case for concise debate on current issues.

7. Orderly conduct

We say that Britain is a country that prides itself in free speech, yet many interruptions in a crowded and excited Chamber are discourteous, offensive or obstructive, and have little place in a civilised democracy. The public rightly condemns loutish behaviour in all its forms, especially within its own Parliament, and MPs need to take note. It is feeble to argue that things were (even) worse in the past. All that tells us is the need for continued reform, and that life in Westminster years ago was beset with terrible weakness. Our past must not be allowed to distort our view of the present, nor to dominate our future.

Most people are appalled by what is happening now and want something quite different. They want to see MPs making proper points instead of political banter, and they want Members to listen to each other. The Speaker has plenty of authority to impose firm order, as outlined in Erskine May, and the power to discipline if necessary by suspension or expulsion, so the fault lies in part in a lack of application by the Speaker.

Some MPs tell me that noise is essential, for without it Speakers will be unable to tell the mood of the House. If that is the case, then they are incompetent and should be silent in the House, since they clearly lack even a basic understanding of how to communicate. I know myself from speaking to tens of thousands of people in large, medium and small groups over the years that it is relatively easy to 'read' any audience, without getting them to yell or grunt or make fatuous comments.

The only exception I would make is in a culture far removed from one's own (eg tribal rural culture in Africa), being interpreted into another language to several thousand people. In such a situation I have been profoundly grateful for local people explaining to me why, for example, they have burst out laughing at what I thought would be a serious moment.

That situation hardly applies to a small to medium size British audience of between thirty and six hundred people in an intimate venue. In such a place body language and facial expression say it all. There is no need whatever for sullen silence, but merely for greater courtesy and common decency.

Some MPs are incapable of coherent speech in the Chamber. Others drone on, reading monotonous speeches without more than a brief glance around the Chamber. They need help but will they be willing to learn? Selection Committees should pay far more attention to oratory skills and personal character than to a track record in mere activism and door knocking.

Unfortunately the impression given by television is that the Chamber is either full of noisy male 'yobs' (the women seem relatively polite and far less boorish), or empty apart from a few who are asleep, picking their fingernails or dealing with correspondence. It is hardly any better if you stand in the strangers' gallery as I have often done.

Ministers can also be bad examples: for reasons of protocol they deliver fixed bland statements with almost zero content. You learn more from a five-minute interview on radio or television than from an hour listening to the same

Minister in the Chamber. In an interview a Minister is forced to abandon fixed text and actually deal with issues. Of course many are skilled at trying to evade this method of getting at the truth.

8. Quorum for debates

One afternoon I went into both the House of Commons and the House of Lords. In the Commons I counted fewer than twenty people including the Speaker – out of 651. There was one representative of the government, who slouched back with his eyes closed as his opposition colleague addressed him. Several others were talking in pairs. Two or three were scribbling away on letters and one was reading a newspaper – both of which activities are technically in breach of the rules. One was talking to the Speaker. I counted only two people who were intently listening to the speech – which I have to say was rambling, bordering on the incoherent, without passion, purpose or conviction. The state of the Lords was similar or worse.

This is no way to supervise the executive of our country. If an MP wants to say something to a Minister, he or she should go and say it, but there is no need to abuse the Chamber in the process. If an MP wishes a statement to go 'on the record', then let a copy be sent to the relevant Department, and hand a copy to *Hansard* recorders. If an MP wishes to be on television, then he or she may be disappointed unless something more interesting is found to say.

This line of thought is traumatic to many back-benchers who seem to live in a world of partial denial. If they face the painful reality, then they are forced to admit to themselves that most of the time when they do actually manage to attract the eye of the Speaker to say something in debate, it is almost a complete waste of time.

One practical way to help revive the Chamber would be to insist on a quorum at all times for debates to continue, but this rule was abolished by Standing Order No 40 in 1971, presumably because MPs were abusing the rule by forcing the Speaker to count and recount the number of Members in debate.

It should be perfectly possible to make a quorum work with strong leadership from the Speaker. Simple electronic counting at the doors would help, with a number displayed on the numerous television screens both inside and outside the Chamber. A quorum would impose a discipline on the length of debates and the number of contributions, and would therefore improve the quality of debates.

When you have sat through an interminable number of dreadful contributions, you can begin to understand why MPs enjoy letting off steam in a noisy manner when they do get together. But the answer is not more animal noises, nor more time for debate, but a new debating culture altogether.

As we have seen, most debates are largely a formality with a fixed outcome. Life is far too short to spend on such nonsense. The timing of debates could be severely cut to three or four set pieces on either side, plus the same number of other contributions, unless there are a sizeable number who wish to continue. The serious work on refining the exact wording of proposed legislation can continue at committee stage or in the House of Lords.

9. *More time for back-bencher motions*

The time saved in this way could be given over to allow back-benchers who think they have a majority in the House to put through particular measures. This is easy to test through collecting more than a set number of signatures on early Day Motions – the parliamentary form of a petition. It is a disgraceful thing indeed when a hardy group of ten or twelve MPs 'talk out' a debate by reading long bogus speeches with the express intent of forcing the Speaker to declare that there is now no time for a vote.

This is a monstrous abuse of the democratic will, especially if there are – say – 300 who would vote in favour against 100. It is hard to imagine a worse use of parliamentary time and energy, and once again confirms an image in the public mind of injustice, abuse and moral decay. There are already sanctions which can be applied by the Speaker to prevent this but they are poorly used. For example, an MP can be stopped for repetition or irrelevance. Again, there is a 'ten-minute rule' on the length of contributions which can be applied at present under certain circumstances. Its use should be extended.

Giving a real chance to back-benchers of carrying through their own legislation would energise the majority who at present feel that their role is marginal. It would also keep government on its toes – more alert to back-bench concerns, to opposition MPs and to public opinion.

10. Reform of debating hours and archaic practices

Further reform of interminable debating hours and voting times would also make it easier for women with young children to become MPs. At present it is almost impossible for a nursing mother to survive life in Westminster. I am convinced that if half of MPs were women, then the whole culture of Parliament would change for the better. If this had been the case ten years ago then I find it hard to imagine that Westminster would be in the same mess today: fewer sex scandals, less financial impropriety and less excessive whipping for a start.

There is another factor in debates which destroys communication and makes every exchange clumsy. As we enter the third millennium it is absurd that MPs cannot talk to each other in debate, but have to address every comment via the Speaker. The result is stilted dialogue, which is unhelpful at a time when the Chamber needs a new breath of life.

Members still describe each other as 'the Honourable Member for . . .'. This archaic form of address has one advantage but many disadvantages. The advantage is that it is a constant reminder to the individual MP that his or her total identity in the House is as a representative of constituents – as if that were needed. One would have thought MPs were more intelligent than that.

However, the disadvantages are not only clumsiness in debate, but also, as far as the public is concerned, a level of confusion about who is saying what. It makes for lifeless exchanges. It would be far better for MPs to say what they mean in direct language. Some MPs are so confused themselves about where MPs are from that they are unable to address them at all other than as 'the Honourable Member'.

11. Voluntary ban on 'propaganda sound-bites'

There are various stock phrases or insults which come out time and time again, which communicate nothing except the lack of creative ability and intelligence of the speaker. They should cease by mutual agreement. For example, '. . . when we win the next election . . .' is a very odd statement indeed, whatever the polls may say. Yet it is a stock phrase that has been repeated hundreds of times by senior MPs of both main parties over the last few years.

In no other walk of life would a professional of any standing use such proud, strange and illogical language. If they did, they would be regarded quite rightly with utter contempt. They might say: 'If I get the job,' or 'If I am offered a place on the board.' This style of posturing is popular with politicians and is carried from the Chamber into many media interviews.

However such repetitive banter is tedious and irritating to listen to. Those who stoop that low come across as arrogant, foolish, deluded or just lacking in integrity.

Many such offending phrases are propaganda sound-bites, designed no doubt to appeal to a television editor who they think is looking for a twenty-five-second quote for the next news bulletin. But they have the opposite effect and insult our intelligence. The first lesson to learn when dealing with the media is the need to interest or entertain, and an over-rehearsed one-line comment may do neither. The sad thing is that tens of thousands of pounds are wasted every year by the main parties on paying people to dream up these catchy but superficial phrases.

An example might be a reply in Question Time when a Conservative might say: 'Labour is the party of great promises and high taxation which always promises and can never deliver,' as a reply to a serious question on the National Health Service. The trouble is, that similar abuse has been heard a hundred times – and may not be true anyway. After all, a revolution has taken place in the Labour Party. Another Conservative jibe has been: 'Labour don't know what they stand for except Tory policies,' or 'They are the party with no policies, no ideas, and no answers.'

This is cheap debating that is itself empty of new ideas and very unattractive. We are far more interested to know what good ideas the speaker has that will help us through situations which we all recognise are very complex. Labour is just as bad. Some praise of the other side would make a welcome change from time to time. Anything else other than broad agreement on many issues looks rather forced since we all know that consensus is alive and well in British politics – so long as you are not in the Debating Chamber or in a media interview 'on the record'.

12. New emphasis on honest consensus

There is no government in recent history that has reversed more than a very small proportion of the legislation passed by the previous administration, even though every measure may have been bitterly opposed at the time. Sometimes the reason is that undoing the damage would only create further chaos, but more usually the reason is lack of integrity in the opposition throughout, rather than sudden conversions. These are very serious issues that we see in almost every debate in Parliament day by day. One can hardly blame the public for concluding beyond all doubt that most politicians are insincere.

How refreshing it would be to hear Tony Blair regularly congratulating John Major on a major speech, or pointing out that New Labour would probably be doing largely the same thing, without being drowned out by mocking Conservative laughter. What a revolution it would be for John Major to agree that Labour have some excellent ideas which he has been discussing with colleagues because they find support with many in the Conservative Party.

Adversarial politics is dead. It has had its day, but the corpse still needs to be buried. It stinks of rotting political flesh. Adversarial politics is dishonest, disreputable, disagreeable and destructive. There is this deep-rooted and warped idea that the only way to get power or to keep it is to rubbish the other side. This is obviously false and morally wrong. It cannot go on. The nation has seen through the years of half-lies and distortions. We are sick and tired of it. If today's politicians do not bury this corpse, then we shall do so through the ballot box, by selecting candidates who will.

Another classic example of lack of integrity is over the abuse of statistics. When two politicians tear into each other on television, one saying that an important trend is rising and the other claiming the opposite, what are we to think? Are they both mad? Are they both liars? Is only one telling one hundred per cent truth? Or have they both plucked out of thousands of figures those that best support their case?

We need an independent source of official statistics on the economy and other areas of national life, which is used by all parties as a common basis for discussion and manifestos – whether on crime, unemployment, economic growth or health or education. Without this we will continue to have a situation where nine out of ten people disbelieve what party leaders are saying. We cannot go on like this and there is an alternative. Radical reform is not only possible but essential.

Every now and then we see a glimpse of reality: when the national interests are threatened or there is risk of war. But why does it take war to make peace in Parliament? Why does it take war to make MPs behave like mature adults instead of hot-headed hooligans? In good Churchillian fashion, compromise, solidarity, mutual respect, positive affirmation and public unity become the order of the day. We saw this in the Falklands and Gulf Wars, and more recently in Bosnia. We have also seen living, warm, powerful consensus over Northern Ireland. Of course there are dissenting voices, because there are genuine, deeply felt disagreements, but the empty rhetoric and point-scoring have largely gone.

We could see a recovery of consensus across the whole of politics almost overnight. It would only take two or three statesmen with the strength of character to do it. National leaders, men and women of calibre and character, are what we need, able to command total respect because of who they are; high achievers from all walks of life with charisma, passion, integrity and utter conviction. Looking across the entire House of Commons today it is hard to see even one person with that kind of leadership.

But where are those kind of people? Where are the nation's leaders? Do they exist or are they a romantic dream? The answer is that I stumble across them in every area of national life, but rarely in politics, although a few do land up in the Lords where they are politely listened to by all the wrong people. Lords do listen to Lords, but the weight of the Lords has something to say to the juvenile House of Commons. It is ridiculous that a Peer cannot address MPs by invitation in debate. Change the constitution, and make it serve us better.

If these leaders of industry, the professions, the church and other walks of life were to enter the House of Commons in significant numbers, the result would indeed be a political revolution. How many would it take to shame the party hacks into order? Between fifty and a hundred MP independent minded leaders would be more than enough to alter radically the whole of national political life. These are not party political issues, but issues of life and death for our democracy as a whole.

Perhaps MPs would be encouraged in a new spirit of consensus and co-operation to sit where they like, without abuse or ridicule, on one side of the House or the other. The rows of benches are an historical and unhelpful accident, maintaining a divisive, sectarian tradition where Parliament first sat in the long, narrow St Stephen's Chapel, part of the old Palace of Westminster, from 1547 until the great fire in 1834. Visitors walk through the Chapel as a mere corridor today.

Open government

So much has been made by the Conservative administration about open government. Indeed, it was an important element of the 1992 manifesto. The truth is that it is now far easier than it was to obtain some kinds of information, notably about the Secret Services. However, our system of government is still built around the principles of blind deference to authority and secrecy; and it is condescending: 'Just trust us because we are wise and powerful and we know best.'

Secrecy serves the status quo very well, and makes effective opposition almost impossible, whichever party is in power. Secrecy may be more tolerable in a 'high trust' environment, but where there is natural suspicion at every level, then secrecy is seen as conspiratorial. It also adds fuel to the righteous fire of investigative journalists who feel constantly cheated of vital information.

Secrecy is clearly necessary from time to time, for example where national security is at risk, or when an interest rate is about to change. Secrecy does also have a useful role in protecting civil servants from exposure when they have done nothing wrong except produce first-class advice on how to implement a third-class ministerial idea.

Freedom of Information Act

Without any protection, civil servants will be unable to maintain so easily a tradition of strict neutrality because it could be assumed that every paper leaving a civil servant's desk contains ideas that he or she agrees with. Nevertheless, the arguments are growing rapidly for a Freedom of Information Act, which would allow every citizen to obtain a vast range of government data.

Critics of openness would say that it will simply lead to civil servants being unwilling to commit important ideas or comments to paper, in case their confidential advice lands up on the front page of a newspaper. I am no great enthusiast of comprehensive Freedom of Information legislation, just as in theory I prefer self-regulation to external controls, but in the current climate I think it is essential to respond with openness rather than continue as in the past. At the moment we need a transparent system of government, as far as is humanly possible. Without it, the current malaise will only get worse. The use of technology should reduce the costs of openness. For example, the *Hansard* records of parliamentary debates should be published on Internet. This will strengthen democracy at a time when newspapers have all but ceased to report Parliament in any detail.

A challenge to the two-party system

We have discussed principles to guide those in public life, external regulation of MPs with sanctions, new restrictions on commercialism of Parliament in return for restructured pay, state funding for political parties and disclosure of major donors, a less tyrannical whipping system, reforms within the Debating Chamber and legislation for openness.

While all these things may help to counteract some of the concerns raised through this book, so long as we are left with a two-party system, it will be harder to establish the consensus and co-operation in which integrity is most likely to flourish in the longer term. It will also be harder to persuade the 'middle ground' leaders in the nation to enter politics, because they will be forced from the outset to polarise into one of two main political camps, or face almost certain political oblivion.

However, there are many people who cannot with integrity force themselves into either mould. One example might be someone with strong socialist compassion, but some other values that might be too 'moralistic' to fit comfortably in the Labour Party. Another might be someone who is strongly anti-European, yet strongly socialist, or someone who has a very liberal view of personal morality, yet is in favour of far less state control.

Why should there only be two models of government, only two ways of seeing the whole nation, only two ways of expressing political vision? The two-party system has provided stable government but at the cost of failing to enfranchise the moderate majority, in favour of party political hacks or extremists. Our adversarial process then magnifies the differences, while the media explode them out of all proportion, because only three things fill news items: 'hard' news events, speculation and conflict; and when the nation is not at war there is not enough of the first.

Electoral reform

One rather controversial option therefore would be to look once again at some reform of the voting system. At present most of the electorate get someone to represent them whom they did not choose, campaigning for policies that the voter may not agree with. For example, in 1974, Labour won a majority with only 39.2 per cent of the vote, and in 1983 the Conservatives won 61 per cent of the seats, a landslide victory, but with only 42 per cent of the votes. In the same election the Liberal and Social Democratic Alliance won 25 per cent of the votes yet only 3 per cent of the seats. In 1987, Labour won 70 per cent of the Scottish seats for 42 per cent of the votes.

These are hardly pictures of democracy at its best. Out of 651 seats, only 170 have majorities of 10 per cent or less from the 1992 election. This means that in 481 seats or 74 per cent of cases, unless there is a swing of more than 10 per cent from one election to the next, there is going to be no alternative to the previous MP.

Many seats offer no choice at all because the area they cover is so heavily weighted towards one party. An example is Riverside in Liverpool, where more than 20,000 out of 27,000 votes were for Labour, or City of London and Westminster South where the Conservative vote was 21,000 out of 35,000. In most constituencies you will find large numbers of voters who would like to vote for moderation, say for the Liberal Democrats, yet know that such a vote will never have the faintest chance of winning.

Proportional representation (PR) would change all that of

course, yet there is very strong opposition to it within the House of Commons, perhaps because so many MPs would have a less certain future. Support for electoral reform is also declining in the nation as a whole. We are told that it is 'not British', yet for many years PR has worked well in Northern Ireland for local government and for the European Parliament, and was used for appointment of university seats until the 1950s. In 1992 Labour adopted the Plant Committee proposals for PR by an additional member system for the proposed Scottish Parliament, but PR has always been opposed by the Conservatives.

It is said that PR means constant coalitions and weak government. People point to Italy which has become so unstable that PR has been abandoned, but West Germany has been governed very successfully with a different form of PR. They have a combined system which allows half the MPs to be elected for single-member constituencies, with a top-up additional member method to correct any imbalance in Parliament.

There is no doubt that the right form of PR could be a revolutionary change which would encourage political, cultural and ethnic diversity, increase the number of parties with MPs, and increase cross-party co-operation. It would end the sterility of the current two-party system and allow people a far wider choice. It would encourage a new generation of men and women to enter public life, who at present feel totally disillusioned with both the main parties and who see the Liberal Democrats as a waste of time because they will never be in power under the current system.

Reforms of the Lords

While there may not be great enthusiasm for such a radical measure as PR, there is far wider agreement that the House of Lords needs an overhaul. Whatever approach is taken is likely to be complex and lengthy to implement. The Upper Chamber has an important role in improving legislation, and in maintaining the general health of Westminster. These roles should continue. There is no need to increase the powers of the Lords. However, at present the Lords is too closely associated with patronage and inherited wealth, despite the fact that many hereditary Peers live on surprisingly low incomes.

1. Abolition of voting Hereditary Peers

The simplest reform would be to abolish the voting rights of all Hereditary Peers and to remove their day subsistence allowances. This would reduce the number of Peers by 758 from 1,204 to just 443. At the same time it would be worth reviewing the status of the 'Lords Spiritual', or those twenty-six members of the Anglican Church who are Lords by virtue only of their appointment as bishops or archbishops. It could be a convenient time to formally disestablish the Anglican Church.

2. Abolition of religious discrimination

The current situation in the Lords is untenable in today's multi-faith society, and is also discriminatory against the majority of Christians in other denominations. It is hard to justify special voting rights for leaders of just one branch of the Protestant faith with a mere 1.5 million members, and not for other Protestants, nor for Catholics, who between them have almost 5 million members.[244] And what about Muslims or other faith groups?

At the same time, restrictions should be abolished which prevent clergy of any denomination becoming elected Members of Parliament, or prevent them being appointed as Peers in the same way as anyone else, on the basis of merit. The 1801 Act says that no person 'ordained to the office of priest or deacon' or who is a minister of the Church of Scotland can be an MP. Roman Catholic priests are also banned by the Roman Catholic Relief Act of 1829.

This is illogical, sectarian, and against every tradition of electoral freedom. People should be able to elect whomever they want, and Christian leaders motivated by faith may be of great help in the House of Commons at such a time as this, particularly if they have general experience in the workplace as well. It is sad that religious intolerance and bigotry in Northern Ireland may have overshadowed the very real contribution that the Christian community could make to the renewal of politics in Britain today.

3. New peerage allocation methods

If the total number in the Lords was partially reduced, say, to 800, then there would be room to create 357 new Peers, some of whom might well be those who had lost their hereditary or religious seats, but whose skills and experience would be greatly missed in the House. The remainder could be selected using the usual methods, although in the light of our review of the patronage system in an earlier chapter it might be appropriate at the same time to reform the peerage allocation methods.

There is already an all-party committee to scrutinise new peerages. There should be a far greater emphasis on merit and usefulness with smaller party and Prime Ministerial lists. Cross-benchers should have a key role in influencing future peerage allocation, since they are independent of party pressures.

Clearly the major political parties would be very anxious to maintain the balance of their representation, although there would seem to be many advantages in making sure that a good number (perhaps a quarter) were non-affiliated cross-benchers, since 170 of the Hereditary Peers are of this category, and have brought a breadth to debate. Labour would be an obvious gainer since at present (1994 figures) 479 Peers say they are Conservative, compared to only 114 supporting Labour. However, 332 of those Conservatives are Hereditary Peers.

4. Overhaul of Peers' allowances

The daily allowances are not large, and insufficient to support 'working Peers' spending at least half the year in the House of Lords, and they are poorly supported with administration. There may be an argument for creating a third level of Peer remuneration, between a government post and an ordinary Peer, for some asked to serve the Upper House by attending a large number of committees and such like.

5. Retirement for elderly or absent Peers

There should be a maximum age beyond which a Peer has to retire to give way to a new peerage of young people – perhaps at seventy-five. The title could continue for life, but after the retirement date, the Peer might be treated as a Hereditary Peer, losing allowances and voting rights but still able to attend and participate in debates.

Peers who do not attend Parliament for several consecutive sessions, or are present on fewer than a minimum number of days in a calendar year without special leave of absence, could be considered by their non-attendance to be retired as from the next session. In this way a more active second Chamber would be maintained.

6. Movement between both Houses

There are many people who may be unable or unwilling to become MPs for family or other reasons, yet could make a valuable contribution to the Lords, either as a cross-bencher or as a party member. Some could be encouraged perhaps, as their situations change, to consider becoming an MP, in which case their peerage could be suspended during their time in the Commons.

Such a flow between the Chambers could help renew the vitality of both Houses, and may be increasingly necessary if the number of Life Peers increases following the abolition of Hereditary voting Peers. A small risk of such traffic between the two places could be that some Lords become tamed by the lure of a seat in the other House, and end up as docile and dependent on the party line as many back-bencher MPs. However this would be a risk worth taking.

7. Recruitment, induction and training

'Politics is perhaps the only profession for which no preparation is thought necessary.' Robert Louis Stevenson (1850–1894)

The proposals above relate to those already shaping public life, but they beg a central question which has recurred throughout this book. What can be done to ensure that a new generation of high calibre men and women with vision and integrity are encouraged to enter politics? While it is true that the reforms as outlined above will make Westminster a far more attractive place to be, there are other steps which need to be taken.

Schools education programme   A national programme of educational visits should be targeted at sixteen- to eighteen-year-olds in schools. The aim should be that wherever possible each school receives a visit from their MP every two years for a talk on how Westminster works, with the chance of a conducted tour of Parliament for those interested. Many MPs already see schools visits as a priority, but these would be more focused, as part of a well-publicised national initiative to help win the interest and respect of a new generation.

Recruitment of national leaders Modest state funding should be given to an all-party group designed to identify and befriend those with outstanding leadership gifts in all walks of life, with the aim of encouraging them to stand as MPs or to be accepted as nominations for the Upper House.

Altered selection criteria Candidates for constituencies should be scrutinised far more closely for their leadership qualities, including their ability to communicate and motivate, their ethics and their lifestyles to help determine if they are worthy of the public trust which will be placed in them. A key test should be whether this candidate is likely to act in a way which could bring public office into disrepute. There should be less emphasis on a long track record of political activism, which by definition will exclude candidates with a fresh interest in politics as a result of recent reform – the very candidates who are needed to bring a transformation to Westminster.

Training for all candidates There should be a standard training course for all prospective candidates, run on an all-party basis, with an emphasis on the eight foundational values listed earlier in this chapter, as well as on working together with those who belong to other parties.

Induction for new MPs and Lords New Members of both Houses should receive an induction programme with an emphasis on expectations and codes of conduct as well as on the need to avoid acting in such a way as might be likely to damage the reputation of public office. There should also be training courses on effective public speaking which Whips might require certain members to attend.

Towards responsible reporting

So far, all the reforms discussed have been directed at the conduct of Parliament and political parties, now and in the future. However, some attention needs to be given to reforms directed at the press and other media. The number of times that individual privacy has been invaded by the press over the last few years are too numerous to mention. At present there is far too little redress for an individual with modest means who thinks that he or she has been libelled or otherwise abused.

We have seen how voluntary regulation has failed miserably to prevent the hounding of those in public life, yet the Conservative Party has had no stomach for a fight because every time there has been a whisper of press controls, another two or three of their MPs have hit the dust over allegations which the press have said would never have been revealed were regulations in force. Hence there is a dilemma.

The need for legislation

Clearly the media have an important democratic role in widening debate and probing behind the scenes, but there must be a better-defined code with proper sanctions which have backing in law, including a French-style right of reply. There will always be a debate about what is or is not in the public interest, but as we have seen, one thing which is clearly not in the public interest is to create a situation where large numbers of excellent potential leaders of this nation are put off entering public life. It is also worrying that so much media power is now owned by a few individuals or companies and great care needs to be taken that such market domination is not encouraged any further.

It is also important to reach agreement with the media that Ministers will make 'no comment' on sensitive matters such as interest rate changes, and that such an answer should be taken at face value. The alternative is that Ministers are forced to continue to lie by denying the truth – creating a vicious circle where they are even less likely to be believed in the future.

In conclusion, then, we have seen that there are many reasons for the public revulsion against politicians and for the widely held mistrust of what they say. We have seen that while politics in Britain has always had its weak points, and while the media have tended to sensationalise, there is widespread agreement that something has gone wrong more recently.

The truth about Westminster is that the institution is in a sad state of decay. Endless point-scoring by politicians has cheapened debate, clouded real issues, and encouraged media over-reaction. The whole system of government from Secretary of State to civil servants is rooted in secrecy and open to great abuse of power.

The truth is that there are far fewer villains than the media make out, and where there have been highly publicised 'misdemeanours', they have sometimes been relatively minor matters or have involved serious but highly complex issues. It is hard for those who have never held office to understand fully the pressures of running a government Department, and the almost inevitable pitfalls. It is probably almost impossible to be a Minister for long under the current system without in some way becoming 'tainted by office'.

However if there are few real villains, there are even fewer heroes: leaders of obvious integrity who command national respect across party divides. As a result there is a crisis of leadership in our nation, which is perhaps the most serious defect of Westminster today. A culture of consensus rather than confrontation could help create positive government, positive opposition, positive leadership, and positive reporting. The alternative is years more dominated by the politics of insecurity, cover-up, denial, fear of exposure, avoidance and aggressive arrogance.

We have seen the growing pressures for change, and the need for reform that goes beyond mere codes of practice, but the answer lies not in mere codes or conventions. During the next century, historians will look back at the last days of this century and no doubt place the British crisis of self-confidence over Westminster in the context of more than fifty years of historical decline from the days of a world empire. They will note too a similar unease in many other developed nations following the end of the Cold War, the collapse of communism, severe economic depression, and deep-rooted problems in society such as the collapse of family life, crime and drug addiction, and the negative view of leadership.

What will they describe beyond the year 2000? Will they record that the same corrupting system grumbled on for a further fifty years until the whole concept of 'the leader worth following' had all but perished? Or will they record a political renaissance as a new generation rose up with fresh ideals and vision, rediscovering the best of our heritage, and rejecting the worst?

If there is no change, I believe Westminster will slowly die over the next fifty years, after gradual delegation to European Parliament on the one hand, to Regional Assemblies, local government and privatised industries on the other, and all the while with loss of economic power to progressive globalisation. However I believe that a change in values is likely to come to Westminster, because the country is hungry for that change, and because there is a strong memory of a 'better way', held particularly in the Upper House. Rapid change in Europe demands that Westminster be in a healthy state.

Some may place their hope in elections and new governments, but changes in government will surely lead to bitter disappointment unless there is a change in heart – which is little to do with policies. Yet a change in heart will only come through a change in vision, and a change in vision will only take root as those with vision take courage to rise above the mocking and ridicule to communicate that vision.

Whether that vision is translated into action will depend on the outcome of an intense and bitter struggle between a tiny minority with power or the hope of it, and a far greater number across this whole nation who believe the nature of that power should fundamentally change.

12

Christians in Politics

*'In the nineteenth century . . . Christians saw slavery
abolished, the hours and conditions of work for women and
children transformed, employment exchanges introduced,
orphanages and leper colonies built and staffed. We can and
we must do it again!' Clive Calver (1949–)*

*'Politics is not the art of the possible. It consists of choosing
between the disastrous and the unpalatable.' J.K. Galbraith
(1908–)*

Is one party more Christian than another? That was the
emotive question raised by Tony Blair in a newspaper article
which described how his own Christian faith had led him to
the Labour Party. Howls of protest erupted from
Conservative MPs, horrified at the suggestion that their party
was any less Christian than his. Some went further. Harry
Greenway wrote in the local press that his own faith had
made him a strong Conservative supporter.

The reality is that a large number of MPs would say that
they are Christians, and many go to church regularly. The total
number could exceed eighty named individuals, according to

informal reports from those with long experience of Westminster.[245] Examples include Alistair Burt, Brian Mawhinney, Simon Hughes, David Alton, David Porter, Robert Key and Tony Blair. While a number of MPs may be wary about being labelled, there are also problems of definition. Christian faith stretches across all party lines and the Parliamentary Prayer Group is an active source of encouragement and support.

Each of these Parliamentarians would no doubt vigorously defend the reasons why their choice of party is consistent with the faith that they have, but does this mean that any attempt to define 'Christian' political values is doomed to failure? Are there any general principles to which most could agree? And is it 'safe' for an MP to risk being labelled 'Christian' – and then 'hypocrite' when it is realised that he or she is all too human. Christians fail too, and the stronger the moral position taken, the more the sense of outrage and condemnation of any fall. The public is often lacking in mercy.

There are other more fundamental questions such as: Is it right for Christians to be involved in politics at all? In the last century there was a very active involvement in politics, with well-known figures William Wilberforce and Lord Shaftesbury as well as many others. Wilberforce campaigned for the abolition of slavery for almost the entire length of his political life. They left a legacy which is still felt in our society today. However most church historians would agree that over the following decades there was a gradual withdrawal by some parts of the church from the political process, particularly among Evangelicals.

At the same time, the mandate for social action was also subdued among Evangelicals, who became suspicious of what they labelled 'the social gospel'. As they saw it, the more liberal wing of the church had lost a clear message and was instead focusing on good works. As a reaction, Evangelicals placed most of their energy into evangelism. There is more balance today, with a growing social conscience, but still only an elementary political awareness. Political action, by such groups as CARE, Evangelical Alliance, the Jubilee Centre, Life and SPUC, has often been based on single-issue campaigning on matters such as euthanasia, abortion, divorce law reform or Sunday trading. This is hardly a substitute for a broad manifesto. While support from some parts of the church has been huge, other believers have felt alienated by the virulence of the campaigning. The abortion issue more than any other has tended to polarise the church.

While it is possible that the majority of churchgoers in the country may well advocate tighter laws regarding late abortion, there are a variety of views about the exact status and value of – say – a fertilised egg, or a pre-implantation ball of cells, or of an eight-week foetus. Many Catholics and Evangelicals may share a strictly pro-life position, but others may not. There is however a far greater degree of consensus over euthanasia, which perhaps helps explain why efforts to legalise it have failed. On many campaigning issues there have been differences in approach between different groups, and sometimes, perhaps, conflicts of interest, where a position taken on one issue could affect other areas.

A Christian view of government

There are many faiths represented in multi-cultural Britain, and I have no doubt that followers of these will have perspectives to bring to help Parliament recover a reputation for integrity. However, the major religion in Britain is still Christianity. So what is a Christian view of government?

Jesus himself taught his disciples to respect authority even if, as was generally perceived then, it was corrupt or morally deficient or lacking in spiritual understanding. The disciples were told to pay taxes and to 'render unto Caesar what is due to Caesar and unto God what is due to God'.[246] While he challenged religious hypocrisy and corruption, and was very outspoken, he did nothing to suggest that his disciples should ignore the government of the day.

Jesus was prepared however to commit an act of angry violence against property as part of a wider protest against corruption, when he overturned the tables of the money-lenders in the Temple courts. He was also prepared to act aggressively towards individuals, threatening them with violence, for the same reason. We are told that he made a whip out of some cords and began threatening them with it in such a way that they fled from the area.[247]

Jesus was abrasive and 'rude' in the language he used against religious leaders (Pharisees), and used collective language so strong that in today's culture it would verge on the libellous if printed in reference to prominent national religious leaders.

'You have neglected the more important matters of the law – justice, mercy and faithfulness . . . Blind guides . . . hypocrites . . . full of greed and self-indulgence . . . blind . . . snakes, brood of vipers . . . how will you escape being condemned . . . I am sending you prophets and wise men . . . some of them you will kill, others crucify . . . you make [people] twice as much sons of hell as you are.' This is extremely inflammatory language to say the least, bordering on accusing certain people of being murderous as well as being morally corrupt.

Scarcely a generation later, the apostle Paul wrote to the church in Rome, suffering under a tyrannical dictatorship and severely persecuted, that authority in all its forms was God given and to be respected. 'It is necessary to submit to the authorities,' and later, 'If you owe taxes, pay taxes.'[248] However, Peter committed an act of civil disobedience when he refused a court order to stop preaching in public places, and was arrested for it.[249] Even afterwards he again defied a court ban.[250]

The picture then is one of great respect for government as

a God-ordained expression of his authority, part of the structure of a healthy society, and of a healthy church, with disobedience as a last resort in extreme circumstances where a 'higher authority' is being violated (abuse of the Temple area, ban on preaching).

Participation in secular government

Then there is the question of whether Christians should get involved in a governmental process that denies or ignores the truths of the Christian faith. Are Christians called to speak in from outside the system, or to step in?

The book of Genesis shows how Joseph was sold into slavery, landed up in prison but found favour with the national leader (Pharaoh). He was offered a post effectively as Prime Minister of Egypt at a time of imminent national crisis. Over a number of years he took control of agricultural production and distribution, and prevented widespread deaths from famine.[251]

Daniel likewise was talent-spotted from a Jewish community which was in exile after being herded in large numbers from their own country to one around 1,000 miles away. He was promoted and gained great influence at governmental level.[252]

Nehemiah was also someone who was drawn into the most senior levels of the government machine, from a community in exile, serving a regime which had an entirely different faith and worldview. This influence was later used by him to obtain a massive government grant to rebuild the wrecked city of Jerusalem. There was no suggestion that all the money should have come from the Jewish community themselves. Nehemiah raised funds aggressively, presented his case effectively to the highest authority in the land, and was given huge state backing as well as guarantees of safe conduct.[253]

There is therefore great biblical precedent for the deepest involvement in national government, for the good of the people. Doors opened in a remarkable way and the opportunities to exercise power in a benevolent way were grasped.

Jesus himself taught that his followers were to be salt and light, salting a whole dish, lighting up the whole area.[254] He also used a picture of yeast: a small amount having a transforming effect on the whole loaf.[255] This implies that he expected that his disciples would, as they grew in number, not only preach a message of good news, with some responding, but would bring a wider impact to the whole of society.

Jesus also challenged injustice, spoke of mercy and compassion, and said that we were to love those around us as much as we cared about ourselves.[256] Since many injustices and other problems in society can be made easier or worse by good or bad government, it seems inevitable that as soon as a Christian community thinks seriously about society as a whole, it is confronted by the need to get involved in exercising power through involvement in government.

Christian policies – can they be defined?

However, once a Christian is in Parliament, or in office, there are other urgent questions. The complexities of modern life are so great, and change so rapidly, that a policy hammered out today may become irrelevant tomorrow.

At the most basic level governments raise money through taxes or borrowing, and spend money on public services or on reallocation of wealth through benefits and rebates of various kinds. The areas of controversy are therefore:

1. How taxes are raised.

2. How much is borrowed.

3. How the 'cake' is sliced in expenditure between Departments.

4. How efficiency and effectiveness are maintained.

The fiercest and most bitter of arguments can be over these four things. However, it can be hard to justify one approach over another in terms of Christian values. In almost every case the debate is not over an absolute, but over subtle differences.

For example, what proportion of the nation's wealth should be taxed and spent by government? What proportion should be income tax or other taxes? What should be the level of 'social taxes' such as a tax on fuel, petrol or alcohol? How much should a government raise through borrowing, risking pressure on exchange rates and interest rate changes, affecting the whole economy?

If more is spent on education and health than can be raised in taxes or borrowing, what government funded jobs in other areas are axed in order to do it? The most vexing questions of all are related to the economy: do we grow a large, low tax economy or a small high tax economy? What will be the effect of – say – a one point cut in interest rates, or of cutting back on road building to pay more teachers?

Efficiency and effectiveness are values that all would support, but how do we achieve them? There are many ways of running a state health service. There are many ways of managing local schools, or of providing other public services. At the end of the day, while we can define certain principles which are Christian, it is not easy to define detailed policy from the Bible or from the historic teachings of the church. The reality is that in an imperfect world every option can have problems attached to it, and there may be no 'ideal' solution that is practical in the foreseeable future.

One may argue that such things as extremes of wealth and poverty are incompatible with Christian values. But how do you define poverty? Until recently, poverty was defined as having an income less than a quarter of the national average, but that definition means that exactly the same level of poverty will always be with us, however affluent or poor our society becomes.

Should poverty be defined in cross-national terms? Is my neighbour a peasant farmer in a small tribal community with no running water? To whom is my lot to be compared in the 'need' stakes? The Christian community may be able perhaps to find a greater degree of consensus over issues such as Sunday trading, but even then there is debate and uncertainty.

Christian principles – a guiding factor

Those in politics face these sorts of issues every day. A secondary position to take is that because it is impossible to write a 'Christian Manifesto' for every aspect of government action, one should rely more on underlying Christian principles, about which most if not all Christians are in agreement. These principles might be such things as respect for the individual, respect for human life, basic human rights, personal responsibility, fairness, justice, compassion, mercy, tolerance of others' views, good stewardship of the earth's resources.

We have already seen a set of principles governing personal conduct in politics, in the previous chapter. These are based very largely on Christian values such as integrity, honesty, loving not only our neighbour but also our enemies,[257] judging others as we ourselves would want to be judged,[258] caring about others as we would want to be cared for if we were in a similar situation.[259]

A Christian party?

The word 'Christian' is already a part of the political process in Europe, and the Christian Democratic tradition is well established. Formed after the Second World War, it has thrived in many other countries, but has never had much support in Britain until now.

In the UK the word 'Christian' is quite emotive, and conjures up all kinds of images in politics, some of which are very negative in the public mind. The continued sectarian problems in Northern Ireland have not helped.

If a party is labelled as Christian then two dangers could result: first there is a danger that those supporting the party will appear to be wanting to occupy the moral high ground, giving the impression that those in other parties may be less Christian in their politics. Secondly, there is a danger that the Christian faith and the mission of the church will be judged by how party members conduct themselves, and by the policies they espouse. It is all too easy to see the 'Christian' label becoming one of abuse – 'Call yourself Christian? How can you if you agree with that?' In fact the label was not one used by the earliest disciples. They were known as 'believers',[260] and not Christians until later.[261]

The same fate following labelling can befall any MP who has a high profile Christian faith, but the pressures on those in a so-called Christian party could be even greater. I am not suggesting that people in politics should hide their faith, but only that a self-confessed Christian party may invite hostile media attention, and may auto-destruct at the first whiff of scandal.

There are other issues too: how do you define the word Christian? Do MPs or all party members have to sign some kind of declaration of faith, or merely assent to a manifesto? Who agrees the manifesto? Who writes the declaration of faith? Are declarations worth the paper they are written on? How can you enforce faith? What happens to those who as part of the pilgrimage of life find that their personal faith fades? What happens over issues of personal morality – are

these also to become part of some statement of intent? These
are all important questions that would have to be addressed.
It is quite possible that agreement could only be reached on
some of these things by alienating a large number within the
Christian community – whether one goes down the 'exclu-
sive' path or within the 'broad stream of sympathisers'.

The Christian Democratic movement in Europe could
hardly be said to be enthusiastically Christian and there are no
statements of faith as such, yet there is a strong Christian influence which has continued over several decades. But if such a
new party were not strongly and unmistakably Christian, what
would be the advantage in calling it Christian at all?

While all these issues may seem rather hypothetical in
today's two-party system, they could rapidly become very
urgent if a referendum on electoral reform voted for proportional representation. At the time of writing, the nearest there
is to a Christian political party is the Movement for Christian
Democracy, only a few years old yet growing fast with a
newspaper whose readership probably exceeds 40,000. But
this is a movement supported by members of all political per-
suasions and is unlikely to turn into a new party.

Practical policies for a Christian party

The simplest way forward for a new party wishing to be a
Christian political influence would be to work through consensus. Otherwise, there is a real danger that such a party
would become known for little more than a rag bag of single
issues on which 'extreme' positions are taken, say over abortion. It is true that proportional representation does allow for
the election of small numbers of people backed by minority
views, but it is no substitute for a coherent political frame-
work.

The consensus route would mean that on most matters, the

policies supported would be those that the majority of the country (and probably also the majority of Christians) would agree over. There would be no embarrassment whatever about appearing to compete with New Labour or the Conservatives for the middle ground. If good government is by the people, for the people, then middle-of-the-road consensus is the only route to it, providing the great majority of voters with what they feel is right.

Such a party would find that there were some positions that seemed more Labour than Conservative, or vice versa. For example, a Christian party would without doubt be strongly pro-family and would place a high value on human life as part of a manifesto, yet would also be strongly in favour of measures to help the disadvantaged, oppressed and marginalised – not forgetting the developing world. In old left–right terms it might appear more right wing in morality and left wing in care and compassion.

A new movement

In all we have seen throughout this book it has become obvious that radical change is needed, and that a deeper transformation of political life will require a change of hearts rather than a code of practice.

Either those already in the system change their values, or others with different values need to take up the challenge, become involved and bring a secondary transformation. Unless proportional representation is introduced in a way which breaks two-party domination, all those wishing to make an impact will be forced to choose between one of the three main parties, or indeed between just two parties if they aim to play a part in government.

I am convinced that it would not take more than sixty-five new MPs with charisma, energy, unshakeable values, unflinching integrity, courage and vision for the future, to change the whole atmosphere in Westminster.

There is little doubt in my mind that it will happen in time. There is already a momentum under way, with new faces taking their first tentative steps into the political process, ranging from canvassing on doorsteps, to standing as local councillors or as parliamentary candidates. They will bring a wind of fresh air, as part of a new political movement that sees leadership, authority and power as a means to serve others, a calling to be held with humility rather than arrogance. Such a group could become a focus for longer-term change beyond the millennium, a rallying point around which many others could gather, backed by tens of thousands of supporters across the UK.

I have no doubt that a significant number of these new faces will be people motivated by a strong faith, drawn from every part of the church. It seems likely that an increasing number will be Evangelicals, who now constitute around half of all Protestants and are a rapidly growing religious force in Britain. The Evangelical Alliance already represents around 1.3 million believers, a potent force. Their press office deals with up to seventy calls a week, with 2,849 churches, 57,600 personal members increasing at 10,000 a year, their member societies number over 735, including major care agencies such as TEAR Fund (UK's fifth largest development agency) with a mailing list of 140,000, the Shaftesbury Society and some branches of the Salvation Army. Another evangelical campaigning group, CARE, has a mailing list of 80,000.[262]

The evangelical community is growing rapidly as some other parts of the church are in decline. Over 100,000 adults attended a fifteen-week enquirers' course all over the country in 1995 (Alpha). Each year around 70,000 church members spend a week of their annual leave at a national Christian residential conference (Spring Harvest), so vast that it has to be repeated several times at up to three different sites in order to pack everyone in. Churches like Kensington Temple in London have grown from around 500 to 6,000 in the last twelve years, planting 100 new congregations across London in the process. In June 1994 70,000 people took part in a prayer march across London, praying for change in society and in national political life. This London-based initiative started originally with 2,500 people in 1987, but by 1994 it had spawned simultaneous prayer marches by 12 million people in almost 100 other nations.[263]

There is a vitality and vibrancy in the evangelical movement which crosses every denominational label and cultural barrier. The Archbishop of Canterbury retains his evangelical persuasion and it is shared by the majority of newly ordained Anglican clergy. The significance of these changes will be long term and should not be underestimated. There is a new sense of confidence as it becomes fashionable in some circles to admit that you too have been 'born again'. At least one Member of Parliament has so indicated in the last couple of years alone.[264]

The national Prayer Breakfasts held at Westminster each year are packed to overflowing with around 1,000 national leaders from every walk of life. One organiser told me recently that he thought there were probably in excess of 3,000 people who would like to attend each year. Places have to be rationed, with most people not permitted to be there for two years in succession. Members of both Houses are heavily represented. A similar prayer breakfast in the City attracts several hundred annually. Both these initiatives are relatively recent and heavily influenced by Evangelicals.

These changes in the British church scene need to be placed in the context of a global spiritual awakening. Every month more people are adopting the Christian faith than has ever happened in any month in the whole of recorded history. The world population continues to grow rapidly at around 1.7 per cent per year, yet the global Christian community is already 1.7 billion in size and growing far faster at 2.3 per cent per year, while Evangelicals are growing at 4.5 per cent per year.[265]

This movement has been frustrated in Britain by the lack of progress on a number of single-issue campaigns. Surely this frustration will now be channelled into a more established political process.

Clive Calver, Director of the Evangelical Alliance, recently wrote this:[266]

> Politics is the art of the possible – God is the author of the impossible. Therefore those two world views will always collide. Rather than disengage from the political world, we need to re-engage with it by carrying the truth within us that God gives, and the hope provides for the possible to be transformed through the life and ministry of his people.
>
> Our world needs to be different, and if we are truly to act as 'salt and light' then we must be active in the political arena. Let us pray for all those who seek to serve God in politics, and also take the opportunities that we are given through our communities and national involvement that God alone can provide.
>
> In the nineteenth century Evangelical Christians saw slavery abolished, the hours and conditions of work for women and children transformed, employment exchanges introduced, orphanages and leper colonies built and staffed. We can and we must do it again!

If between now and 2010 just one in a hundred of more than 6 million regular churchgoers in Britain (11 per cent of the population) were to become in some way involved in the political process, then 60,000 people would become involved, most for the first time. It would only take one in a thousand of these to end up in Parliament to make a very signficant impact in the future.

How can I get involved?

1. Vote at elections and encourage others to do so.

2. Write to your MP regularly about your concerns, and go and visit if necessary. Your opinion will be listened to and does have an influence.

3. Join a party.

4. Visit Parliament while in session. See what goes on. This is a public right. There is rarely a queue for the Lords but the Commons can be very busy, so contact your MP first and ask for a pass, or go later in the evening.

5. If you are a church-goer, you might like to consider joining a denominational group that has a political wing, or interdenominational groups that have a voice. Examples might include Evangelical Alliance, the Diocesan Board for Social Action, the Christian Medical Fellowship, CARE, the Jubilee Centre, or the Movement for Christian Democracy. By joining you are adding the weight of your own voice to the organisation, and informing yourself too.

6. Create or support a local constituency group, perhaps working with other groups such as local churches. For example CARE tries to ensure that all candidates in every area are asked to meetings with churchgoers so that they can be asked where they stand on particular issues.

7. Support with practical help and prayer those already in local or national government. Life can be very tough and lonely, especially for spouses and children.

8. Take opportunities to speak about political issues.

9. Get involved in government, whether at the level of such things as school governing bodies, or local government or national government, perhaps by helping as part of an administration or campaign team, or by standing for Parliament – somebody has to, so why not you?

10. Invite an MP to speak in your church or at a celebration event or ecumenical gathering of some kind.

11. Include political issues in your publications.

12. Keep an open attitude to others with different views.

Notes

1. See later interview.
2. Quoted in *The Daily Telegraph*, 15 May 1995.
3. Gallup Poll, May 1995, reported in *The Daily Telegraph*, 9 June 1995.
4. Gallup Poll, *The Daily Telegraph*, 9 June 1995.
5. Poll quoted in 'Standards in Public Life', First Report of the Nolan Committee, May 1995.
6. 66 per cent to be exact.
7. Gallup Poll quoted in 'Standards in Public Life', First Report of the Nolan Committee, May 1995.
8. Gallup Poll, *The Daily Telegraph*, 9 June 1995.
9. 'Britain cannot look on the bright side', *The Daily Telegraph*, 23 June 1995.
10. 'It's all over for the constitution', *The Independent*, 30 May 1995. MORI poll sponsored by the Joseph Rowntree Foundation.
11. Personal interview, House of Lords, 4 April 1995.
12. 'Murky past puts cash row in shade', *The Guardian*, 26 October 1994.
13. 'When the going gets rough some hapless ministers try to rough it out', *The Guardian*, 26 October 1994.

14. 'When the going gets rough some hapless ministers try to rough it out', *The Guardian*, 26 October 1994.

15. 'Murky past puts cash row in shade', *The Guardian*, 26 October 1994.

16. 'When the going gets rough some hapless ministers try to rough it out', *The Guardian*, 26 October 1994.

17. Lecture given to the Carlton Club, quoted in *The Independent*, 20 May 1995.

18. Personal interview, 7 Millbank, Westminster, 10 May 1995.

19. Personal interview, 7 Millbank, Westminster, 21 March 1995.

20. Personal interview, 7 Millbank, Westminster, 1 February 1995.

21. Personal interview at his offices in Victoria, 16 February 1995.

22. 'Standards in Public Life', First Report of the Nolan Committee, May 1995.

23. Report of Committee of Privileges, Vol II, 3 April 1995.

24. Report of Committee of Privileges, Vol I, 3 April 1995.

25. 'Tories block open inquiry on MPs' cash', *The Daily Telegraph*, 1 November 1994.

26. 'Defiant Benn produces his "boring" report', *The Independent*, 2 November 1994.

27. 'Tories block open inquiry on MPs' cash', *The Daily Telegraph*, 1 November 1994.

28. Telephone interview, 31 June 1995.

29. Personal interview, House of Lords, 4 April 1995.

30. Personal interview in Vauxhall, 7 April 1995.

31. Personal interview, 7 Millbank, Westminster, 19 January 1995.

32. Personal interview, 7 Millbank, Westminster, 10 May 1995. New measure introduced 1996.

33. Personal interview at Westminster Central Hall, 26 January 1995.

34. Personal interview at Richmond House, Whitehall, 20 February 1995.

35. 'Standards in Public Life', First Report of Lord Nolan's Committee, 1995.

36. 'State of the Nation' MORI Poll, *The Independent*, 30 May 1995.

37. 'Lobbying's high priest admitted paying MPs', *The Times*, 21 October 1994.

38. *Ibid*.

39. *Ibid*.

40. 'Lobbyist says he believes there is little sleaze at Westminster', *The Guardian*, 21 October 1994.

41. Ian Greer, 'Right to be heard', 1985.

42. 'Lobbying's high priest admitted paying MPs', *The Times*, 21 October 1994.

43. 'When pious Hattersley was "MP for hire"', *Evening Standard*, 27 October 1994.

44. *Ibid*.

45. 'Top Tory quits rail link lobby company', *The Independent*, 28 October 1994 and 'Rumbold resigns from lobby firm', *The Daily Telegraph*, 28 October 1994.

46. 'Rumbold resigns from lobby firm', *The Daily Telegraph*, 28 October 1994.

47. 'Top Tory quits rail link lobby company', *The Independent*, 28 October 1994.

48. Oral evidence to Nolan Inquiry, 18 January 1995.

49. 'Rumbold resigns from lobby firm', *The Daily Telegraph*, 28 October 1994.

50. 'Top Tory quits rail link lobby company', *The Independent*, 28 October 1994.

51. *The Observer*, 26 February 1994.
52. Personal interview, The Treasury, Whitehall, 25 April 1995.
53. Evidence to the Committee of Privileges, published 3 April 1995, Vol II.
54. Personal interview, 7 Millbank, Westminster, 10 May 1995.
55. Personal interview, House of Lords, 20 February 1995.
56. Personal interview, House of Lords, 20 February 1995.
57. Personal interview, 7 Millbank, Westminster, 1 February 1995.
58. Paul Halloran and Mark Hollingsworth, *A Bit on the Side* (Simon and Schuster, 1994).
59. Register of Members' Interests, 31 March 1996.
60. Research by Gill Howarty, Public Information Office, House of Commons, January 1995.
61. *Ibid*.
62. *Ibid*.
63. *Ibid*.
64. *Ibid*.
65. *Ibid*.
66. *Ibid*.
67. Exact figure was 69.8p per mile in 1995.
68. Personal interview, Millbank, 10 May 1995.
69. Anonymous MP's comments to me.
70. 1994 figure.
71. Research by Gill Howarty, Public Information Office, House of Commons, January 1995.
72. 'MPs angry at "puny" pay award, *Sunday Times*, 6 August 1995.
73. Personal interview at Richmond House, Whitehall, 20 February 1995.
74. 'MPs' expenses under Nolan scrutiny', *The Independent*, 10 June 1995.

75. *Ibid.*
76. *Ibid.*
77. Personal communication, April 1995.
78. 'Full House puts Lords £6 million in pocket', *The Daily Telegraph*, 18 April 1995.
79. *Ibid.*
80. Personal communication, House of Lords, May 1995.
81. Personal interview, House of Lords, 4 May 1995.
82. Personal interview, House of Lords, 4 May 1995.
83. Erskine May, *Parliamentary Practice*, 21st edition published by Butterworths and confirmed in discussion with the House of Lords Information Office, 15 February 1996.
84. Personal communication.
85. 'Jobs bonanza for ex-ministers', *The Independent*, 2 May 1995.
86. Personal interview, House of Lords, 4 May 1995.
87. Interview in South West London, 8 June 1995.
88. Written submission, 11 January 1995.
89. Cabinet Office figures 1989. The most recent edition of *Public Bodies* gives a total of 43,000, a discrepancy explained by the fact that the *Public Bodies* figure is of public bodies, not ministerial appointments.
90. Parliamentary written answers.
91. Public Appointments Unit 1993 figures.
92. Paragraphs 49 and 50.
93. Figures from Tony Wright's submission to the Nolan Inquiry. He acknowledges the help of Robin Clarke.
94. From article he wrote for *Countryside Commission News*, March 1991.
95. Quoted in *Independent on Sunday*, 28 March 1993.
96. Official Report, 18 January 1994.
97. From *The Independent*, 17 March 1994.
98. Report in *The Observer*, 4 July 1994.

99. 'Patronage decides who serves at the top', *Financial Times*, 14 January 1993.

100. 'Sir Paul makes light of media's bite', *The Independent*, 2 November 1994.

101. *Here and Now*, BBC television, 2 November 1994.

102. I am grateful to Tony Wright MP whose paper submitted to the Nolan Inquiry on 11 January 1995 is the source of much of this material.

103. Personal interview, House of Lords, 4 May 1995.

104. Tony Wright's submission to the Nolan Inquiry, 11 January 1995.

105. 'Patronage in British Government', 1963, p 257.

106. MORI 'State of the Nation' poll, *The Independent*, 30 May 1995.

107. Special investigation by the *Sunday Times*, 27 September 1992.

108. Tony Wright quoting *The Times*, March 1992.

109. Tony Wright MP quoting a study by Richards in 1963.

110. Personal interview, London, 21 March 1995.

111. Submission to Lord Nolan, 11 January 1995.

112. Personal interview, 7 Millbank, Westminster, 1 February 1995.

113. Personal interview, 7 Millbank, Westminster, 21 March 1995.

114. Personal interview, London, 21 March 1995.

115. Personal interview, House of Commons, 18 January 1995.

116. 'Tories condemn secret donations', *The Times*, 20 May 1993.

117. *Ibid*.

118. 'Conservatives given £7 million by foreign donors', *The Guardian*, 29 April 1993.

119. *Ibid*.

120. Annual Report and Accounts from Conservative Central Office years ending 31 March 1993 and 1994.

121. *Ibid*.

122. *Ibid*.

123. *Ibid*.

124. Annual Report and Accounts from Conservative Central Office years ending 31 March 1995.

125. Telephone conversation, 26 October 1995.

126. Annual Report and Accounts from Conservative Central Office, year ending 31 March 1995.

127. Paul Whiteley, Patrick Seyd and Jeremy Richardson, *True Blues* (Oxford University Press, 1994).

128. 'Aging Tory membership threat to funding', *The Guardian*, 10 October 1994 and Labour Party information.

129. 'MPs funding local parties with up to £11,000 a year', *The Times*, 11 October 1995.

130. Jeremy Hanley, Chairman of the Conservative Party – personal interview – stated in May 1995 that the 1994–5 accounts would show a rise in constituency income.

131. 'MPs funding local parties with up to £11,000 a year', *The Times*, 11 October 1995.

132. *Ibid*.

133. *Ibid*.

134. *Ibid*.

135. *Ibid*.

136. 'Tories back in the black to fight election', *The Daily Telegraph*, 25 August 1996.

137. Headline from *The Independent*, 22 September 1989.

138. *Ibid*.

139. *Ibid*.

140. Minority Report on Party Financing of the Home Affairs Committee of the House of Commons, 9 March 1995.

141. Personal interview, The Treasury, Whitehall, 25 April 1995.

142. Personal interview, Richmond House, Whitehall, 27 April 1995.

143. Personal interview, House of Lords, 4 May 1995.

144. Personal interview in Vauxhall, 7 April 1995.

145. Personal interview in Victoria, 22 February 1995.

146. Personal interview, Conservative Central Office, 17 May 1995.

147. 'State of the Nation', MORI poll, *The Independent*, 30 May 1995.

148. 'Blair mystery cash', *Daily Express*, 24 February 1995.

149. Personal interview at his London home, 17 May 1995.

150. 'Labour will get secret cash help', *The Independent*, 15 May 1995.

151. Personal interview, 7 Millbank, Westminster, 1 February 1995.

152. Committee of Privileges Report, 3 April 1995, Vol II.

153. Figures from interview with Labour Party press officer, 4 July 1995.

154. 'One thing after another', *The Guardian*, 21 October 1994.

155. 'Sleaze fatigue', *Evening Standard*, 27 October 1994.

156. Personal interview at his London home, 17 May 1995.

157. Interviews with various well-known people in politics and show business.

158. 'Hugh blows it with £15 hooker', *Daily Mirror*, 28 June 1995.

159. Personal interview, 7 Millbank, Westminster, 21 March 1995.

160. Telephone interview, 3 July 1995.

161. 'Blackmail by Whips exposed', *The Times*, 18 May 1995.

162. Personal interview, 7 Millbank, Westminster, 21 March 1995.

163. Theresa Gorman, *The Bastards* (Pan, 1993), quoted with her permission.
164. Personal interview, House of Lords, 4 April 1995.
165. Personal interview, House of Commons, 18 January 1995.
166. Personal interview, 7 Millbank, Westminster, 19 January 1995.
167. Personal interview, 7 Millbank, Westminster, 21 March 1995.
168. 'Dirt book whips rebels into line', *The Daily Telegraph*, 18 May 1995.
169. *Ibid*.
170. *Ibid*.
171. Personal interview, House of Lords, 4 May 1995.
172. Personal interview, Conservative Central Office, 17 May 1995.
173. Personal interview, House of Lords, 20 February 1995.
174. Personal interview in Victoria, 16 February 1995.
175. *Hansard*, 29 November 1994.
176. *Christian Democrat*, June/July 1995.
177. Oral evidence to Scott Inquiry, Day 48, 8 December 1993.
178. Oral evidence to Scott Inquiry, Day 55, 17 January 1994.
179. Personal interview, Richmond House, Whitehall, 27 April 1995.
180. Personal interview, House of Lords, 4 April 1995.
181. 'New rules for Ministers on "evading truth"', *The Daily Telegraph*, 31 October 1995.
182. Personal interview at Richmond House, Whitehall, 20 February 1995.
183. Personal interview, Richmond House, Whitehall, 27 April 1995.
184. Personal interview, House of Lords, 4 May 1995.
185. Personal interview, 7 Millbank, Westminster, 21 March 1995.

186. Personal interview, House of Lords, 4 April 1995.
187. Personal interview, London, 7 June 1995.
188. Personal interview, 7 Millbank, Westminster, 1 February 1995.
189. Personal interview, House of Lords, 20 February 1995.
190. Telephone interview, 30 January 1995.
191. *Britain: 1994*, an Official Handbook, HMSO.
192. *Ibid.*
193. 'Ministers accused of fictional arms export policy', *The Times*, 20 June 1995.
194. 'Public pays Scott Ministers' legal bill', *The Independent*, 13 June 1995.
195. Personal interview in Victoria, 16 February 1995.
196. 'Whitehall and Ministers blamed for inquiry delay', *The Independent*, 6 June 1995.
197. 'The court cases that cost firms their reputations', *The Independent*, 6 June 1995.
198. Scott Report, D5.13.
199. 'One thing after another', *The Guardian*, 21 October 1994.
200. 'Ministers fought on different fronts', *The Guardian*, 21 June 1995.
201. 'The court cases that cost firms their reputations', *The Independent*, 6 June 1995.
202. *Ibid.*
203. *Ibid.*
204. *Ibid.*
205. 'Damage Limitation', *Sunday Times*, 11 June 1995.
206. Personal interview, House of Lords, 4 May 1995.
207. Personal interview, House of Lords, 4 April 1995.
208. Personal interview at his home, 17 May 1995.
209. 'Parliament must not be run by outsiders', *The Independent*, 20 May 1995 – text of speech to the Carlton Club.

210. Personal interview, House of Lords, 4 April 1995.

211. Granada Television, *This Morning*, interview reported in *The Daily Telegraph*, 4 November 1995.

212. Personal interview, 7 Millbank, Westminster, 10 May 1995.

213. Personal interview, House of Lords, 4 April 1995.

214. Personal interview, House of Commons, 22 February 1995.

215. Personal interview, The Treasury, Whitehall, 25 April 1995.

216. Personal interview, House of Lords, 4 May 1995.

217. Personal interview, Richmond House, Whitehall, 27 April 1995.

218. Personal interview in Victoria, 16 February 1995.

219. Personal interview, 7 Millbank, Westminster, 19 January 1995.

220. Personal interview, Conservative Central Office, 17 May 1995.

221. Personal interview, House of Commons, 26 January 1995.

222. Personal interview, Conservative Central Office, 17 May 1995.

223. 'Tony Blair admits to Question Time fears', *The Daily Telegraph*, 4 November 1995.

224. 'Press "courted with Harrods cards"', *The Independent*, 3 November 1994.

225. *Ibid*.

226. *Ibid*.

227. *Ibid*.

228. 'MPs unite to condemn editor over forged fax', *The Times*, 3 November 1994.

229. *Ibid*.

230. 'Aitken's wars on newspaper "lies"', *The Times*, 12 April 1995.

231. 'Why he is wrong to sue', *The Times*, 12 April 1995.
232. 'Backbench demands for curbs on the press', *The Independent*, 12 April 1995.
233. Quoted by Lord Thompson in questioning Peter Preston, editor of *The Guardian*, Nolan Inquiry, 25 January 1995.
234. 'Revealed – too late for us to care', *The Independent*, 10 April 1995.
235. Personal interview, West London, 1 July 1995.
236. 'Standards in Public Life', First report of the Committee on Standards in Public Life, Vol 1. May 1995.
237. Erskine May, *Parliamentary Practice* (Butterworths, 1989, 21st Edition).
238. *Ibid.*
239. *Ibid.*
240. *Ibid.*
241. *Ibid.*
242. Erskine May, *Parliamentary Practice* (Butterworths), various editions.
243. Standards in Public Life, First Report of Lord Nolan's Committee, 1995.
244. Figures for attendance, not nominal adherence. *Operation World* (OM Publishing, 1993).
245. Personal communications.
246. Mark 12:17.
247. John 2:14–16 and Mark 11:15.
248. Romans 13:1–7.
249. Acts 4:18–20.
250. Acts 5:17–29.
251. Genesis 37–47.
252. Daniel 1:1–21.
253. Nehemiah 1:1–2:20.
254. Matthew 4:13–16.
255. Matthew 13:33.

256. Luke 10:27.
257. Matthew 5:44.
258. Matthew 7:1–2.
259. Matthew 19:19.
260. Acts 2:44; 4:32.
261. Acts 11:26.
262. Figures from Tear Fund, CARE and the Evangelical Alliance.
263. Figures from the Evangelical Alliance, Kensington Temple and March for Jesus.
264. Personal communication from the MP concerned.
265. Patrick Johnstone, *Operation World* (OM Publishing, 1993).
266. *Compass Magazine*, Volume 2, 1, July 1996.

A Short Bibliography

Parliamentary Practice, Erskine May, Twenty First Edition (Butterworths, 1989).

The Constitution in Flux, Philip Norton (Blackwell, 1982).

'Standards in Public Life', First Report of the Committee on Standards in Public Life, Chairman Lord Nolan, Volume 1, HMSO 1995.

The Downing Street Years, Margaret Thatcher (Harper Collins, 1995).

Livingstone's Labour, Ken Livingstone (Unwin, 1989).

'A Written Constitution for the United Kingdom', Institute for Policy Research (Mansell, 1993).

Politics, Bill Jones (editor) (Harvester Wheatsheaf, 1991).

'Britain 1994', Official Handbook, HMSO.

The End of an Era, Tony Benn diaries (1980–90) (Arrow, 1994).

Mackintosh's *The Government and Politics of Britain*, Peter Richards, 7th edition (Unwin, 1988).

Inside the House of Commons, John Biffen (Grafton Books, 1989).

Faith in Britain, David Alton (Hodder and Stoughton, 1991).

Vacher's Parliamentary Companion, November 1994, Vacher Publications.

Parliamentary Companion, PMS, January 1995, PMS Publications.

Biographical Guide, PMS, 1994/5, PMS Publications.

Relational Justice, Jonathan Burnside and Nicola Baker (Waterside Press, 1994).

The Times Guide to the House of Commons, April 1992, Times Books.

Dodd's *Parliamentary Guide*, 1989, Dodd.

The Bastards, Teresa Gorman (Pan, 1993).

A Bit on the Side, Paul Halloran and Mark Hollingsworth (Simon and Schuster, 1994).